✿✿✿✿✿✿✿✿✿✿✿✿✿✿✿✿✿✿✿✿✿✿✿✿✿✿✿✿✿✿✿✿✿✿✿✿✿✿✿

GERMAN-AMERICAN COOKERY

✿✿✿✿✿✿✿✿✿✿✿✿✿✿✿✿✿✿✿✿✿✿✿✿✿✿✿✿✿✿✿✿✿✿✿✿✿✿✿

HERE IS A BOOKFUL of simple and absolutely authentic do-it-yourself recipes for all of the good old-fashioned dishes that have made German cookery so popular throughout the world—good substantial food, filling and full of flavor, distinctive and eminently satisfying.

Who hasn't, and who wouldn't, relish the taste of pfeffernuesse, stollen, and spritz cookies; spice, cheese and marble cakes; sweet and sour meats; hasenpfeffer, sauerbraten, chicken fricassee, fried liver and onions, schnitzel, sauerkraut and frankfurters; potato pancakes and kartoffelsalat?

The author, born and brought up in Germany, now the wife of an American GI, tells precisely and with remarkable clarity, in both English and German, exactly how to prepare these and many more traditional German dishes.

D1710506

GERMAN-AMERICAN COOKERY

A Bilingual Guide

By BRIGITTE SCHERMER SIMMS

CHARLES E. TUTTLE COMPANY : PUBLISHERS

Rutland, Vermont   Tokyo, Japan

Representatives
Continental Europe: BOXERBOOKS, INC., Zurich
British Isles: PRENTICE-HALL INTERNATIONAL, INC., London
Australasia: BOOK WISE (AUSTRALIA) PTY. LTD.
104-108 Sussex Street, Sydney 2000

Published by the Charles E. Tuttle Company, Inc.
of Rutland, Vermont & Tokyo, Japan
with editorial office at
Suido 1–chome, 2–6, Bunkyo-ku, Tokyo, Japan

Copyright in Japan, 1967, by
The Charles E. Tuttle Company, Inc.
All rights reserved
First edition, 1967
Eleventh printing, 1983

Book design by Roland A. Mulhauser

Library of Congress Catalog Card No. 67–20948

International Standard Book No. 0-8048-0206-8

PRINTED IN JAPAN

DEDICATION

To my dear Father with love
WILLI V. SCHERMER
Bensheim, Germany

ACKNOWLEDGMENT

I would like to express sincerest thanks to:

MY WONDERFUL HUSBAND, James A. Simms, Jr., who gave me the idea to write this book and who was ever so encouraging.

MY DARLING DAUGHTER Eveline R. Simms, 11 years old, without whose help I would not have had time to write this book.

MY SISTER Marita S. Spartas and MY DEAR FRIENDS Mariko Zemla, Dagmar Nichols, Elise Self, and Johanna Goodman who were kind enough to compliment my cooking.

TABLE OF CONTENTS

GERMAN-AMERICAN COOKERY

****

KUCHEN, TORTEN, DESSERTS

****

OBSTTORTE

1½ Tasse Mehl
¼ Tasse und 1 Essloeffel Zucker
7 Essloeffel Magarine
1 Eigelb
1 Teeloeffel Vanille
1 Essloeffel Milch

Mehl und Zucker werden einer mittelgrossen Schuessel vermengt. Die Magarine kommt hinzu und wird mit einer Gabel gut vermengt. Dann gibt man Eigelb, Vanille und Milch hinzu und knetet es gut durch. Der Teig kommt in eine 9" oder 10" grosse Springform, die nur am Rande gefettet wird. Er wird auf den Boden und etwa 1" am Rande hochgedrueckt. Der Boden wird bei 375 F, 20 Minuten gebacken, danach laesst man ihn auskuehlen. Der Rand wird vorsichtig entfernt und der Tortenboden wird auf einen Teller gehoben.
Fuellung: 2 Pfund frisches oder eingemachtes Obst. Pfirsiche, suesse Kirschen, Aprikosen, Blaubeeren oder gemischtes Obst. Bei Erdbeeren eignen sich nur Frische, sie werden mit einer extra Tasse Zucker bestreut und muessen einige Zeit stehen, dann kommen sie in ein Sieb zum Abtropfen. Der Saft wird zur Glasur verwendet.

2 Essloeffel Staerkemehl
1 Tasse Fruchtsaft
½ Tasse Zucker
einige Tropfen Farbstoff

Staerkemehl und ¼ Tasse des Saftes werden in einem Topf verruehrt. Der Zucker, restliche Saft und Farbstoff kommen hinzu und werden 5 Minuten bei staendigem Ruehren gekocht, dann gekuehlt. ::: Die Frucht wird auf den Tortenboden gelegt und die Glasur kommt essloeffelweise darueber. Die Torte laesst man kuehlen. Die Obsttorte wird mit suesser Schlagsahne serviert.

CAKES, PASTRIES AND DESSERTS

FRUIT TORTE

Mix flour and sugar, cut in margarine. Add egg yolk, vanilla and milk, using hands to mix ingredients. Smooth dough into a 9" or 10" spring form pan greased on sides only. Push up on side for 1". ::: Bake at 375 F for 20 minutes. Cool on wire rack. Release ring of pan carefully, and with a large knife transfer crust onto cake plate.

Filling: Use 2 pounds fresh or canned fruit such as peaches, sweet cherries, apricots, or blueberries. Drain well, save juice. When using strawberries, use fresh ones only and add 1 extra cup of sugar poured over the berries, and let soak. Drain and save juice.

1½ cups flour
5 tablespoons sugar
7 tablespoons soft margarine
1 egg yolk
1 teaspoon vanilla
1 tablespoon milk

In small saucepan combine cornstarch, ¼ cup of the juice, stir until smooth. Add sugar, remaining juice and food coloring. Bring to a boil, stirring constantly, cook for 5 minutes, cool for 10 minutes. ::: Arrange fruit on baked, cooled crust. Spoon juice mixture over fruit, chill. Serve with sweetened whipped cream.

2 tablespoons cornstarch
1 cup fruit juice
½ cup sugar
Few drops of food coloring

BISMARKEICHE

4 Eier
¼ Teeloeffel Cream of Tartar
1 Tasse Zucker
1 Teeloeffel Rum Aroma
1 Tasse gesiebtes Mehl
¼ Teeloeffel Salz

Das Eiweiss wird schaumig geschlagen und Cream of Tartar kommt hinzu und wird zu festem Schnee geschlagen. Die Haelfte des Zuckers ½ Tasse, wird allmaehlich zugegeben. ::: Eigelb wird geschlagen, bis eine kremartige Masse entsteht, dazu kommt der Rest des Zuckers und Rum Aroma. Das Ganze wird gut geschlagen. Der Eigelbkrem wird auf den Eiweissschnee gegeben und vorsichtig untergehoben. Danach hebt man Salz und Mehl unter den Teig. ::: Der Teig wird auf ein mit Aluminium Papier ausgelegtes Backblech 15″ × 10″ × 1″ gestrichen und bei 375 F, 20 Minuten gebacken. ::: Nach dem Backen wird das Backblech auf ein mit Zucker bestreutes Kuechenhandtuch gestuerzt und sofort vom Papier befreit, dann von der langen Seite her aufgerollt und 1 Stunde lang kaltgestellt. Die ausgekuehlte Rolle wird vorsichtig auseinander gerollt und mit eine der unten angegebenen Fuellungen bestrichen. Rum Krem Fuellung, Seite 30; Butter Krem Fuellung, Seite 30.

KAESETORTE

1 Rezept Tortenboden, Seite 18
4 Eier separiert
2 Pfund Krem Kaese
¾ Tasse Milch
1½ Tassen Zucker
2 Essloeffel Zitronensaft
1 geriebene Zitronenschale
2 Essloeffel Mehl
½ Tasse Rosinen

Der zubereitete Tortenboden wird kaltgestellt. Eiweiss wird steifgeschlagen und beiseite gestellt. ::: Der Kaese wird mit der Milch glattgeruehrt. Man gibt Eigelb, Zucker, Zitronensaft, Rinde und Mehl darunter und schlaegt es gut durch. Dann ruehrt man die Rosinen drunter. Der steife Eierschnee wird vorsichtig unter das Ganze gezogen und in die zubereitete und mit Teig ausgelegte Springform gegeben. ::: Die Kaesetorte wird bei 450 F fuer 20 Minuten gebacken, dann bei 250 F noch eine Stunde laenger. Nach dem Backen laesst man die Torte noch 30 Minuten im Ofen auskuehlen, dann stuerzt man sie auf ein Rost, wo sie eine weitere Stunde kuehlen muss.

BISMARK LOG

Beat egg whites until foamy, add cream of tartar and beat until stiff. Gradually add ½ cup of sugar. ::: Beat egg yolks until thick, add the remaining ½ cup of sugar and rum. Fold egg yolk mixture into egg whites. Sift flour with salt and fold into egg mixture. Pour into foil-lined 15"×10"×1" jelly roll pan. Bake in moderate oven at 375 F for 20 minutes. ::: When baked, turn out on towel sprinkled with granulated sugar, remove foil from cake. Roll cake up, starting at the longest part and wrap in towel. Chill 1 hour, unroll carefully and fill with Rum Cream Filling on page 31, or Butter Cream Filling on page 31.

4 eggs separated
¼ teaspoon cream of tartar
1 cup sugar
1 teaspoon rum
1 cup sifted flour
¼ teaspoon salt

CHEESE CAKE

Make crust, chill. Beat egg whites until stiff, set aside. ::: Cream cheese with milk until smooth. Add egg yolks, sugar, lemon juice, rind, and flour; beat well. Stir in raisins, then carefully fold in egg whites and pour into prepared crust. ::: Bake in hot oven at 450 F for 20 minutes. Reduce heat to 250 F and bake 1 hour. Turn off heat and leave cake in oven for 20 minutes. Remove from oven and carefully remove sides of pan. Let cool for 30 minutes. Turn over on wire rack and cool for 1 hour.

1 recipe cookie crust on page 19
4 eggs separated
2 pounds cream cheese
¾ cup milk
1½ cups sugar
2 tablespoons lemon juice
1 grated lemon rind
2 tablespoons flour
½ cup raisins

GEWUERZKUCHEN

¾ Tasse Magarine
1½ Tasse Zucker
4 Eier
1 Teeloeffel Vanille
¼ Teeloeffel Mandel Aroma
¼ Teeloeffel Rum Aroma
½ Teeloeffel Salz
⅛ Teeloeffel Nelken
⅛ Teeloeffel Muskatnuss
2 Teeloeffel Zimt
3½ Teeloeffel Backpulver
3 Tassen Mehl
¾ Tasse Milch
5 Essloeffel Kakao

Das Fett wird schaumig geruehrt, man gibt Zucker hinzu. Die Eier werden einzeln zugefuegt und schaumig geschlagen. Dann werden die Gewuerze und der Kakao untergeruehrt. Das Mehl wird mit dem Backpulver gesiebt und abwechselnd mit der Milch unter den Teig geruehrt. Der Teig wird in eine gefettete und bemehlte Napfkuchen oder Kastenform gefuellt. ::: Er wird bei 375 F, 1 Stunde gebacken. Der Kuchen wird auf ein Rost gestuerzt und ausgekuehlt, er kann mit Puderzucker bestreut werden. Der Gewuerzkuchen kann in Scheiben geschnitten werden und mit suesser Schlagsahne serviert werden.

MARMORKUCHEN

1 Tasse Butter oder Magarine
1¼ Tasse Zucker
3 Eier
1 Teeloeffel Vanille
1½ Teeloeffel Rum
¼ Teeloeffel Salz
2¼ Tassen Mehl
2 Teeloeffel Backpulver
½ Tasse Milch
3 Essloeffel Kakao
3 Essloeffel Zucker
2–3 Essloeffel Milch

Die Butter wird schaumig geruehrt, Zucker und Eier kommen hinzu und werden gut geschlagen. Vanille, Rum und Salz werden miteingeruehrt. Das Mehl wird mit dem Backpulver gesiebt und abwechselnd mit der Milch unter den Teig gegeben. ::: Die Haelfte des Teiges wird in eine gefettete und mit Mehl bestaeubte Napfkuchenform gefuellt. Unter den Rest des Teiges ruehrt man Kakao, Zucker und Milch. Der dunkle Teig wird auf den Hellen gefuellt und mit einer Gabel wird der Teig 2 Mal rundherum durchgezogen. ::: Der Kuchen wird bei 375 F, 65 Minuten gebacken. Er wird auf ein Rost gestuerzt und nach dem Erkalten mit Puderzucker bestreut.

SPICE CAKE

Cream margarine, add sugar and one egg at a time and beat until fluffy. ::: Add all the spices and cocoa, blend well. Sift flour with baking powder and add alternately with the milk until well blended. Pour batter into a greased and floured ring mold or bread pan. ::: Bake at 375 F for 1 hour. Turn out on wire rack and cool. Dust with confectioners sugar. Delicious, if sliced and topped with sweetened whipped cream.

¾ cup margarine
1½ cups sugar
4 eggs
1 teaspoon vanilla
¼ teaspoon almond flavor
¼ teaspoon rum flavor
½ teaspoon salt
⅛ teaspoon nutmeg
⅛ teaspoon cloves
2 teaspoons cinnamon
5 tablespoons cocoa
3½ teaspoons baking powder
3 cups flour
¾ cup milk

MARBLE CAKE

Cream butter, add sugar, eggs and beat well. Add vanilla, rum and salt. Sift flour and baking powder, add alternately with milk. ::: Pour half of batter into greased and floured tube pan. To the rest of batter add cocoa, sugar and milk, stir until well blended, pour into pan. Run a fork through batter twice around pan. ::: Bake at 375 F for about 65 minutes. When cooled, dust with confectioners' sugar.

1 cup butter or margarine
1¼ cups sugar
3 eggs
1 teaspoon vanilla
1½ teaspoons rum
¼ teaspoon salt
2¼ cups flour
2 teaspoons baking powder
½ cup milk
3 tablespoons cocoa
3 tablespoons sugar
2–3 tablespoons milk

DELIKATER TOPFENKUCHEN

3 Tassen Mehl
¼ Teeloeffel Soda
1 Tasse Butter
3 Tassen Zucker
5 Eier
1 Teeloeffel Vanille
1 Teeloeffel Zitronensaft
1 Tasse saure Sahne

Mehl und Soda werden miteinander gesiebt. ::: Die Butter wird schaumig geruehrt und den Zucker gibt man allmaehlich hinzu. Die Eier gibt man einzeln hinzu, dann Vanille und Zitronensaft. Das Ganze muss 10 Minuten lang geschlagen werden. Die saure Sahne und das Mehl werden dann vorsichtig unter den Teig gezogen. ::: Der Teig wird in eine gutgefettete und mit Mehl bestaeubte Napfkuchenform gefuellt und bei 325 F, 1½ Stunden lang gebacken. ::: Dieser Kuchen bedarf keiner Glasur, kann aber nach Belieben mit Schokoladenguss auf Seite 30 bestrichen werden.

SANDKUCHEN

¾ Tasse Butter oder Magarine
4 Eier, separiert
¾ Tasse Zucker
1 Teeloeffel Vanille
1 Teeloeffel Rum
1 Tasse Mehl
1 Teeloeffel Backpulver

Die Butter wird schaumig geruehrt. Man gibt Zucker und Eigelb hinzu und schlaegt es schaumig. Mehl und Backpulver werden zusammengesiebt und unter den Teig geruehrt. ::: Eiweiss wird zu steifem Schnee geschlagen und unter den Rest des Teiges gezogen. Der Teig wird in eine gefettete mit Waxpapier ausgelegte Kastenform gefuellt und bei 300 F, 50 Minuten gebacken. ::: Der Kuchen wird 15 Minuten auf einem Rost gekuehlt, dann aus der Form gestuerzt und vom Waxpapier befreit. ::: Der Sandkuchen wird mit Schokoladenguss bestrichen, Seite 30.

TORTENBODEN

½ Tasse Magarine
½ Tasse Zucker
1 Ei
½ Teeloeffel Vanille
1½ Tassen Mehl
1 Teeloeffel Backpulver
Etwas Milch

Man ruehrt die weiche Magarine schaumig, gibt Zucker, Ei und Vanille hinzu und schlaegt bis es schaeumt. Dann kommen Mehl und Backpulver hinzu. Der Teig wird gut verknetet. Man nimmt nur genug Milch um den Teig geschmeidig zu machen. Der Teig muss fest bleiben und wird dann 1 Stunde kaltgestellt. ::: Die Haelfte des Teiges, wird in einer 9″ grossen gefetteten und mit Mehl bestaeubten Springform ausgerollt. Aus dem Rest formt man 2 Rollen und legt sie an den Rand des Bodens und drueckt sie an dem Rande der Springform hoch. ::: Der Tortenboden wird dann bis zum Backen kaltgestellt.

DELICIOUS POUNDCAKE

Sift flour with soda. ::: Cream butter, add sugar gradually.
Add one egg at a time, vanilla and lemon juice, beat for 10
minutes. Stir in sour cream. Add flour and pour into a well-
greased and floured tube pan. ::: Bake at 325 F for 1½ hours.
::: This cake needs no frosting, but a chocolate frosting may
be used if so desired.

3 cups flour
¼ teaspoon baking soda
1 cup butter, very soft
3 cups sugar
5 eggs
1 teaspoon vanilla
1 teaspoon lemon juice
1 cup sour cream

SANDLOAF

Cream butter, add egg yolks, sugar, vanilla and rum, beat until
fluffy. Sift flour with baking powder and blend into batter. :::
Beat egg whites until stiff, fold into batter. Pour into a greased
and waxpaper-lined loafpan. ::: Bake at 300 F for 50 minutes.
Cool for 15 minutes, turn out on wire rack. Remove pan and
waxpaper and let cool completely. ::: Frost with Chocolate
Frosting on page 31.

¾ cup butter or margarine
4 eggs separated
¾ cup sugar
1 teaspoon vanilla
1 teaspoon rum
1 cup flour
1 teaspoon baking powder

COOKIE CRUST

Have margarine at room temperature, cream well. Add sugar,
egg and vanilla and beat until fluffy. Gradually add flour and
baking powder. Use milk sparingly and knead dough with
hands. Dough should be stiff, chill 1 hour. ::: Grease and flour
a 9″ spring form pan, line bottom of pan with ½ of the dough.
Divide rest of dough and shape into 2 rolls. Line sides of pan
with these, using hands to push dough up on sides. ::: Chill
until ready to use.

½ cup margarine
½ cup sugar
1 egg
½ teaspoon vanilla
1½ cups flour
1 teaspoon baking powder
Some milk

SUESSER HEFETEIG

2 Beutel trockene Hefe
¼ Tasse lauwarmes Wasser
¾ Tasse Milch
¾ Tasse Zucker
1 Teeloeffel Vanille
½ Teeloeffel Salz
½ Tasse Magarine
5 Tassen Mehl
2 Eier

Die Hefe wird in dem lauwarmen Wasser aufgeloesst. Die Milch erhitzt. In die Milch gibt man Zucker, Vanille, Salz und Magarine und laesst es kuehlen. ::: In die lauwarme Milch gibt man 3 Tassen Mehl und verruehrt gut. Hefe und Eier gibt man hinzu und schlaegt, bis der Teig Blasen wirft. Dann kommt der Rest des Mehls hinzu. Der Teig wird auf einer mit Mehl bestaeubten Flaeche verknetet, bis er geschmeidig ist. Dann kommt er in eine gefettete Schuessel, wird mit einem Handtuch bedeckt und laesst ihn am warmen Ort stehen, bis er etwa doppelt so hoch ist, ungefaehr 1½ Stunden. ::: Der Teig ist dann fertig zum Gebrauch von Gebaecken verschiedener Art. Rezepte finden Sie auf den folgenden Seiten. Nach der Zubereitung muss der Teig nochmals 1 Stunde gehen.

MOHNBROETCHEN

½ Rezept suesser Hefeteig, Seite 20
1 Ei und 1 Essloeffel Wasser, leicht geschlagen
Mohnsamen

Der Teig wird in 12 Portionen geteilt, man formt jedes Teil in ein Broetchen. Sie werden auf ein gefettetes Backblech gelegt, mit einem Handtuch bedeckt und man laesst sie an einem warmen Ort gehen, bis sie doppelt so hoch sind. ::: Die Broetchen werden bei 425 F ungefaehr 20 Minuten gebacken.

NAPFKUCHEN

⅔ Rezept suesser Hefeteig, Seite 20
¾ Tasse Rosinen
¼ Tasse Orangeat
¼ Tasse Zitronat
½ Tasse gehackte Mandeln
Schale einer geriebenen Zitrone

Orangat und Zitronat werden kleingeschnitten. Der Teig kommt in eine grosse Schuessel, Rosinen, Orangat, Zitronat, Mandeln und Zitronenschale, werden mit dem Teig verknetet. Der Teig kommt in eine gefettete Napfkuchenform, wird mit einem Handtuch bedeckt und muss an einem warmen Ort 1½ Stunden gehen. ::: Der Napfkuchen wird bei 350 F, 35–40 Minuten gebacken. Nach dem Auskuehlen wird er mit Puderzucker bestreut.

BASIC SWEET DOUGH

Soften yeast in lukewarm water. Scald milk, add sugar, vanilla, salt and margarine and let cool to lukewarm. ::: To this milk mixture add 3 cups flour and stir well. Add yeast and eggs, beat until bubbles appear. Add remaining flour, knead on floured surface until satiny. Put into large greased bowl, cover with a clean towel and let rise in warm place until double, about 1½ hours. ::: Shape into cakes or sweet rolls of various types. Recipes are on the following pages. ::: Let rise again for the time indicated and bake.

½ ounce active dry yeast
¼ cup lukewarm water
¾ cup milk
¾ cup sugar
1 teaspoon vanilla
½ teaspoon salt
½ cup margarine
5 cups flour
2 eggs

POPPY SEED ROLLS

Divide dough into 12 portions and shape into oblong rolls. Arrange on greased baking sheet, cover and let rise until double. ::: Brush with egg and water mixture and sprinkle with poppy seeds. ::: Bake at 425 F for 20 minutes.

½ recipe basic sweet dough, page 21
1 egg and 1 tablespoon water, slightly beaten
Poppy seeds

EASY FRUIT CAKE

Put dough into a large bowl, add raisins, orange peel, lemon peel, almonds and grated lemon rind. Knead well. Put dough into a greased tube or ring mold pan. Pat dough evenly into pan. Cover and let rise in warm place for 1½ hours. ::: Bake at 350 F for 35–40 minutes. Cool, sprinkle with confectioners' sugar.

⅔ recipe basic sweet dough, page 21
¾ cup raisins
¼ cup candied orange peel, chopped
¼ cup candied lemon peel, chopped
½ cup chopped almonds
1 grated lemon rind

PECAN SCHNECKEN

⅓ Rezept suesser Hefeteig, Seite 20
1 Tasse Pecans, gemahlen
½ Tasse Zucker
1 Teeloeffel Vanille
1 Eiweiss
3 Essloeffel Magarine
2 Essloeffel Buechsenmilch
3 Essloeffel Zucker

Die Fuellung wird folgendermassen hergestellt: Pecans, Zucker, Vanille und Eiweiss werden miteinander verruehrt. ::: Der Teig wird auf einer bemehlten Flaeche in ein Viereck von 9″ × 9″ ausgerollt, mit der Magarine bestrichen und die Fuellung wird gleichmaessig darauf verteilt. Der Rand wird mit Wasser angefeuchtet und dann aufgerollt. Die Enden werden etwas zusammengedrueckt. Die Rolle wird in 1″ breite Stuecke geschnitten. Die Schnecken werden auf ein gefettetes Backblech gelegt, ungefaehr 1″ auseinander, mit der Hand etwas flach gedrueckt, dann mit der Buechsenmilch bestrichen und mit Zucker bestreut. Mit einem Handtuch bedeckt, laesst man sie am warmen Ort 1 Stunde gehen. ::: Die Schnecken werden bei 350 F, 15 Minuten lang gebacken.

HASELNUSS KAFFEEKUCHEN

⅓ Rezept suesser Hefeteig, Seite 20
1 Tasse Haselnuesse, gemahlen
½ Tasse Zucker
1 Teeloeffel Mandel Aroma
1 Ei
3 Essloeffel Wasser
2 Essloeffel Buechsenmilch

Der Teig wird auf einer mit Mehl bestaeubten Flaeche in der Groesse von 12″ × 6″ ausgerollt. ::: Die Fuellung wird folgendermassen hergestellt: Haselnuesse, Zucker, Mandel Aroma, Ei und Wasser werden gut verruehrt, bis eine geschmeidige Masse entsteht, die auf den ausgerollten Teig gestrichen wird. Den Rand laesst man ungefaehr ½ inch frei. Der Rand wird mit etwas Wasser bestrichen. Der Teig wird von der langen Seite her eingerollt. Die Rolle wird etwas in die Laenge gezogen und auf ein gefettetes Backblech, in die Form eines U oder Kranzes gelegt und mit der Buechsenmilch bestrichen. Mit einer Schere schneidet man mehrere Kreuzschnitte in die Oberflaeche. ::: Der Kuchen wird bedeckt und muss am warmen Ort, 1 Stunde gehen, er wird bei 350 F, 35 Minuten gebacken.

PECAN ROLLS

Combine pecans, sugar, vanilla and egg white, blend well. ::: On floured surface roll dough into a square 9″ × 9″, brush with margarine and spread with the filling. Moisten rims of dough with a little water and roll up like a jelly roll, pinch edges firmly together. Slice into 1″ pieces and put on greased cookie sheet about 1″ apart. Brush with milk and lightly flatten rolls, sprinkle with sugar. Cover and let rise in warm place for 1 hour. ::: Bake at 350 F for about 15 minutes.

⅓ recipe basic sweet dough, page 21
1 cup finely ground pecans
½ cup sugar
1 teaspoon vanilla
1 egg white
3 tablespoons melted margarine
2 tablespoons canned milk
3 tablespoons sugar

FILBERT COFFEE CAKE

On floured surface roll dough into a rectangle 12″ × 6″. ::: Combine filberts, sugar, almond flavor, egg and water. Stir until smooth. Spread evenly onto rolled-out dough, bringing filling within ½ inch of edge. Moisten edge with a little water. Roll up from the widest part. Slightly stretch roll, pinch ends firmly together and place on greased baking sheet. Shape into a circle. With scissors make several cross incisions on top of cake. Brush with milk. ::: Cover and let rise in warm place for 1 hour. Bake at 350 F for 35 minutes.

⅓ recipe basic sweet dough, page 21
1 cup chopped filberts
½ cup sugar
1 teaspoon almond flavor
1 egg
3 tablespoons water
2 tablespoons canned milk

STOLLEN

1 Rezept suesser Hefeteig, Seite 20
1 Tasse Rosinen
½ Tasse gehackte Haselnuesse
½ Tasse gehackte Mandeln
½ Tasse Orangat, gewuerfelt
½ Tasse Zitronat, gewuerfelt
3 Essloeffel zerlassene Butter

Der Teig wird mit den 5 folgenden Zutaten gut verknetet und in 2 Haelften geteilt. ::: Jede Haelfte wird in ein Oval von 10″×8″ geformt und mit Butter bestrichen. Dann wird Jedes einmal uebergeklappt um einen Stollen zu formen und nochmals mit Butter bestrichen. Die beiden Stollen werden auf ein gefettetes Backblech gelegt, mit einem Handtuch bedeckt, sie muessen 1½ Stunden am warmen Ort gehen. ::: Man backt die Stollen bei 375 F, 35–40 Minuten. Nach dem Erkalten bestreut man sie mit Puderzucker.

ROSINEN ZOPF

⅓ Rezept suesser Hefeteig, Seite 20
1 Tasse Rosinen
2 Essloeffel Buechsenmilch

Der Teig und die Rosinen werden auf einer mit Mehl bestreuten Flaeche gut verknetet, dann in 3 Teile geschnitten. Aus jedem Teil formt man eine 9″ Rolle. ::: Die Rollen werden auf ein gefettetes Backblech gelegt, die Enden etwas angefeuchtet und zusammengedrueckt. Man flechtet einen Zopf daraus. Der Zopf wird mit der Milch bestrichen, mit einem Handtuch bedeckt. Er muss 1 Stunde am warmen Ort gehen. ::: Man backt ihn bei 350 F, 35 Minuten. Nach dem Erkalten, wird er mit Puderzucker bestreut.

PFLAUMENKUCHEN

⅓ Rezept suesser Hefeteig, Seite 20
2 Pfund frische Pflaumen
½ Tasse Zucker

Der Teig wird auf dem Boden einer gefetteten 10″ Springform ausgerollt. An den Seiten wird der Teig etwas hochgedrueckt, damit ein Rand entsteht. ::: Die Pflaumen werden gewaschen und in 4 Teile geschnitten und auf den Teig gedrueckt, sodass sie in Reihen zu stehen kommen. Der Kuchen wird mit einem Handtuch bedeckt und man laesst ihn an einem warmen Ort 1 Stunde gehen. ::: Er wird bei 350 F, 25 Minuten gebacken. Der noch heisse Pflaumenkuchen wird mit dem Zucker bestreut, man laesst ihn dann abkuehlen.

STOLLEN

Combine dough with following 5 ingredients and knead well. Divide dough into 2 portions. ::: Shape each into an oval about 10″ × 8″, brush with butter, fold each over once the long way to form a Stollen. Brush again with butter. Place on greased baking sheet and let rise for 1½ hours. ::: Bake at 375 F for 35–40 minutes. Cool and dust with confectioners' sugar.

1 recipe basic sweet dough, page 21
1 cup raisins
½ cup chopped filberts
½ cup chopped almonds
½ cup candied orange peel, chopped
½ cup candied lemon peel, chopped
3 tablespoons melted butter

RAISIN BRAID

On floured surface knead raisins into dough. Cut into 3 pieces. Out of each form a 9″ roll. ::: Put rolls side by side onto a greased baking sheet. Carefully braid. Moisten ends and pinch firmly together. Brush with milk. Cover and let rise in warm place for 1 hour. ::: Bake at 350 F for 35 minutes. Place on wire rack to cool. Sprinkle with confectioners' sugar.

⅓ recipe basic sweet dough, page 21
1 cup raisins
2 tablespoons canned milk

PURPLE PLUM COFFEE CAKE

Pat dough into bottom of 10″ spring form pan, bring dough up on sides for 1″. ::: Wash plums, cut into quarters lengthwise, stick pieces into dough in rows, so each piece is standing up. Cover and let rise for 1 hour. ::: Bake at 350 F for 25 minutes. While still hot sprinkle with the ½ cup sugar, let cool.

⅓ recipe basic sweet dough, page 21
2 pounds fresh purple plums
½ cup granulated sugar

APFELKUCHEN MIT KAESEBELAG

⅓ Rezept suesser Hefeteig, Seite 20
5 Backapfel
8 ounces Kremkaese
½ Tasse Zucker
1 Ei
3 Essloeffel Milch
2 Essloeffel Staerkemehl
2 Essloeffel Zitronensaft

Der Hefeteig wird auf den Boden einer 10″ grossen Springform angedrueckt, an den Seiten etwa 1″ hochgedrueckt. ::: Die Aepfel werden geschaelt, entkernt und in Scheiben geschnitten. Sie werden auf den Teig gelegt, sodass sie mit der glatten Seite nach oben zu stehen kommen. ::: Der weiche Kaese wird mit den restlichen 5 Zutaten verruehrt und etwas geschlagen. Der Kaesekrem wird auf die Aepfel gefuellt. ::: Der Kuchen muss am warmen Ort 1 Stunde gehen. Er wird bei 350 F, 30 Minuten gebacken und nach dem Erkalten mit Puderzucker bestreut.

BERLINER PFANNKUCHEN

⅓ Rezept suesser Hefeteig auf Seite 20
1 Eiweiss, geschlagen
⅓ Tasse beliebige Marmelade

Der Teig wird auf einem mit Mehl bestaeubtem Brett leicht geknetet und 3/8″ dick ausgerollt. Mit einem Glas, sticht man Plaetzchen aus. ::: Der Rand von Jedem wird mit etwas Eiweiss bestrichen. Die Haelfte der Plaetzchen werden in der Mitte mit 1 Teeloeffel Marmelade bedeckt, die restlichen Plaetzchen legt man darueber und drueckt die Raender etwas zusammen. Sie werden auf ein bemehltes Backblech gelegt, mit einem Handtuch bedeckt und an einen warmen Ort, gestellt bis sie doppelt so hoch sind. ::: Oel oder Schmalz werden in einem elektrischen Bratentopf auf 370 F erhitzt und einige der Pfannkuchen werden in das heisse Fett gegeben und 3–6 Minuten gebraten. Sie werden nur einmal gewendet. Man laesst sie auf Papierhandtuecher abtropfen und rollt sie in Zucker.

WEISSBROT PUDDING

1½ Tassen Dosenmilch
1½ Tassen Wasser
½ Tasse Zucker
1 Teeloeffel Mandel Aroma
3 Essloeffel Butter
8 Scheiben altes Weissbrot, gewuerfelt
1 Ei, geschlagen
½ Tasse Rosinen

Milch und Wasser laesst man kurz aufkochen. Man gibt Zucker, Mandelaroma und Butter hinzu. ::: Die Brotwuerfel kommen in eine gefettete Kastenform, darueber gibt man die Milch, Ei und Rosinen und verruehrt es gut. ::: Der Pudding wird bei 350 F, 70 Minuten gebacken. Der Pudding wird mit Vanille Pudding Sosse serviert, Seite 28.

APPLE CAKE WITH BAKED-ON CHEESE TOPPING

Pat dough into bottom of 10″ spring form pan, push dough up on sides of pan for 1″. ::: Peel, core and slice apples. Arrange slices on dough, standing smooth side up. ::: Have cream cheese at room temperature. Combine all 6 ingredients, beat well and pour over apples. ::: Let rise in warm place for 1 hour. ::: Bake at 350 F for 30 minutes, cool. Sprinkle with confectioners' sugar.

⅓ recipe, basic sweet dough, page 21
5 cooking apples
8 ounces cream cheese
½ cup sugar
1 egg
3 tablespoons milk
2 tablespoons cornstarch
2 tablespoons lemon juice

BERLIN FRIED CAKES

Knead dough on lightly-floured surface a few times. Roll to 3/8″ thickness. With medium large glass, dipped in flour, cut dough into rounds. ::: Brush edge of each round with egg white, place 1 teaspoon of jam in center of half of the rounds. Top with rest of rounds. Pinch edges firmly together. Place on floured cookie sheet, cover and let rise until double in size and light to the touch. ::: Heat oil or lard in deep fryer to 370 F. Place a few cakes into heated fat, fry on both sides until golden brown, turn only once. Frying time is from 3 to 6 minutes. Repeat with rest of rounds. Lift out of fat and drain on paper towels. Roll in granulated sugar.

⅓ recipe basic sweet dough, page 21
1 egg white slightly beaten
⅓ cup jam

BREAD PUDDING

Scald milk and water. To this add sugar, almond flavor and butter. ::: Grease a bread pan and put bread cubes into it, add milk mixture, egg and raisins and stir lightly. ::: Bake at 350 F for 70 minutes. Serve with cooled Pudding Sauce, page 29.

1½ cups canned milk
1½ cups water
½ cup sugar
1 teaspoon almond flavor
3 tablespoons butter
8 slices stale bread cubed
1 egg, beaten
½ cup raisins

WINDBEUTEL

½ Tasse Wasser
¼ cup Magarine
½ Tasse Mehl
¼ Teeloeffel Salz
2 Eier

Das Wasser wird in einem kleinen Topf zum Kochen gebracht. Die Magarine kommt dazu und wird mitgekocht, bis sie zerlaufen ist. Man dreht die Flamme klein, gibt Mehl und Salz hinzu und ruehrt, bis sich der Teig von den Seiten des Topfes loest und fest ist. Man nimmt den Topf von der Flamme und gibt die Eier einzeln hinzu, und schlaegt die Masse 2 Minuten. ::: Mit 2 nassen Teeloeffeln wird der Teig in kleine Haeufchen auf ein gefettetes und bemehltes Backblech gesetzt. Man formt 8 runde Haeufchen und setzt sie 2½ inches auseinander. ::: Sie werden bei 450 F, 12 Minuten gebacken, danach verringert man die Backhitze auf 375 F und backt sie nochmals 30 Minuten. Nach dem Erkalten, schneidet man Deckel ab und fuellt sie mit Rum Krem Fuellung Seite 30, oder mit gekochtem Pudding. Danach werden sie mit Puderzucker bestaeubt.

PUDDING SOSSE

½ Paeckchen Puddingpulver
1¾ Tassen Milch

Das Puddingpulver wird mit etwas von der Milch glattgeruehrt, dann gibt man den Rest der Milch hinzu und bringt die Masse zum Kochen. Die Sosse wird bei staendigem Ruehren 5 Minuten gekocht, dann abgekuehlt. Die Puddingsosse wird zu Brotpudding auf Seite 26 gereicht.

GUGELHOPF

1 Beutel trockene Hefe
1 Tasse lauwarme Milch
¾ Tasse Butter oder Magarine
¾ Tasse Zucker
3 Eier
1 Teeloeffel Vanille
1 Teeloeffel Zitronensaft
Schale einer geriebenen Zitrone
4 Tassen Mehl
¾ Tasse Rosinen
½ Tasse Zitronat, gewuerfelt
½ Tasse Mandeln, gehackt

Die Hefe wird in der lauwarmen Milch aufgeloest. ::: Butter und Zucker werden schaumig geruehrt. Die Eier kommen einzeln hinzu, dann Vanille, Zitronensaft und Rinde. Die Hefe und das Mehl werden abwechselnd hinzugegeben. Der Teig wird gut geruehrt. Dann hebt man Rosinen. Zitronat und die Haelfte der Mandeln unter den Teig und giesst ihn in eine gefettete und mit dem Rest der Mandeln ausgestreute Napfkuchenform. ::: Man stellt ihn an a einen warmen Ort, bedeckt mit einem Handtuch und laesst ihn gehen, bis der Teig doppelt oder fast am Rande der Form ist. ::: Er wird bei 375 F, 50 Minuten gebacken.

CREAM PUFFS

In small saucepan bring water to a boil, add margarine, boil until melted. Turn heat low, add flour and salt. Stir with spoon until dough leaves side of pan, which will take only a very little while. Remove from heat and beat in eggs one at a time, until each is well blended. Beat dough for 2 minutes. ::: With 2 wet spoons, heap dough onto a greased and lightly floured baking sheet. Make 8 heaping rounds, set 2½" apart. ::: Bake at 450 F for 12 minutes, reduce heat to 375 F and bake 30 minutes longer. Remove to wire rack and cool. ::: With sharp knife slice off tops of puffs and fill with Rum Cream Filling, page 31, or any prepared pudding filling. Dust with confectioners' sugar.

½ cup water
¼ cup margarine
½ cup flour
¼ teaspoon salt
2 eggs

PUDDING SAUCE

Combine pudding mix with a little of the milk, stir until smooth. Add rest of milk and bring to a boil. Stirring constantly, cook for 5 minutes, cool. Serve over Bread Pudding, page 27.

½ package Pudding Mix of any desired flavor
1¾ cups milk

GUGELHOPF

Soften yeast in lukewarm milk. ::: Cream butter and sugar, add eggs, one at a time. Stir in vanilla, lemon juice and rind. Add yeast alternately with flour, mixing well. Stir in raisins, citron and half of the chopped almonds. ::: Grease mold or angel food pan, sprinkle with rest of almonds and pour batter into pan. Cover and let rise in warm place until dough has risen to top of pan. About 1¼ hours. ::: Bake at 375 F for 50 minutes.

¼ ounce active dry yeast
1 cup milk, scalded
¾ cup butter or margarine
¾ cup sugar
3 eggs
1 teaspoon vanilla
1 teaspoon lemon juice
1 grated lemon rind
4 cups flour
¾ cup raisins
½ cup finely cut citron
½ cup chopped almonds

CAKES, PASTRIES AND DESSERTS ✦ 29

RUM GLASUR

1½ Tassen Puderzucker
1 Teeloeffel Rum Aroma
3–4 Essloeffel kochendes Wasser

Zucker, Rum und kochendes Wasser werden verruehrt, bis eine geschmeidige nicht zu duenne Masse entsteht.

RUM KREM FUELLUNG

2 Tassen Sahne zum Schlagen
½ Tasse Puderzucker
1 Teeloeffel Rum Aroma
½ Teeloeffel Vanille

Die Sahne wird mit dem Zucker, Rum Aroma und Vanille geschlagen, bis eine steife Masse entsteht. ::: Soll die Fuellung fuer die Bismarkeiche verwendet werden, dann wird die Haelfte der Fuellung auf die ausgekuehlte und auseinander gerollte Rolle gestrichen, wieder aufgerollt und mit dem Rest der Fuellung bestrichen. Man stellt die Bismarkeiche bis zum Verzehr kalt.

SCHOKOLADEN GUSS

1 Tasse Puderzucker
3 Essloeffel Kakao
2–3 Essloeffel kochendes Wasser
½ Teeloeffel Rum Aroma

Zucker und Kakao werden vermischt, man gibt das kochende Wasser hinzu und ruehrt, bis eine geschmeidige Masse entsteht, dann wird Rum Aroma untergeruehrt. Das Rezept reicht fuer einen Sandkuchen.

BUTTER KREM FUELLUNG

6 Essloeffel Butter oder Magarine
¾ Tasse Puderzucker
⅛ Teeloeffel Rum Aroma
1 Eigelb

Die Butter wird schaumig geruehrt und der Zucker wird allmaehlich hinzugegeben, dann Rum Aroma. Die Masse wird schaumig geschlagen, danach gibt man das Eigelb hinzu und schlaegt nochmals kurz durch. ::: Das Rezept ergibt ½ Tasse. ::: Soll es fuer die Bismarkeiche verwendet werden, dann verdreifacht man das Rezept. Die Haelfte davon wird auf die gut ausgekuehlte Rolle gestrichen, die dann wieder zusammengerollt und mit dem Rest des Butterkrems verziert wird. Die Bismarkeiche soll moeglichst im Kuehlschrank aufbewahrt werden, da diese Fuellung bei sehr warmen Wetter zu weich wird.

RUM GLAZE

Combine sugar, rum and boiling water, stir until smooth. Glaze should not be too thin.

1½ cups confectioners sugar
1 teaspoon rum
3–4 tablespoons boiling water

RUM CREAM FILLING

Beat whipping cream with confectioners' sugar until stiff, add rum and vanilla and beat again. ::: If used for Bismark Log, unroll cake carefully and fill with half of the Rum Cream Filling, reroll. Frost with remaining frosting. Chill until serving time.

2 cups whipping cream
½ cup confectioners' sugar
1 teaspoon rum
½ teaspoon vanilla

CHOCOLATE FROSTING

Combine sugar and cocoa, add boiling water and rum and mix well until smooth. This recipe will frost one cake layer or one sandloaf.

1 cup confectioners sugar
3 tablespoons cocoa
2–3 tablespoons boiling water
½ teaspoon rum

BUTTER CREAM FILLING OR FROSTING

Cream butter until fluffy, gradually add sugar and rum, beat well. Add egg yolk and beat until smooth. ::: Makes ½ cup. ::: For use in Bismark Log, triple the recipe. Carefully unroll cake, spread with half of the Butter Cream, re-roll. Frost with remaining Butter Cream. This cake should be kept under refrigeration, since the fillings tends to soften in warm weather.

6 tablespoons butter or margarine
¾ cup confectioners' sugar
⅛ teaspoon rum
1 egg yolk

KLEINGEBAECK

PFEFFERNUESSE

4 Tassen Mehl
1 Teeloeffel Backpulver
1 Essloeffel Zimt
1 Teeloeffel Nelken, gemahlen
1 Teeloeffel Muskat, gemahlen
1 Teeloeffel Cardamon
1 Teeloeffel Anisamen, gemahlen
¼ Teeloeffel schwarzer Pfeffer
1¼ Tasse Honig
2 Essloeffel Butter
2 Eier
¼ Tasse Orangat, gewuerfelt
¼ Tasse Zitronat, gewuerfelt
¼ Tasse Mandeln, gehackt

Die trockenen Zutaten werden zusammengesiebt. Honig und Butter werden etwas gewaermt. Man schlaegt die Eier in den Honig, gibt die gesiebten Zutaten, Zitronat, Orangat und Mandeln hinzu und verruehrt den Teig gut. Er wird ½ Stunde kaltgestellt. ::: Mit bemehlten Haenden formt man 1″ grosse Baelle aus dem Teig. Sie werden auf ein gefettetes Backblech gelegt und bei 350 F, 15 Minuten gebacken. ::: Nach dem Erkalten werden sie mit 1¾ Tasse Puderzucker, welches mit 2–3 Essloeffeln heissem Wasser verruehrt wird, bestrichen.

BUTTERGEBAECK

½ Tasse Schmalz
1 Tasse Butter
2 Tassen Zucker
5 Eigelb
1 Teeloeffel je Rum und Vanille Aroma
2 Tassen Mehl, gesiebt mit
3 Teeloeffel Backpulver
¼ Tasse Mandeln, gehackt

Schmalz und Butter werden schaumig geruehrt. Man gibt Zucker hinzu. Die Eigelbs werden einzeln unter den Teig geruehrt, dann Rum und Vanille. Mehl und Backpulver werden unter den Teig geknetet, dann die Mandeln. ::: Der Teig wird 25 Minuten kalt gestellt. ::: Er wird auf einer bemehlten Flaeche ¼ inch dick ausgerollt und in beliebige Formen ausgestochen. ::: Die Plaetzchen werden bei 400 F goldbraun gebacken.

COOKIES

PFEFFERNUESSE

Sift dry ingredients. ::: Heat honey and butter until lukewarm.
::: Beat in eggs. Add dry ingredients, lemon and orange peel
and almonds. Stir until blended. Refrigerate ½ hour. ::: With
floured hands shape dough into 1″ balls. Put on greased cookie
sheet. ::: Bake at 350 F for 15 minutes. Cool. ::: Frost with
1¾ cups confectioners' sugar, which has been blended with
2–3 tablespoons hot water.

4 cups flour
1 teaspoon baking powder
1 tablespoon cinnamon
1 teaspoon ground cloves
1 teaspoon ground nutmeg
1 teaspoon cardamon
1 teaspoon ground aniseed
¼ teaspoon black pepper
1¼ cup honey
2 tablespoons butter
2 eggs
¼ cup candied orange peel
¼ cup candied lemon peel
¼ cup chopped almonds

BUTTER COOKIES

Cream lard and butter until fluffy. Add sugar and egg yolks,
one at a time, cream well. With hands, knead in flour and baking powder, then almonds. ::: Chill for 25 minutes. ::: Roll
out on floured board, ¼″ thick and cut into desired shapes.
::: Bake at 400 F until golden brown.

½ cup lard
1 cup butter
2 cups sugar
5 egg yolks
1 teaspoon each rum, vanilla
2 cups flour, sifted with
3 teaspoons baking powder
¼ cup grated almonds

KOKOSNUSS MAKRONEN

5 Eiweiss
1 Tasse Zucker
1¼ Teeloeffel Mandel Aroma
1½ Tasse Kokosraspeln

Die Eiweisse werden zu steifem Schnee geschlagen. Zucker, Mandel Aroma und Kokosraspeln hebt man vorsichtig unter den Eierschnee. ::: Mit 2 Teeloeffeln werden kleine gerundete Teighaeufchen auf ein gefettetes Backblech gesetzt. ::: Die Makronen werden bei 275 F, 25–30 Minuten goldgelb gebacken.

SPRITZGEBAECK

2½ Tassen Mehl
1 Teeloeffel Backpulver
1 Tasse weiche Butter
¾ Tasse Zucker
4 Eigelb
1 Teeloeffel Vanille
½ Teeloeffel Mandel Aroma

Das Mehl wird mit dem Backpulver gesiebt. Die Butter wird schaumig geruehrt, der Zucker wird hinzugegeben und gut geruehrt. Man gibt die Eigelb einzeln hinzu, dann Vanille und Mandel Aroma. Danach gibt man das Mehl hinzu und ruehrt den Teig gut durch. ::: Der Teig kommt in eine Gebaeck-spritze und man spritzt verschiedene Formen auf ein ungefettetes Backblech. ::: Die Plaetzchen werden bei 375 F, 12 Minuten gebacken.

❖❖❖❖❖❖❖❖❖❖❖❖❖❖❖❖❖❖❖

COCONUT MACAROONS

Beat egg whites until stiff. Fold in sugar, almond flavor and coconut. ::: Drop by rounded teaspoons onto greased cookie sheet. ::: Bake at 275 F for about 25–30 minutes, until golden brown.

5 egg whites
1 cup sugar
1¼ teaspoons almond flavor
1½ cups shredded coconut

SPRITZ COOKIES

Sift flour with baking powder. ::: Cream butter, add sugar and cream well. Add egg yolks one at a time and vanilla and almond flavor. Beat well. Blend in flour and mix well. ::: Put dough into cookie press and shape cookies on ungreased cookie sheet. ::: Bake at 375 F for 12 minutes.

2½ cups flour
1 teaspoon baking powder
1 cup soft butter
¾ cup sugar
4 egg yolks
1 teaspoon vanilla
½ teaspoon almond flavor

GEFLUEGEL GERICHTE

GEBACKENES HUHN

2 kleine Brathuehner halbiert
½ Tasse aufgeloeste Magarine
Salz
Pfeffer

Die Huehner werden gewaschen und gut getrocknet, mit der Magarine bestrichen und auf ein Backblech gelegt und mit Salz und Pfeffer bestreut. Sie werden bei 400 F, 20 Minuten gebacken, dann gewendet, mit Magarine bestrichen und nochmals 30 Minuten gebacken. ::: Gebackenes Huhn kann zu Petersilien Kartoffel, Seite 76 und zu Gurkensalat, Seite 80 gereicht werden. ::: Das Rezept reicht fuer 4 Personen.

GEBRATENE GANS

1 Gans von ungefaehr 8 Pfund,
kochfertig
Salz
Gaenseklein Fuellung, Seite 38
Gaenseklein Sosse, Seite 42

Die Gans wird gewaschen und gut abgetrocknet. Sie wird von innen und aussen gesalzen, gefuellt mit Gaenseklein Fuellung. Die Keulen werden zusammen gebunden. Die Gans wird in eine flache Bratschale gelegt und zwar muss sie auf dem Ruecken liegen. Mit einer Gabel sticht man mehrere Male in die Fettpolster. Sie wird mit Aluminium Papier bedeckt und bei 325 F, etwa 3–3½ Stunden gebacken. Nach dem Backen wird die Fuellung entfernt und kommt in eine separate Schuessel. Ist die Gans sehr fett, dann backt man sie ohne Fuellung. Die Fuellung kann in einer Backschale mitgebacken werden. ::: Die Gans wird zu Rotkohl Seite 88, Kartoffelkloesse Seite 74 und zu Gaenseklein Sosse Seite 38 gereicht. ::: Das Rezept reicht fuer 6 Personen.

POULTRY DISHES

ROAST CHICKEN

Wash and dry fryers, brush with margarine all over, arrange halves on a baking pan. Sprinkle with salt and pepper. ::: Bake at 400 F for 20 minutes, turn chicken once and brush with margarine. Bake 30 minutes longer. Arrange on platter. ::: Serves **4**. ::: Serve with Parsley Boiled Potatoes and Cucumber Salad.

2 small fryers, cut into halves
½ cup melted margarine
Salt and pepper

ROAST GOOSE

Rinse Goose and dry well. Rub inside and outside with salt, stuff and close body openings. Tie legs together. ::: Put into shallow baking pan, prick with fork through fat layers. Cover with aluminium foil and bake at 325 F for 3–3½ hours. ::: When done, drumstick meat will be very soft to the touch. Transfer goose to a platter, remove stuffing and put into separate serving dish. If goose is very fat, do not stuff. Bake stuffing in a separate pan. ::: Make gravy. ::: Serves 6. ::: Serve with Red Cabbage and Potato Dumplings.

1 Goose about 8 pounds, ready for
  cooking
Giblet Stuffing, page 39
Giblet Gravy, page 43
Salt

GEBRATENE PUTE

1 Pute von ungefaehr 8–10 Pfund,
kochfertig
Celery Fuellung, Seite 42
Sosse Seite 42
¼ cup zerlassene Magarine

Die Pute wird gewaschen und gut abgetrocknet, dann mit der Celery Fuellung gefuellt. Sie wird in eine flache Bratschale gelegt und mit der Magarine bestrichen. Sie wird mit Aluminium Papier bedeckt und bei 325 F, ungefaehr 3–3½ Stunden gebacken. Die Pute wird waehrend des Backens oefters mit Magarine bestrichen. ::: 20 Minuten, ehe die Backzeit um ist, wird die Pute vom Aluminium Papier befreit, man laesst sie unbedeckt bis zum Ende der Backzeit schmoren. ::: Die Pute ist ausreichend fuer 6 Personen.

GAENSEKLEIN FUELLUNG

½ Tasse Butter oder Magarine
½ Tasse Zwiebeln, ghackt
½ Tasse Celery, gehackt
2 Essloeffel Petersilie gehackt
1 Teeloeffel Gefluegelgewuerz
½ Teeloeffel Salz
¼ Teeloeffel Pfeffer
½ Rezept Gaenseklein, Seite 42
7 Tassen Weissbrot gewuerfelt
½ Tasse Milch

Die Butter wird in einem grossen Topf zerlassen und man gibt die 6 folgenden Zutaten hinzu. Es wird gut durchgeruehrt und zugedeckt 12 Minuten schwach gekocht. Dann gibt man ½ Rezept Gaenseklein hinzu und kocht es nochmals 2 Minuten mit. ::: Die Brotwuerfel und die Milch werden zugegeben und die Masse wird gut vermengt. Die Fuellung wird dann in die Gans gegeben. ::: Fuellung fuer Huhn und Pute: Wird wie oben hergestellt, statt des Gaensekleins, nimmt man Herz, Magen und Leber von Huhn oder Pute.

HUEHNER FRIKASSEE

1 Suppenhuhn von ungefaehr 4–5
Pfund
6 Tassen kochendes Wasser
½ Tasse Karotte, kleingeschnitten
⅓ Tasse Zwiebel, gehackt
¼ Tasse Celery, kleingeschnitten
½ Pfund gefrorener Spargel
½ Tasse Pilze, gewuerfelt
2 Essloeffel Zitronensaft
1 Essloeffel Zucker
1 Ei, geschlagen
Salz

Das Huhn wird zerlegt, gewaschen und in einen grossen Kochtopf gelegt. Man giesst Wasser, Karotte, Zwiebel hinzu und laesst es zugedeckt garkochen. Celery, Spargel und Pilze werden zur Suppe gegeben und 20 Minuten lang leicht gekocht. ::: In einem kleinen Topf ruehrt man ¼ Tasse Mehl mit ½ Tasse kaltem Wasser an, gibt 1½ Tassen von der Huehnerbruehe hinzu und laesst es bei dauerndem Ruehren aufkochen. Dieses wird in das Huehnerfricassee gegeben. ::: Man gibt Zitronensaft, Zucker, Ei und Salz hinzu und schmeckt es ab. ::: Das Huehnerfricassee wird ueber Reis serviert. ::: Das Rezept reicht fuer 6 Personen.

ROAST TURKEY

Rinse and dry turkey. Stuff with Celery Stuffing. Place in shallow baking pan and brush with melted margarine, cover with foil and put into preheated oven of 325 F. Roasting time is about 30 minutes per pound, baste often. 20 minutes before roasting time is up, remove foil. ::: When turkey is done, remove to preheated platter, remove stuffing and place in separate serving dish. ::: Make Giblet Gravy. ::: Makes 6 servings.

8- to 10-pound turkey, ready for cooking
Celery Stuffing, page 43
Giblet Gravy, page 43
¼ cup melted margarine

GIBLET STUFFING

In large saucepan melt butter, add the 6 following ingredients, stir to blend. Cover and let simmer for 12 minutes. Add giblets, simmer 2 more minutes. Then add bread cubes and milk and toss well. Stuff bird.

½ cup butter or margarine
½ cup minced onion
½ cup chopped celery
2 tablespoons chopped parsley
1 teaspoon poultry seasoning
½ teaspoon salt
¼ teaspoon pepper
½ recipe Cooked Giblets, page 43
7 cups cubed bread
½ cup milk

CHICKEN FRICASSEE

Cut chicken into serving pieces, wash and put into a large kettle. Add boiling water, carrots, onions. Cover and simmer until tender. ::: Add celery, asparagus and mushrooms, simmer 20 minutes more. ::: In small saucepan combine ¼ cup flour and ½ cup cold water, stir well, let come to a boil. Remove from heat and stir into the chicken fricassee. ::: Add lemon juice, sugar, beaten egg and salt to taste, stir well. ::: Arrange over boiled white rice. ::: Makes 6 servings.

4- to 5-pound broiling chicken
6 cups boiling water
½ cup sliced carrots
⅓ cup minced onions
¼ cup celery, diced
½ pound frozen asparagus spears
½ cup sliced mushrooms
2 tablespoons lemon juice
1 tablespoon sugar
1 egg, slightly beaten
Salt

1 Bratenhuhn von ungefaehr 2½
Pfund
¾ Tasse Mehl
1½ Teeloeffel Salz
¼ Teeloeffel Pfeffer
⅔ Tasse Schmalz

Das Huhn wird in Stuecke zerlegt, gewaschen und gut abgetrocknet. Mehl, Salz und Pfeffer kommen in eine Tuete und werden gut durchgeschuettelt. Man legt die Huhnstuecke in die Tuete und schuettelt bis das Fleisch gut bemehlt ist. ::: Das Schmalz wird in einer grossen Bratpfanne erhitzt und die Huhnstuecke werden darin bei hoher Flamme auf beiden Seiten gut gebraeunt. Die Flamme wird auf klein gestellt und die Pfanne mit einem Deckel bedeckt. Man laesst das Huhn 40 Minuten schwach schmoren. Danach entfernt man den Deckel, dreht die Flamme ganz auf und laesst das Huhn 3 Minuten auf jeder Seite braeunen, bis es knusperig ist. ::: Das Rezept reicht fuer 4 Personen. ::: Man reicht es zu Petersilie Kartoffel, Seite 76, Blumenkohl in Butter, Seite 84, und Tomatensalat, Seite 80.

½ Pfund Huehnerleber, gehackt
¼ Tasse Zwiebel, gehackt
etwas Pfeffer
1 Essloeffel Butter
½ Teeloeffel Salz
5 Eier
2 Essloeffel Milch
1 Teeloeffel Salz
1 Essloeffel Butter

OMELET WITH HUEHNERLEBER FUELLUNG

Fuellung: Leber und Zwiebeln werden in der heissen Butter gebraeunt. Man gibt Salz und Pfeffer hinzu und schmort es 5 Minuten.

Omelet: Eier, Milch und Salz werden gut verschlagen. Die Butter wird in einer grossen Pfanne erhitzt, die Eier werden in die Pfanne gegeben. Man laesst sie bei kleiner Flamme braten, bis die Unterseite braun ist. Die Oberseite muss weich bleiben, aber gesetzt sein. Die Fuellung wird auf die Haelfte des Omelets gegeben und die andere Haelfte vorsichtig darueber geklappt. Das fertige Omelet wird auf eine Platte geschoben. ::: Das Rezept reicht fuer 2 Personen.

FRIED CHICKEN

Cut fryer into serving pieces. Wash and dry. Into a paper bag put flour, salt, pepper and shake well. Put chicken pieces into bag and shake until well coated. Heat lard in large skillet. Over high heat fry chicken pieces, until well browned on both sides. Reduce heat, cover with a lid and simmer for 40 minutes. Turn heat to high, remove lid and fry chicken for 3 minutes on each side. ::: Serve with Parsley Boiled Potatoes, page 77, Buttered Cauliflower, page 85, and Tomato Salad, page 81. ::: Makes 4 servings.

2½-pound fryer
¾ cup flour
1½ teaspoon salt
¼ teaspoon pepper
⅔ cup lard or bacon grease

OMELET WITH CHICKEN LIVER FILLING

Filling: Heat butter in small skillet, add liver and onions, fry until well browned, add salt and pepper and saute 5 minutes.

Omelet: Break eggs into bowl, add milk, salt and pepper and beat until blended. In large skillet heat butter, pour in egg mixture. Fry over medium heat until bottom is brown, top firm, but soft. Arrange Chicken liver filling over half of omelet. Loosen edges and carefully fold other half over. Slide onto plate. ::: Serves 2.

1 tablespoon butter
½ pound chicken livers, diced
¼ cup minced onion
Dash of pepper
½ teaspoon salt
5 eggs
2 tablespoons milk
1 teaspoon salt
1 tablespoon butter

CELERY FUELLUNG

Wird wie Gaenseklein Fuellung hergestellt. Statt ½ Tasse Celery, nimmt man 1 Tasse Celery und laesst, Herz, Magen und Leber aus.

GAENSEKLEIN SOSSE

1 Gaensemagen, Herz und Leber,
gehackt
2½ Tassen Wasser
⅓ Tasse Zwiebelscheiben
¼ Tasse Celery, gehackt
2 Boullionwuerfel
Salz und Pfeffer

Man gibt Herz, leber und Magen in einen kleinen Topf, giesst Wasser hinzu, dann Zwiebel und Celery und kocht es zugedeckt gar. Man hebt etwa die Haelfte des Gaensekleins, Zwiebeln und Celery aus der Bruehe und hebt es fuer die Gaenseklein Fuellung auf, Seite 38. ::: In die Bruehe gibt man die Boullionwuerfel und laesst es nochmals auf kochen. Die Sosse wird mit 1 Essloeffel Staerkemehl und 2 Essloeffel Wasser angebunden und mit Salz und Pfeffer abgeschmeckt. ::: Sosse fuer Gebratene Pute oder Huhn wird wie oben hergestellt. Statt des Gaenskleins, nimmt man Herz, magen und Leber von Pute oder Huhn.

CELERY STUFFING

Prepare as Giblet Stuffing, increase celery to 1 cup and leave out giblets.

GIBLET GRAVY

Put giblets into a small saucepan, add water, onions and celery. Cover and simmer until tender. ::: Remove half of giblets, onions and celery from broth and save for Giblet Stuffing page 39. To the broth add boullion cubes and let come to a boil. Thicken gravy with 1 tablespoon cornstarch, which has been blended with 2 tablespoons water. Add salt and pepper to taste.

Giblets (gizzard, heart and liver), chopped
2½ cups water
⅓ cup sliced onions
¼ cup celery, diced
2 boullion cubes
Salt and pepper to taste

WILD UND HASE

⅓ Tasse gewuerfelter Speck
1 Hase zerlegt von ungefaehr 2 Pfund
½ Tasse Zwiebeln gehackt
2 Essloeffel Mehl
1½ Tassen Wasser
½ Tasse Rotwein
1 Essloeffel Zucker
Salz und Pfeffer

Der Speck wird in einer grossen Pfanne leicht gebraeunt, man gibt das Fleisch und die Zwiebeln hinzu und laesst Beides gut braeunen. Ofters wenden. Man staeubt das Mehl darueber und ruehrt es mit durch und gibt das Wasser hinzu. Gut durchruehren, damit keine Klumpen entstehen. ::: Das Fleisch muss bedeckt 1 Stunde leicht kochen, oder bis es zart ist. ::: Danach gibt man Rotwein, und Zucker hinzu und schmeckt es mit Salz und Pfeffer ab. ::: Das Rezept reicht fuer 4 Personen. Der Hasenpfeffer wird ueber gekochten Nudeln serviert.

GEBACKENER HASE

1 zerlegter Hase von ungefaehr 2 Pfund
1½ Teeloeffel Salz
Pfeffer
½ Tasse Mehl
½ Tasse Speck, gewuerfelt
⅓ Tasse Zwiebeln, gehackt
2¼ Tassen heisses Wasser
½ Tasse saure Sahne
Salz und Pfeffer

Der gut gewaschene und abgetrocknete Hase wird mit Salz und Pfeffer bestreut und in dem Mehl gewendet. ::: Speck und Zwiebeln werden in einem Bratentopf etwas gebraeunt, dann aus dem Fett entfernt und fuer spaeter aufgehoben. ::: Der Hase wird in demselben Fett auf beiden Seiten gebraeunt. Das Wasser wird dazu gegossen, dan gibt man den gebraeunten Speck und Zwiebeln hinzu. Der Topf wird bedeckt und in den vorgeheizten Backofen von 350 F geschoben, und 1 Stunde geschmort. ::: Danach giesst man die sauere Sahne ueber das Fleisch und laesst bei offenem Topf nochmals 10 Minuten schmoren. ::: Die Sosse wird mit 1 Essloeffel Staerkemehl und 2 Essloeffel Wasser angebunden und mit Salz und Pfeffer abgeschmeckt. ::: Das Rezept reicht fuer 4 Personen.

44 ✦ WILD UND HASE

GAME AND RABBIT

HASENPFEFFER

Wash rabbit, dry well. ::: In large skillet fry bacon until lightly browned and add rabbit and onions to this. Brown well on both sides. Sprinkle with flour and stir. Add the water slowly, a little at a time, stirring constantly until blended. ::: Cover and simmer for about 1 hour or until meat is tender. ::: Add wine, sugar, and salt and pepper to taste. ::: Makes 4 servings. Serve over Boiled Noodles.

⅓ cup bacon cubed
2-pound rabbit, cut into serving pieces
½ cup onion chopped
2 tablespoons flour
2½ cups water
½ cup red wine
1 tablespoon sugar
Salt and pepper to taste

BAKED RABBIT

Wash and dry rabbit. Sprinkle with salt and pepper and roll in flour. ::: In Dutch oven or heavy skillet fry bacon and onions until lightly browned. Remove onions and bacon, set aside for later use. ::: Brown rabbit in same grease, evenly on both sides. Add water to meat, and already-browned onions and bacon. Cover and bake in oven at 350 F for 1 hour. ::: Pour sour cream over meat and bake uncovered for 10 more minutes. ::: Remove meat to platter. Add salt and pepper to gravy, bring to a boil. Blend 1 tablespoon cornstarch with 2 tablespoons water. Stir into boiling liquid, simmer for 3 minutes. ::: Makes 4 servings.

2-pound rabbit, cut into serving pieces
1½ teaspoons salt
Pepper
½ cup flour
½ cup bacon, chopped
⅓ cup onions, chopped
2¼ cups hot water
½ cup sour cream
Salt and pepper to taste

REH RAGOUT

2 Pfund junges Rehfleisch
2½ Tassen Wasser
1½ Teeloeffel Salz
¼ Teeloeffel Paprika
3 Nelken
2 Lorbeerblatt
5 Pfefferkoerner
½ Tasse Karotte in Scheiben
¼ Tasse Butter, ½ Tasse Zwiebeln
2 Essloeffel Mehl
2 Essloeffel Zitronensaft
2 Essloeffel Rotwein
1 Essloeffel Zucker

Das Fleisch wird in kleine Wuerfel geschnitten. Das Wasser bringt man in einem grossen Topf zum Kochen und gibt das Fleisch und die 6 folgenden Zutaten dem Wasser hinzu. Man laesst es zugedeckt langsam, 2 Stunden kochen. 2 Tassen der Bruehe werden abgemessen und fuer die Zubereitung der Sosse aufgehoben. ::: In einem seperaten Kochtopf wird die Butter erhitzt und die Zwiebeln werden darin hellgelb gebraten, das Mehl wird darueber gestaeubt und mitgebraeunt. Unter staendigem Ruehren gibt man die 2 Tassen Bruehe hinzu, laesst kurz aufkochen und gibt dieses dem Fleisch hinzu. Danach gibt man Zitronensaft, Rotwein und Zucker hinzu, ruehrt durch und laesst 10 Minuten leicht kochen. Es wird mit Salz und Pfeffer abgeschmeckt. ::: Das Rezept reicht fuer 4 Personen. ::: Das Rehragout wird ueber gekochten Reis serviert.

YOUNG DEER RAGOUT

Cut meat into cubes. In large saucepan bring water to a boil, add meat and following 6 ingredients, cover and cook slowly for about 2 hours. Pour off 2 cups of the broth and save for gravy. ::: In another pan heat butter, add onions and fry until golden brown, add flour, stir and let brown lightly. Add the 2 cups of broth to this, stirring constantly, while it thickens. Pour over meat. Stir in lemon juice, wine and sugar, simmer 10 minutes. Add salt and pepper to taste. ::: Makes 4 servings. ::: Serve over Boiled Rice.

2 pounds young deer meat
2½ cups water
1½ teaspoons salt
¼ teaspoon paprika
3 cloves
2 bay leaves
5 peppercorns
½ cup sliced carrots
¼ cup butter
½ cup onions, chopped
2 tablespoons flour
2 tablespoons lemon juice
2 tablespoons red wine
1 tablespoon sugar

RINDFLEISCH GERICHTE

RINDERFILLET MIT PILZE

4 Rinderfillets oder Tenderloin
Salz und Pfeffer
2 Essloeffel Butter
½ Tasse gehackte Zwiebeln
1 Tasse frische oder eingemachte ganze Pilze

Die Fillets werden mit Salz und Pfeffer bestreut und in der Butter, auf beiden Seiten gut gebraeunt. Man gibt die Zwiebeln hinzu und laesst sie 5 Minuten, bei kleiner Flamme mitschmoren. Die Zwiebeln werden dann auf das Fleisch gehoben, die Pilze darueber gegeben und das Ganze wird zugedeckt, 25 Minuten lang geschmort. ::: Das Rezept reicht fuer 4 Personen.

RINDERBRATEN MIT GEMUESE

5 Pfund Chuck Roast, oder Beliebiges Rindfleisch
4 Essloeffel Fett
1 Pfund geschaelte Karotten
½ Pfund halbierte Zwiebeln
3 Pfund Kartoffel, geschaelt und in Viertel geschnitten
1½ Pfund Weisskohl
Salz und Pfeffer
2½ Tassen heisses Wasser

Das Fett wird in einem grossen Schmortopf erhitzt und das Fleisch darin auf allen Seiten gut gebraeunt, dann mit Salz und Pfeffer bestreut. Man giesst 1 Tasse Wasser hinzu und laesst es zugedeckt schmoren, bis es fast gar ist. Die Schmorzeit dauert von 4 bis 5½ Stunden, die Laenge, haengt von der Qualitaet des Fleisches ab. ::: Danach gibt man Karotten und Zwiebeln zu dem Fleisch, dann das restliche Wasser und laesst es 20 Minuten leicht kochen. dann gibt man Kartoffeln und Weisskohl hinzu, bestreut es mit Salz und Pfeffer und kocht es nochmals 20 Minuten. ::: Das fertige Fleisch wird auf eine grosse Platte gehoben und das Gemuese wird rundherum gelegt. ::: Die Sosse stellt man her, indem man 1 Essloeffel Staerkemehl mit 3 Essloeffel Wasser anruehrt, dieses unter Ruehren in die kochende Fluessigkeit gibt. Die Sosse wird mit Salz und Pfeffer abgeschmeckt. ::: Das Rezept reicht fuer 6 Personen.

BEEF DISHES

BEEF FILLETS WITH MUSHROOMS

Sprinkle fillets with salt and pepper. ::: In large skillet heat butter and brown fillets on both sides. Push meat to one side of skillet, add onions, saute 5 minutes. Spoon onions over fillets. Pour mushrooms on top, cover and simmer for 25 minutes. ::: Makes 4 servings.

4 Beef fillets or tenderloins
Salt and pepper
2 tablespoons butter
½ cup chopped onions
1 cup fresh or canned whole mushrooms

BEEF ROAST WITH VEGETABLES

In Dutch oven or heavy skillet heat fat, add roast and brown well on all sides. After meat is well browned, sprinkle with salt and pepper, add 1 cup water, cover and simmer until meat is almost tender, which may take from 4 to 5½ hours, depending upon type of meat. Add carrots and onions and the remaining 1½ cups of water. Cook for 20 minutes, then add potatoes and cabbage and cook for 20 more minutes. ::: Remove roast to heated platter and arrange vegetables around it. ::: Make gravy by combining 1 tablespoon cornstarch with 3 tablespoons water and stir into boiling liquid, add salt and pepper to taste. ::: Makes 6 servings.

5-pound chuck roast, or any inexpensive cut of roast
4 tablespoons fat
1 pound whole pared carrots
½ pound onions, cut in halves
3 pounds potatoes, peeled and cut into fourths
1½ pounds white cabbage, cut into wedges
Salt and pepper
2½ cups hot water

RINDSROULADEN

2 Pfund Round Beef ¼" dick
Salz und Pfeffer
2 Teeloeffel Senf
1 Tasse Zwiebel, gehackt
2 Saure Gurken, gewuerfelt
⅓ Pfund Speck oder Bacon, gewuerfelt
3 Essloeffel Fett
1 Essloeffel Staerkemehl
2 Essloeffel Wasser
2 Tassen Wasser
Salz und Pfeffer

Das Fleisch wird in 4 Scheiben geschnitten ungefaehr 8" × 4" gross, etwas geklopft, mit Senf bestrichen und mit Salz und Pfeffer bestreut. Zwiebel, Gurken und Bacon kommen in eine Schuessel und werden gut vermengt. Auf jede Fleischscheibe wird ein Viertel der Zwiebelmischung gehaeuft. Das Fleisch wird zusammen gerollt und mit Faden umrollt. ::: Das Fett wird in einem Schmortopf erhitzt und die Fleischrollen werden darin gut von allen Seiten gebraeunt. Danach gibt man die 2 Tassen Wasser hinzu und laesst das Fleisch zugedeckt, 2 Stunden schwach kochen. ::: Das fertige Fleisch kommt auf eine Platte und die Sosse wird zum Aufkochen gebracht. Das Staerkemehl wird mit dem Wasser verruehrt und in die kochende Sosse gegeben, die dann mit Salz und Pfeffer abgeschmeckt wird. ::: Das Rezept reicht fuer 4 Personen. Zu den Rouladen reicht man Kartoffelbrei und Gruene Bohnen.

ROSENKOHL CASSEROLE

¼ Pfund Speck, Bacon, gewuerfelt
½ Tasse gehackte Zwiebeln
3 Tassen rohe Kartoffelscheiben
¾ Pfund Hackfleisch
2 Eier
Salz und Pfeffer
etwas Muskatnuss, gerieben
1 Essloeffel gehackte Petersilie
1 Pfund Rosenkohl
2 Tassen Rindfleischbruehe

Der Speck wird mit den Zwiebeln etwas gebraeunt. Der Boden einer Backschale wird mit einem Teil der Kartoffelscheiben ausgelegt. ::: In einer grossen Schuessel vermengt man Hackfleisch, Zwiebel, Speck und Eier. Der Teig wird mit Muskatnuss und Petersilie bestreut und mit Salz und Pfeffer abgeschmeckt. ::: Ein Teil des Fleischteiges wird ueber die Kartoffeln gegeben, darueber gibt man einen Teil des gewaschenen Rosenkohls. Das Ganze wird mehrere Male wiederholt, sodass mehre Schichten entstehen. Die Rindfleischbruehe wird darueber gegossen und die Backschale wird in den vorgeheizten Backofen geschoben und bei 375 F 1½ Stunde gebacken. ::: Das Rezept reicht fuer 4 Personen.

BEEF ROULADEN

Cut beef into 4 strips 8"×4", use meat pounder to flatten slightly. Sprinkle with salt and pepper, spread with mustard. In small bowl combine onions, pickles and bacon, toss well. Divide into 4 portions and place each onto a strip of meat. Roll up tightly and secure with string or skewers. In Dutch oven heat fat, add Rouladen and brown well on all sides. Add 2 cups water, cover and let simmer for 2 hours. ::: Make gravy by blending cornstarch with 2 tablespoons water and stir into boiling liquid. Simmer for 5 minutes, add salt and pepper to taste. ::: Serve with Mashed Potatoes and Green Beans. Makes 4 servings.

2 pounds round beef, ¼ inch thick
Salt and pepper
2 teaspoons mustard
1 cup minced onions
2 sour pickles, cubed
⅓ pound bacon, cubed
2 cups water
3 tablespoons fat
1 tablespoon cornstarch
2 tablespoons water
Salt and pepper

BRUSSELS SPROUTS CASSERROLE

Fry bacon and onions until lightly browned. Arrange part of potato slices in bottom of baking dish. ::: In large bowl combine ground beef, fried onions, bacon and eggs. Sprinkle with salt, pepper, nutmeg and parsley and mix well. ::: Spread some of the meat mixture over potatoes, top with a layer of Brussels sprouts. Repeat in this order, potatoes, meat, Brussels sprouts. Pour beef broth over this and bake at 375 F for 1½ hours. ::: Makes 4 servings.

¼ pound bacon, cut into cubes
½ cup minced onions
3 cups raw, sliced potatoes
¾ pound ground beef
2 eggs
Salt and pepper
A little nutmeg
1 tablespoon parsley
1 pound Brussels sprouts
2 cups canned beef broth

GEBRATENE LEBER MIT ZWIEBELN

1½ Pfund Rinderleber oder 6
Scheiben
Salz und Pfeffer
Etwas Mehl
1 Tasse Zwiebelscheiben
4 Essloeffel Fett

Die Leber wird mit Salz und Pfeffer bestreut und in Mehl gewendet. Das Fett wird in einer grossen Pfanne erhitzt und die Leber darin auf beiden Seiten gut gebraeunt. Die Zwiebelscheiben werden rund um die Leber gelegt. Man laesst das Ganze 8 Minuten schmoren. Die Zwiebeln werden oefters gewendet. ::: Die Leber wird auf eine Platte gelegt und die Zwiebelscheiben gibt man darueber. ::: Das Rezept reicht fuer 6 Personen. Man reicht Gebratene Kartoffelplaetzchen und Radischensalat dazu.

RUMSTEAK ODER GEBRATENES SIRLOIN STEAK MIT ZWIEBEL

1 Sirloin Steak ¾" dick
1 Tasse Zwiebelscheiben
5 Essloeffel Butter
Salz und Pfeffer

Die Butter laesst man in einer grossen schweren Bratpfanne heiss werden und braeunt das Steak darin, bis es auf der einen Seite gut braun ist. Es wird gewendet und mit Salz und Pfeffer bestreut. Es wird bei kleiner Flamme langsam auf der anderen Seite geschmort. Man hebt es etwas an und legt die Zwiebelscheiben unter das Fleisch und laesst es 10 Minuten schmoren. Die insgesamte Bratenzeit ist ungefaehr 16 Minuten. ::: Wenn das Steak gar ist, legt man es auf eine Platte und bedeckt es mit den Zwiebelscheiben. ::: Das Rezept reicht fuer 2 Personen. Man reicht es zu Bratkartoffel, Gruenen Butterbohnen und Gruenem Salat.

FRIKADELLEN

2½ Tassen gekochtes Rindfleisch
oder Bratenreste
1 Tasse milde Wurstpastete Sausage
⅓ Tasse gehackte Zwiebel
⅔ Tasse Semmelmehl
1 Ei
1 Essloeffel gehackte Petersilie
¾ Teeloeffel Salz
3 Essloeffel Fett

Das Fleisch wird durch einen Wolf oder Fleischmaschine gedreht und mit den folgenden 6 Zutaten vermengt. Aus dem Teig formt man 6 Frikadellen, man stellt sie 1 Stunde kalt. ::: Das Fett wird in einer grossen Bratpfanne erhitzt und die Frikadellen werden langsam darin gebraeunt. Sie werden einmal gewendet, dann zugedeckt und 25 Minuten schwach geschmort. ::: Das Rezept reicht fuer 6 Personen. Die Frikadellen reicht man zu Petersilie Kartoffel und zu Gurkensalat.

FRIED LIVER WITH ONIONS

Wash and dry liver, remove tubes and skin. Sprinkle with salt and pepper and coat with flour. ::: In large skillet heat fat, add liver, and brown well on both sides. Arrange onion slices around liver and saute for 8 minutes. Arrange liver on heated platter and top with onions. ::: Serve with Fried Potato Cakes and Radish Salad. Makes 6 servings.

1½ pounds beef liver or 6 slices
Salt and pepper
Flour
1 cup sliced onions
4 tablespoons fat

RUMSTEAK OR FRIED SIRLOIN STEAK WITH ONIONS

In large heavy skillet heat butter until very hot. Arrange steak in butter and fry until well browned on one side. Sprinkle with salt and pepper and turn steak over. Reduce heat and slowly brown other side. With large spoon dip out butter and pour over steak, keeping it well basted. Sprinkle with salt and pepper. Lift steak with a fork and arrange onions on bottom of skillet, cover with the steak and saute for 10 minutes. ::: When steak is done, put on heated platter and spoon onions over steak. ::: Serve with Fried Potatoes, Buttered Green Beans, and Green Salad. Makes 2 servings.

2 pounds sirloin steak ¾" thick
1 cup sliced onions
5 tablespoons butter
Salt and pepper

FRIKADELLEN

Put beef through food chopper and mix with following 6 ingredients. Shape into 6 patties and chill for 1 hour. ::: Heat fat and brown Frikadellen slowly, turn only once. Cover and let simmer for 25 minutes. ::: Serve with Parsley Boiled Potatoes and Cucumber Salad. Makes 6 servings.

2½ cups cooked beef or leftover roast beef
1 cup mild sausage
⅓ cup minced onions
⅔ cup breadcrumbs
1 egg
1 tablespoon chopped parsley
¾ teaspoon salt
¼ cup fat

1 Pfund Round Beef in 1" grosse
Wuerfel
½ Pfund Schweinefleisch oder 2
Porkchops in Wuerfel
¾ Tasse gehackte Zwiebel
1½ Teeloeffel Paprika
2 Teeloeffel Salz
Pfeffer
3 Tassen Wasser
2 Essloeffel Staerkemehl
4 Essloeffel Wasser
3 Essloeffel Magarine

Die Magarine wird im Schmortopf erhitzt und die Fleisch-wuerfel darin gebraeunt. Die Zwiebeln gibt man hinzu und braeunt sie leicht an. Dann werden Paprika, Salz und Wasser zugegeben und bei zugedecktem Topf, 1½ Stunden geschmort. Das Staerkemehl wird mit den 4 Essloeffeln Wasser angeruehrt und in die kochende Masse geruehrt. Man laesst es 5 Minuten leicht kochen. Der Gulasch wird mit Pfeffer abgeschmeckt. ::: Man reicht ihn ueber gekochten Nudeln. Das Rezept reicht fuer 4 Personen.

HACKBRATEN

2 Pfund Hackfleisch
⅓ Tasse gehackte Zwiebel
2 Eier
5 Scheiben Weissbrot, eingeweicht
3 Essloeffel Tomatenmark
½ Tasse Paprikaschoten in kleine
Stuecke
2 Teeloeffel Salz
½ Teeloeffel Pfeffer
1 Paprikaschote in Scheiben
⅓ Tasse Tomatenmark

Das Hackfleisch wird mit den folgenden 7 Zutaten vermengt, man formt einen Fleischteig daraus und formt es in 2 gleiche Ovale. Sie werden auf ein Bratrost gelegt und bei 375 F, 40 Minuten gebacken. Danach legt man die Schotenscheiben ueber das Fleisch, begiesst es mit dem restlichen Tomatenmark und laesst es nochmals 20 Minuten backen. ::: Das Rezept reicht fuer 4 Personen.

RINDFLEISCH HASCHEE

1½ Tassen gekochtes kleingesch-
nittenes Rindfleisch, oder Braten-
reste
3 Tassen rohe, gewuerfelte Kartoffel
½ Tasse gehackte Zwiebel
2 Essloeffel gehackte Petersilie
Salz und Pfeffer
4 Essloeffel Dosenmilch
3 Essloeffel Fett

Das Fleisch wird in eine grosse Schuessel gelegt und mit den Kartoffeln, Zwiebeln und Petersilie gut vermengt. Man gibt Salz, Pfeffer und die Milch hinzu und ruehrt es gut durch. ::: Das Fett wird in einer grossen Bratpfanne erhitzt, und das Haschee gibt man in die Pfanne und drueckt es mit einem Loeffel glatt. Es wird bedeckt und bei kleiner Flamme 20 Minuten gekocht. Es wird einmal gewendet, sodass die ge-braeunte Seite nach oben kommt und es wird nochmals 20 Minuten gekocht. ::: Das Rezept reicht fuer 4 Personen. Man reicht Salat dazu.

GOULASH

In Dutch oven or heavy skillet heat margarine, add meat cubes and brown well, add onions and brown well, stir often. Add paprika, salt and water, cover and let simmer for 1½ hours. ::: Blend cornstarch with water and stir into boiling Goulash, cook for 5 minutes. Add pepper to taste. ::: Serve over Boiled Noodles. Makes 4 servings.

1 pound round beef, cut into 1" cubes
½ pound or 2 boneless pork chops, cubed
3 tablespoons margarine
¾ cup minced onions
1½ teaspoons paprika
2 teaspoons salt
3 cups water
2 tablespoons cornstarch
4 tablespoons water
Pepper to taste

MEATLOAF

In large bowl combine ground beef with following 7 ingredients, mix well and shape into 2 loaves. Put in baking dish and bake at 375 F for 40 minutes. Arrange pepper slices on loaves, baste with ketchup and bake 20 minutes longer. ::: Makes 4 servings.

2 pounds ground beef
⅓ cup chopped onions
2 eggs
5 slices bread, cubed and moistened with water
3 tablespoons ketchup
½ cup green peppers, chopped fine
2 teaspoons salt
½ teaspoon pepper
1 green pepper sliced in rings
⅓ cup ketchup

ROAST BEEF HASH

In large bowl, combine beef, potatoes, onions and parsley and toss well. Add salt pepper and milk, toss well. ::: In large skillet heat fat, pour in hash and spread over entire bottom of skillet. Cover and cook over low heat for about 20 minutes. Turn hash once. Cover and cook 20 more minutes. ::: Serve with a Salad. Makes 4 servings.

1½ cups leftover roast beef, chopped
3 cups raw diced potatoes
½ cup minced onions
2 tablespoons minced parsley
Salt and pepper
4 tablespoons canned milk
3 tablespoons fat

1½ Tassen Essig
1½ Tassen Wasser
2 Lorbeerblaetter
5 Pfefferkoerner
3 ganze Nelken
3 Pfund Rindfleisch
1 Teeloeffel Salz
1 Tasse Zwiebel in Scheiben
1½ Tassen warmes Wasser
½ Tasse Fett
1 Essloeffel Staerkemehl
2 Essloeffel Wasser

3 Tage zuvor, gibt man die ersten 5 Zutaten in eine grosse Glasschuessel, legt das Fleisch hinein, bestreut es mit Salz und legt die Zwiebel darueber. Man bedeckt es und laesst es 3 Tage lang im Kuehlschrank stehen. Es wird taeglich einmal gewendet. ::: Das Fett wird in einem grossen Schmortopf erhitzt und das genuegend marinierte und gut abgetropfte Fleisch wird in dem Fett von allen Seiten gut gebraeunt. ⅓ Tasse der Marinade wird dem Fleisch beigegeben, dann giesst man das warme Wasser hinzu und laesst es etwa 2 Stunden schmoren, oder bis es zart ist. Die Sosse wird mit dem mit Wasser angeruehrten Staerkemehl angebunden, dann mit Salz abgeschmeckt. Das Fleisch wird einige Male in der Sosse gewendet und auf einer Platte angerichtet und mit Gurkenscheiben verziert. ::: Das Rezept reicht fuer 4 Personen. Kartoffelkloesse und Rotkohl werden zu dem Sauerbraten gereicht.

SAUERKRAUT MIT WUERSTCHEN

½ Tasse Schmalz
¾ Tasse gehackte Zwiebel
2 Pfund Sauerkraut
1¼ Tasse Wasser
8 Wuerstchen

Das Schmalz wird in einem grossen Topf erhitzt, man gibt Zwiebel hinzu und braeunt sie hellgelb, dann gibt man das Sauerkraut hinein. Man laesst es zugedeckt 30 Minuten leicht kochen. Die Wuerstchen werden ueber das Sauerkraut gelegt und man laesst nochmals 15 Minuten leicht kochen. ::: Das Rezept reicht fuer 4 Personen. Man reicht Stampfkartoffel oder Gebratene Kartoffel dazu.

SAUERBRATEN

3 days before serving, combine first 5 ingredients in large bowl. Do not use plastic bowl. Set beef into this mixture, sprinkle with salt and minced onions, cover and refrigerate for 3 days. Turn meat over each day, so both sides will be marinated. ::: Lift meat out of marinade and dry well. In Dutch oven or heavy skillet heat fat, add meat and brown well on all sides. Strain ⅓ cup of the marinade and add to the meat, cover and simmer for 5 minutes. Add warm water and simmer for 2 hours or until meat is tender. ::: Blend cornstarch and water and stir until smooth, slowly stir into boiling liquid. Add salt to taste. Turn meat several times so it will be well coated with gravy. Then transfer meat to heated platter, slice and decorate with sliced pickles. ::: Serve with Potato Dumplings and Red Cabbage. Makes 4 servings.

1½ cups cider vinegar
1½ cups water
2 bay leaves
5 peppercorns
3 whole cloves
3 pounds rump beef
1 teaspoon salt
1 cup minced onions
⅓ cup fat
1½ cups warm water
1 tablespoon cornstarch
2 tablespoons water

SAUERKRAUT WITH FRANKFURTERS

In large sauce pan heat lard, add onions and fry until golden brown. Add sauerkraut, cover and simmer 5 minutes. ::: Add water and cook slowly for 30 minutes. Arrange frankfurters over sauerkraut, cover and simmer for 15 minutes. ::: Serve with Mashed or Fried Potatoes. Makes 4 servings.

½ cup lard
¾ cup onions, chopped
2 pounds sauerkraut
1¼ cups water
8 frankfurters

1 Kopf Weisskohl, ungefaehr 3
Pfund
1½ Pfund Hackfleisch
½ Tasse gehackte Zwiebel
2 Eier
½ Tasse Semmelmehl
2 Essloeffel Tomatenmark
2 Teeloeffel Salz
½ Teeloeffel Pfeffer
3 Essloeffel Magarine
2½ Tassen Wasser

Der Weisskohl wird mit kochendem Wasser uebergossen, man laesst ihn 30 Minuten ziehen. Dann wird er vorsichtig von den Blaettern befreit. 3 Blaetter fuer je eine Roulade, man legt 6 Portionen zurecht. ::: Das Hackfleisch wird mit den folgenden 6 Zutaten vermengt. Aus dem Teig formt man 6 Portionen und legt sie auf die vorbereiteten Blaetter, rollt sie zusammen und bindet sie mit Faden fest zu. ::: Das Fett wird in einem grossen Topf erhitzt und die Rouladen werden darin von allen Seiten gut gebraeunt, an den Rand giesst das Wasser und laesst sie zugedeckt 45 Minuten schwach kochen. ::: Die Sosse wird mit 2 Essloeffel Staerkemehl und 3 Essloeffel Wasser angebunden und mit Salz und Pfeffer abgeschmeckt. ::: Das Rezept reicht fuer 4 Personen.

GEFUELLTE PAPRIKASCHOTEN

6 gruene Paprikaschoten
1½ Pfund Hackfleisch
⅓ Tasse gehackte Zwiebel
1 Ei
½ Tasse Semmelmehl
2 Teeloeffel Salz
¼ Teeloeffel Pfeffer
¼ Teeloeffel Paprika
¼ Tasse Magarine
1½ Tassen Wasser
1 Tasse Tomatensosse
Salz und Pfeffer

Die gewaschenen Paprikaschoten werden am Stielende etwa ½ inch abgeschnitten, und das Kerngehaeuse entfernt. ::: Das Hackfleisch wird mit den folgenden 6 Zutaten zu einem Teige verarbeitet, die Schoten werden damit gefuellt. ::: Die Magarine wird in einem grossen Topf erhitzt und die Paprikaschoten werden darin auf der Unterseite leicht gebraeunt. Wasser und Tomatensosse giesst man hinzu und laesst es zugedeckt 50 Minuten leicht duensten. ::: Die Paprikaschoten werden auf eine Platte gelegt und die Sosse wird mit 1 Essloeffel Staerkemehl und 2 Essloeffeln Wasser angebunden, dann mit Salz und Pfeffer abgeschmeckt. ::: Das Rezept reicht fuer 6 Personen. Die Paprikaschoten werden ueber gekochten Reis gereicht.

STUFFED CABBAGE ROLLS

Immerse cabbage in a pan of very hot water, let soak for 30 minutes. Remove from water and gently separate leaves. There should be 18 leaves, divide into 6 portions, 3 leaves to a roll. ::: Combine ground beef with following 6 ingredients, mix well and divide into 6 portions. Place portions on prepared leaves, roll each tightly, making sure meat is well covered. Tie together with string. ::: In large skillet heat margarine, add cabbage rolls and fry until almost dark brown. Add 2½ cups water, cover and simmer 45 minutes. Add salt and pepper to taste. ::: Make gravy by combining 2 tablespoons cornstarch with 3 tablespoons water, stir into boiling liquid, simmer 5 minutes. ::: Makes 4–6 servings.

1 large cabbage, about 3 pounds
1½ pounds ground beef
½ cup minced onions
2 eggs
½ cup breadcrumbs
2 tablespoons ketchup
2 teaspoons salt
½ teaspoon pepper
3 tablespoons margarine
2½ cups water

STUFFED PEPPERS

Wash peppers, cut off ½ inch of stem end, and remove seeds. ::: Combine ground beef with the following 6 ingredients. Stuff pepper with this meat mixture. ::: In Dutch oven or heavy skillet heat margarine, add peppers standing upright, let brown lightly on bottom only. Add water and tomato sauce, cover and let simmer for 50 minutes. Add salt and pepper to taste. ::: Lift peppers out of liquid and arrange on platter. Make gravy by combining 1 tablespoon cornstarch with 2 tablespoons water, stir into boiling liquid. ::: Serve over Boiled White Rice. Makes 6 servings.

6 large green peppers
1½ pounds ground beef
⅓ cup minced onions
1 egg
½ cup breadcrumbs
2 teaspoons salt
¼ teaspoon pepper
¼ teaspoon paprika
¼ cup margarine
1½ cups water
1 cup tomato sauce
Salt and pepper

8 grosse feste Tomaten
1½ Pfund Hackfleisch
⅓ Tasse gehackte Zwiebeln
1 Ei
½ Tasse Semmelmehl
2 Teeloeffel Salz
¼ Teeloeffel Pfeffer
¼ Teeloeffel Paprika
¼ Tasse Magarine
1¼ Tasse Wasser
1 Tasse Tomatensosse
Salz und Pfeffer

Von den gewaschenen Tomaten, schneidet man die Deckel ab, entfernt das Kerngehaeuse und den Saft und hebt es fuer spaetere Verwendung auf. Das Hackfleisch wird mit den folgenden 6 Zutaten zu einem Teige verarbeitet und die Tomaten damit gefuellt. ::: Die Magarine wird in einem grossen Topf erhitzt und die Tomaten werden darin auf der Unterseite leicht gebraeunt. Man giesst den Saft und das Kerngehaeuse hinzu und laesst es bedeckt 10 Minuten leicht duensten. Dann gibt man Wasser, Tomatensosse etwas Salz und Pfeffer hinzu und laesst es nochmals 15 Minuten leicht kochen. ::: Die Tomaten werden auf eine Platte gelegt und die Sosse wird mit 1 Essloeffel Staerkemehl und 2 Essloeffeln Wasser angebunden. ::: Das Rezept reicht fuer 4–6 Personen. Die Gefuellten Tomaten werden ueber gekochten Spagetti serviert.

SUESS-SAURE NIEREN

2 Rindernieren
3 Essloeffel Fett
½ Tasse gehackte Zwiebeln
2–3 Essig
1 Essloeffel Zucker
⅛ Teeloeffel Pfeffer
2 Teeloeffel Salz
2 Tassen heisses Wasser
1 Essloeffel Staerkemehl
2 Essloeffel Wasser

Die Nieren werden von allem Fett und Roehren befreit und in kleine Scheiben geschnitten. Das Fett wird in einem mittelgrossen Topf erhitzt und die Nierenscheiben werden darin gut gebraeunt. Dann gibt man Zwiebeln hinzu und laesst sie kurz mitbraeunen. ::: Danach gibt man Essig, Zucker, Pfeffer, Salz und das heisse Wasser hinzu und laesst es zugedeckt 1½ Stunden lang leicht kochen. ::: Die Sosse wird mit dem Staerkemehl und den 2 Essloeffeln Wasser angebunden. ::: Das Rezept reicht fuer 4–6 Personen. Die Suess-sauren Nieren werden zu gekochten Nudeln und gruenem Salat gereicht.

STUFFED TOMATOES

Wash tomatoes and slice off top. Remove seeds and juices, save for later use. Combine ground beef with following 6 ingredients. Stuff tomatoes with the meat filling. ::: In Dutch oven or heavy skillet heat margarine, add tomatoes and stand them upright. Let brown lightly on bottom, reduce heat, add seeds and juices, cover and simmer for 10 minutes. Add water, tomato sauce, and salt and pepper to taste. Cover and let simmer 15–20 minutes more. ::: Arrange sutffed tomatoes on platter and make gravy by combining 1 tablespoon cornstarch with 2 tablespoons water. Stir into boiling liquid. ::: Serve over Boiled Spagetti. Makes 4–6 servings.

8 large firm tomatoes
1½ pounds ground beef
⅓ cup minced onions
1 egg
½ cup breadcrumbs
2 teaspoons salt
¼ teaspoon pepper
¼ teaspoon paprika
¼ cup margarine
1¼ cups water
1 cup tomato sauce
Salt and pepper

SWEET AND SOUR KIDNEYS

Free meat of all fat and gristle and cut into small slices. ::: In Dutch oven or heavy skillet heat fat, add kidney slices and brown well. Add onions, stir and brown lightly. Add vinegar, sugar, pepper, salt and hot water, cover and simmer for 1½ hours. ::: Thicken gravy with cornstarch, blended with 2 tablespoons water, stir into boiling kidneys. ::: Serve over boiled noodles and with a green salad. Makes 4–6 servings.

2 beef kidneys
3 tablespoons fat
½ cup minced onions
1 tablespoon vinegar
2–3 tablespoons sugar
⅛ teaspoon pepper
2 teaspoons salt
2 cups hot water
1 tablespoon cornstarch
2 tablespoons water

SUESS-SAURE KLOPSE

1 Pfund Hackfleisch
1 Ei
½ Tasse Semmelmehl
½ Tasse gehackte Zwiebeln
1½ Teeloeffel Salz
¼ Teeloeffel Pfeffer
2 Essloeffel gehackte Petersilie
1 Essloeffel Milch
2 Essloeffel Fett
2 Essloeffel Mehl
2 Tassen Wasser
2 Essloeffel Zitronensaft
2 Teeloeffel Zucker
Salz und Pfeffer

Das Hackfleisch wird mit den folgenden 7 Zutaten gut ver-mengt. Aus dem Teig formt man kleine Klopse. ::: Das Fett wird in einer Pfanne erhitzt, das Mehl wird darueber gestreut und man laesst es leicht braeunen. Unter staendigem Ruehren gibt man die 2 Tassen Wasser hinzu, Die Klopse werden vor-sichtig in die Sosse gegeben, man gibt Zitronensaft und Zucker hinzu und laesst es zugedeckt 25 Minuten leicht kochen. Die Sosse wird mit Salz und Pfeffer abgeschmeckt. ::: Das Rezept reicht fuer 4 Personen. Zu den Suess-sauren Klopsen reicht man Petersilie Kartoffel.

SCHWEIZER STEAKS

2 Pfund Round Steak
Salz und Pfeffer
¾ Tasse Mehl
3 Essloeffel Fett
2½ Tassen Wasser
2 Teeloeffel Fleisch Extrakt
Salz und Pfeffer
1 Essloeffel Staerkemehl
3 Essloeffel Wasser

Das Fleisch wird in 6 gleichgrosse Stuecke geschnitten und zu ½ inches dick geklopft. Es wird mit Salz und Pfeffer bestreut und im Mehl gewendet. Das Fett wird in einer grossen Pfanne erhitzt und die Steaks werden darin auf beiden Seiten ge-braeunt. Man giesst das Wasser hinzu und laesst es bedeckt 2 Stunden leicht kochen. ::: Wenn die Steaks gar sind, werden sie auf eine Platte gelegt. Man gibt Fleisch Extrakt, Salz und Pfeffer in die Sosse und bindet sie mit dem Staerkemehl und Wasser an. ::: Das Rezept reicht fuer 4–6 Personen. Zu den Schweizer Steaks reicht man Stampfkartoffel und Gruene Butterbohnen.

SWEET AND SOUR MEATBALLS

Combine ground beef with following 7 ingredients, mix well and shape into meatballs. ::: In large skillet heat fat, stir in flour and brown lightly. Stirring constantly, slowly add the 2 cups water. Drop in meatballs, add lemon juice and sugar, cover and let simmer for 25 minutes. Add salt and pepper to taste. ::: Serve over Parsley Boiled Potatoes. Makes 4 servings.

1 pound ground beef
1 egg
½ cup fine breadcrumbs
½ cup minced onions
1½ teaspoons salt
¼ teaspoon pepper
2 tablespoons chopped parsley
1 tablespoon milk
2 tablespoons fat
2 tablespoons flour
2 cups water
2 tablespoons lemon juice
2 teaspoons sugar
Salt and pepper to taste

SWISS STEAK

Cut meat into small steakettes and flatten each with a meat pounder to ½ inch thickness. Sprinkle with salt and pepper, coat with flour, rub in well on both sides. ::: In large skillet heat fat, brown each steakette on both sides until well browned. Add water, cover and simmer for 2 hour or until meat is tender. Add meat sauce, salt and pepper, stir well. Remove meat to platter. Blend cornstarch with water and stir into boiling liquid. ::: Serve with Mashed Potatoes and Buttered Green Beans. Makes 4–6 servings.

2 pounds round steak
Salt and pepper
¾ cup flour
3 tablespoons fat
2½ cups water
2 teaspoons thin meat sauce
Salt and pepper to taste
1 tablespoon cornstarch
3 tablespoons water

SCHWEINEFLEISCH

SCHINKENROLLEN

2 Pfund gekochter Schinken, in ⅓ inch dicke Scheiben
1 Ei, geschlagen mit
2 Essloeffel Milch
Semmelmehl
Salz und Pfeffer
3 Essloeffel Fett

Die Schinkenscheiben werden in Ei getaucht, dann in Semmel-mehl gerollt und mit Salz und Pfeffer bestreut. Das Fett wird in einer Pfanne erhitzt und die Schinkenscheiben werden darin goldbraun gebraten. 2 Minuten auf jeder Seite. Jede Scheibe wird aufgerollt und mit einem Zahnstocher zusammengehalten. ::: Das Rezept reicht fuer 4 Personen. Zu den Schinkenrollen reicht man Spargel mit Butter und Stampfkartoffel.

GEBRATENE SCHINKENKARTOFFEL

⅓ Tasse Magarine
½ Tasse gehackte Zwiebel
3 Pfund gekochte Kartoffel, abgezogen und in Scheiben
3 Eier, etwas geschlagen
1 Essloeffel Schnittlauch
Salz und Pfeffer
1½ Tasse gekochter Schinken, gewuerfelt

Die Zwiebeln werden im heissen Fett hellgelb gebraten, man gibt die Kartoffel hinzu und bratet sie bis sie knusperig sind. Oefters wenden. Die Eier, Schnittlauch, Salz und Pfeffer gibt man darueber und ruehrt gut durch. Man laesst kurze Zeit braten, bis die Eier festgeworden sind, danach ruehrt man den Schinken darunter. ::: Das Rezept reicht fuer 4–6 Personen. Zu den Schinkenkartoffel reicht man Rosenkohl in Butter und beliebigen Salat.

GESCHMORTE SCHWEINEKOTTLETS

8 magere Schweinekottlets
2 Essloeffel Fett
½ Tasse gehackte Zwiebeln
1 Teeloeffel Majoran
1½ Teeloeffel Salz
¼ Teeloeffel Pfeffer
2½ Tassen heisses Wasser
2 Essloeffel Fett
1 Teeloeffel Fleischextrakt

Das Fett wird in einer grossen Pfanne erhitzt und die Koteletts darin gut auf beiden Seiten gebraeunt. Man gibt Zwiebel hinzu und braeunt sie leicht mit. Dann gibt man Wasser, Majoran, Salz, Pfeffer und Fleischextrakt hinzu und laesst es bedeckt 45 Minuten leicht kochen. ::: Das Fleisch wird auf eine Platte gelegt und die Sosse wird mit 1 Essloeffel Staerkemehl und 2 Essloeffeln Wasser angebunden. Dann mit Salz und Pfeffer abgeschmeckt. ::: Das Rezept reicht fuer 4–6 Personen.

PORK DISHES

HAM ROLLS

Dip ham slices into egg mixture, then roll in breadcrumbs. Sprinkle with salt and pepper. ::: In large skillet heat fat and fry ham slices until golden brown, 2 minutes on each side. Roll each slice up and hold with toothpick. ::: Serve with Buttered Asparagus and Mashed Potatoes. Makes 4 servings.

2 pounds cooked ham, in ⅓" thick slices
1 egg slightly beaten with
2 tablespoons milk
Breadcrumbs
Salt and pepper
3 tablespoons fat

HAM FRIED POTATOES

In large skillet heat margarine, add onions and brown lightly, add potatoes and fry until brown, turn often. Pour beaten eggs, chives, salt and pepper over potatoes and fry until eggs are firm. Add ham and stir well. ::: Serve with Buttered Brussels Sprouts and salad of choice. Makes 4–6 servings.

⅓ cup margarine
½ cup onions, chopped
3 pounds boiled potatoes, peeled and sliced
3 eggs, beaten
1 tablespoon chives, finely cut
Salt and pepper to taste
1½ cups cooked ham, cubed

BRAISED PORK CHOPS

In large skillet heat fat and brown pork chops on both sides. Add onions and brown well. Reduce heat add water, marjoram, salt, pepper and meat sauce. Cover and cook slowly for 45 minutes. ::: Remove pork chops to platter. Blend 1 tablespoon cornstarch with 2 tablespoons water, stir into boiling liquid, add salt and pepper to taste. ::: Makes 4 servings.

8 lean pork chops
2 tablespoons fat
½ cup minced onions
1 teaspoon marjoram
1½ teaspoons salt
¼ teaspoon pepper
1 teaspoon bottled meat sauce
2½ cups hot water

SCHINKEN MIT SAUERKRAUT

½ Tasse Schmalz
¾ Tasse gehackte Zwiebel
2 Pfund Sauerkraut
1¼ Tasse Wasser
2 Pfund gekochter Schinken
Salz

Das Schmalz wird in einem grossen Topf erhitzt und die Zwiebeln darin goldgelb gebraten. Das Sauerkraut kommt hinzu und wird zugedeckt 5 Minuten leicht gekocht. Dann gibt man Wasser und Schinken hinzu und laesst es 45 Minuten schwach kochen. Es wird mit Salz abgeschmeckt. ::: Der Schinken wird in Scheiben geschnitten und auf eine Platte gelegt, das gut abgetropfte Sauerkraut wird rundherum um den Schinken gelegt. ::: Das Rezept reicht fuer 4 Personen. Zum Schinken mit Sauerkraut reicht man Bratkartoffel.

PORK CHOP SCHNITZEL

6 Magere Schweinekottlets
Salz Pfeffer und Paprika
2 Essloeffel Mehl
1 Ei und 3 Essloeffel Milch geschlagen
¾ Tasse feines Semmelmehl
⅓ Tasse Magarine
1 Zitrone in 6 Scheiben

Die Pork Chops werden etwas geklopft und mit Salz, Pfeffer und Paprika bestreut. Dann im Mehl gewendet, in das mit Milch verschlagene Ei getaucht und im Semmelmehl gewendet. ::: Sie werden in der heissen Magarine 8 Minuten auf jeder Seite gebraten. Die Pork Chop Schnitzel werden auf eine Platte gelegt und mit den Zitronenscheiben garniert. ::: Das Rezept reicht fuer 4–6 Personen. Zu den Pork Chop Schnitzel reicht man Bratkartoffel und Gruenen Salat.

SCHWEINEBRATEN

4 Pfund Center Loin Roast
2 Teeloeffel Salz
3 Essloeffel Fett
¾ Tasse gehackte Zwiebel
2 Tassen Wasser
1 Teeloeffel Majoran
Salz und Pfeffer
2 Essloeffel Staerkemehl
4 Essloeffel Wasser

Man reibt Salz in das Fleisch. Das Fett wird in einem grossen Schmortopf erhitzt und das Fleisch darin auf allen Seiten gut gebraeunt. Man gibt die Zwiebel hinzu und braeunt sie leicht mit. Das Wasser wird an den Rand des Fleisches gegossen, man laesst es bedeckt 3–3½ Stunden schmoren. Dann gibt man Majoran Salz und Pfeffer hinzu und laesst es nochmals 15 Minuten schmoren. ::: Der Schweinebraten wird in Scheiben zerlegt und auf einer Platte arrangiert. ::: Die Sosse bindet man mit 2 Essloeffel Staerkemehl und 4 Essloeffel Wasser an. ::: Das Rezept reicht fuer 6 Persoen. Zu dem Schweinebraten reicht man Kartoffelkloesse, Rotkohl und Gruenen Salat.

HAM WITH SAUERKRAUT

In Dutch oven or large saucepan heat lard, add onions and brown lightly. Add Sauerkraut, cover and simmer for 5 minutes. Add water and ham and cook over low heat for 45 minutes. Add salt to taste. ::: Lift sauerkraut from liquid and drain. Put ham on heated platter and slice, arrange sauerkraut around ham. ::: Serve with either Mashed or Fried Potatoes. Makes 4 servings.

½ cup lard
¾ cup minced onion
2 pounds sauerkraut
1¼ cups water
2 pounds canned or precooked ham
Salt

PORK CHOP SCHNITZEL

Flatten pork chops with a meat pounder just a little. Sprinkle with salt, pepper and paprika. Coat with flour, dip into milk and egg mixture and roll in breadcrumbs. ::: Fry in hot margarine over medium heat 8 minutes on each side. Turn only once. ::: Arrange on platter, top each pork chop with 1 lemon slice. ::: Serve with Fried Potatoes and Green Salad. Makes 4–6 servings.

6 lean pork chops
Salt, pepper and paprika
2 tablespoons flour
1 egg and 3 tablespoons milk beaten together
¾ cup fine breadcrumbs
⅓ cup margarine
1 lemon cut into 6 slices

PORK POT ROAST

Rub meat with 2 teaspoons salt. In Dutch oven heat fat and brown roast well on all sides. Add onions and brown well. Add 2 cups water, cover and cook slowly for 2–2½ hours. ::: Add marjoram, salt and pepper to taste and simmer 15 minutes more. ::: Slice roast and arrange on platter. ::: Blend cornstarch with 4 tablespoons water and stir into boiling liquid. ::: Serve with Potato Dumplings, Red Cabbage and Green Salad. Makes 6 servings.

4 pounds center loin roast
2 teaspoons salt
3 tablespoons fat
¾ cup minced onions
2 cups water
1 teaspoon marjoram
Salt and pepper to taste
2 tablespoons cornstarch
4 tablespoons water

SUPPEN UND EINTOPF

BOHNENSUPPE

2 Tassen beliebige getrocknete Bohnen
1½ Tassen gekochter Schinken, in Wuerfel
¾ Tasse gehackte Zwiebeln
½ Tasse Karotte, in Scheiben
6 Tassen Wasser
2 Boullionwuerfel
Salz und Pfeffer

Die gewaschnen Bohnen, Schinken, Zwiebeln, Karotte und Wasser werden in einem grossen Topf zum Kochen gebracht, Dann zugedeckt 3 Stunden schwach gekocht. Man gibt Boullionwuerfel zur Suppe und schmeckt sie mit Salaz und Pfeffer ab und laesst nochmals 15 Minuten leicht kochen. ::: Das Rezept reicht fuer 4–6 Personen.

KOHL EINTOPF

2 Pfund Weisskohl, zerschnitten
1 Tasse Zwiebel gehackt
6 Tassen Wasser
2 Pfund Rindfleisch, in Wuerfel
2 Essloeffel Butter
1½ Tassen rohe kleingeschnittene Kartoffel
1 Essloeffel Salz
1 Teeloeffel Kuemmel

Die Butter wird in einem grossen Topf erhitzt und die Zwiebeln darin leicht gebraeunt. Man giesst heisses Wasser hinzu, gibt das Fleisch hinzu und laesst es zugedeckt 2 Stunden schwach kochen. Danach gibt man Weisskohl, Kartoffel, Salz und Kuemmel hinzu und kocht es nochmals 30 Minuten. ::: Das Rezept reicht fuer 6 Personen.

GRUENE BOHNEN EINTOPF

2 Essloeffel Butter
¾ Tasse Zwiebeln gehackt
4 Tassen Wasser
2½ Pfund frische gruene Bohnen, gebrochen
1 Pfund roher Schinken in Wuerfel
1½ Pfund Kartoffel in Viertel geschnitten
Salz und Pfeffer

Die Butter wird in einem grossen Topf erhitzt, man gibt die Zwiebeln hinzu und braeunt sie leicht an. Dann giesst man das heisse Wasser hinzu, gibt Bohnen, Schinken und Kartoffel hinzu und laesst es zugedeckt 1½ Stunden leicht kochen. Der Eintopf wird mit Salz und Pfeffer abgeschmeckt. ::: Das Rezept reicht fuer 4 Personen.

SOUPS AND STEWS

BEAN SOUP

Put washed beans, ham, onions, carrots and water into a large kettle, bring to a boil. Cover and cook over low heat for 3 hours until beans are tender. Cooking time varies according to type of beans used. ::: Add boullion cubes, salt and pepper and cook 15 minutes more, stir well. ::: Makes 4–6 servings.

2 cups dried beans
1½ cups cubed ham
¾ cup diced onions
½ cup sliced carrots
6 cups water
2 boullion cubes
Salt and pepper

CABBAGE STEW

In large kettle heat butter, add onions and brown lightly. Add hot water, stewmeat, cover and boil gently for 2 hours. Add cabbage, potatoes, salt and caraway seeds. Cover and cook 30 minutes more. ::: Makes 6 servings.

2 tablespoons butter
1 cup minced onions
6 cups water
2 pounds stew meat, cubed
2 pounds white cabbage cut into
  small wedges
1½ cups diced raw potatoes
1 tablespoon salt
1 teaspoon caraway seeds

GREEN BEAN STEW

In large kettle heat butter, add onions and brown lightly. Add hot water, green beans, ham and potatoes, cover and boil gently for 1½ hours. Add salt and pepper to taste. ::: Makes 4 servings.

2 tablespoons butter
¾ cup chopped onions
4 cups water
2½ pounds fresh green beans, broken into small pieces
1 pound ham cut into cubes
1½ pounds white potatoes, cut into
  fourths
Salt and pepper

BLUMENKOHLSUPPE

1½–2 Pfund Blumenkohl, in Roeschen zerteilt
7 Tassen Wasser
3 Teeloeffel Salz
2 Boullionwuerfel
2 Essloeffel Butter
3 Essloeffel Gries
Salz

Der gewaschene und zerteilte Blumenkohl wird in einem grossen Topf mit dem Wasser zum Kochen gebracht. Man laesst ihn zugedeckt leicht kochen, bis er zart ist. Man gibt Boullion- wuerfel und Butter hinzu und bringt die Suppe zum Kochen, der Gries wird bei dauerndem Ruehren beigegeben. Man laesst 5 Minuten leicht kochen und schmeckt mit Salz ab. ::: Das Rezept reicht fuer 4 Personen.

HAMBURGERSUPPE

1 Pfund Hackfleisch
1 Tasse gehackte Zwiebel
1 Knolle gehackter Knoblauch
1½ Tassen kleine Makaroni
1 Tasse Tomatensuppe in Dosen
3 Essloeffel Tomatenmark
Salz und Pfeffer
7 Tassen Wasser

Hackfleisch, Zwiebel, Knoblauch und Wasser werden in einem grossen Topf zum Kochen gebracht, dann bedeckt und 1 Stunde leicht gekocht. Man gibt die Makaronis hinzu und kocht, bis sie gar sind. Tomatensuppe und Tomatenmark wer- den in die Suppe geruehrt und mit Salz und Pfeffer abgesch- meckt und nochmals kurz zum Aufkochen gebracht. ::: Das Rezept reicht fuer 4–6 Personen.

ERBSENSUPPE MIT SCHINKEN

1½ Tasse getrocknete, halbierte
Erbsen
1½ Tassen Schinken, gewuerfelt
7 Tassen Wasser
½ Tasse Karotte, in Scheiben
¾ Tasse gehackte Zwiebel
3 Boullionwuerfel
Salz und Pfeffer
2 Essloeffel Magarine
⅓ Tasse Sellerie, gewuerfelt
1 Essloeffel gehackte Petersilie

Die gewaschenen Erbsen, Schinken, Wasser, Karotte und die Haelfte der Zwiebeln, werden in einem grossen Topf zum Kochen gebracht. Man laesst es zugedeckt 2½ Stunden schwach kochen. Die Boullionwuerfel werden in die Suppe gegeben und sie wird mit Salz und Pfeffer abgeschmeckt. ::: Sellerie, Petersilie und der Rest der Zwiebeln, werden in der Magarine leicht gebraeunt. Man gibt es in die Suppe, ruehrt gut durch und laesst es 10 Minuten leicht kochen. ::: Das Rezept reicht fuer 6–8 Personen.

CAULIFLOWER SOUP

Wash and separate cauliflower and put into a large kettle, add water and salt and bring to a boil. Cover and simmer until very tender. Add boullion cubes and margarine, bring to a boil, stir in cream of wheat, cook 5 minutes. Add salt to taste. ::: Makes 4–6 servings.

1 large head cauliflower, separated, into small flowerettes
7 cups water
3 teaspoons salt
2 boullion cubes
2 tablespoons butter or margarine
3 tablespoons Cream of Wheat
Salt to taste

HAMBURGER SOUP

In large kettle combine hamburger meat, onions, garlic and water, bring to a boil. Cover and cook over low heat for 1 hour. ::: Add macaroni and cook until done. Add tomato soup, ketchup, salt and pepper and serve. ::: Makes 4–6 servings.

1 pound hamburger or ground beef
1 cup minced onions
1 clove garlic, minced
7 cups water
1½ cups elbow macaroni
1 cup canned tomato soup
3 tablespoons ketchup
Salt and pepper to taste

SPLIT PEA SOUP WITH HAM

Put washed peas, ham, water, carrots and ½ of the minced onions into a large kettle, cover and gently boil for 2½ hours. Add boullion cubes, salt and pepper. ::: In small frying pan heat margarine, add celery, parsley and rest of onions, fry until onions are golden brown. Add this to the soup and boil gently for 10 minutes. ::: Makes 6–8 servings.

1½ cups dried split peas
1½ cups diced ham
7 cups water
½ cup sliced carrots
¾ cup minced onions
3 boullion cubes
Salt and pepper to taste
2 tablespoons margarine
⅓ cup diced celery
1 tablespoon minced parsley

RINDFLEISCH EINTOPF

1 Pfund Stewmeat, in Wuerfel
1 Tasse Karotte in Scheiben
1 Tasse gehackte Zwiebel
2½ Tassen Wasser
½ Pfund Kartoffel in Wuerfel
½ Pfund Weisskohl, geschnitten
2 Pfund frische oder eingemachte Tomaten
Salz und Pfeffer

Rindfleisch, Karotten und Zwiebel gibt man einen grossen Topf, giesst Wasser hinzu und bringt es zum Aufkochen und laesst es zugedeckt 2 Stunden schwach kochen. Dann gibt man Kartoffel, Weisskohl und Tomaten hinzu, laesst 15 Minuten leicht kochen und schmeckt mit Salz und Pfeffer ab. ::: Der Eintopf reicht fuer 4 Personen. Zum Rindfleisch Eintopf reicht man heisse Mohnbroetchen.

HUEHNER EINTOPF

1 Suppenhuhn von etwa 2½ Pfund
7 Tassen Wasser
2 Teeloeffel Salz
2 Essloeffel gehackte Petersilie
½ Tasse Karotte in Scheiben
⅓ Tasse Celery, kleingeschnitten
½ Tasse gehackte Zwiebel
½ Pfund gefrorene Erbsen
½ Pfund breite Nudeln

Man bringt Wasser und Salz zum Kochen. Das Huhn, Petersilie, Karotte, Celery und Zwiebel werden in das kochende Wasser gegeben und zugedeckt 3½ Stunden leicht gekocht. ::: Man entfernt das Huhn aus der Bruehe, und entfernt die Knochen. Das Fleisch wird kleingeschnitten und wieder in die Bruehe gegeben. Man gibt Erbsen und Nudeln in die Suppe und kocht es 15 Minuten. Die Suppe wird mit Salz abgeschmeckt. ::: Das Rezept reicht fuer 4–6 Personen.

LINSEN EINTOPF

1½ Tassen getrocknete Linsen
8 Tassen Wasser
1½ Tassen gekochter oder roher Schinken, gewuerfelt
¼ Tasse Celery, gewuerfelt
2 Teeloeffel Salz
1½ Tassen rohe gewuerfelte Kartoffel

Die Linsen werden gut gewaschen. Man schuettet sie in einen grossen Topf und giesst das Wasser darueber. Man laesst sie ueber Nacht weichen. Am naechsten Tag, bringt man die Linsen zum Kochen, gibt Schinken, Celery und Salz hinzu und laesst sie zugedeckt 3½ Stunden langsam weichkochen. Dann gibt man die Kartoffel hinzu und die Suppe wird nochmals 45 Minuten gekocht, dann mit Salz abgeschmeckt. ::: Das Rezept reicht fuer 6 Personen.

BEEF STEW

Put meat, carrots and onions into a large kettle, add water, cover and gently boil for 2 hours. Add potatoes and cabbage and cook 25 minutes more. Add tomatoes plus juices, let simmer 15 minutes and add salt and pepper to taste. ::: Serve with Poppy Seed Rolls. Makes 4 servings.

1 pound stew meat, cubed
1 cup sliced carrots
1 cup minced onions
2½ cups water
½ pound diced raw potatoes
½ pound white cabbage, shredded
2 pounds canned tomatoes
Salt and pepper

CHICKEN STEW

Wash chicken. In large kettle bring water and salt to a boil, add chicken, parsley, carrots, celery and onions to boiling water, cover and boil gently until meat is tender, about 3½ hours. Lift chicken out of broth, remove bones and cut meat into small cubes. Return meat to broth, bring to a boil. Add peas and noodles, cover and boil gently for 15 minutes. Add salt to taste. ::: Makes 4–6 servings.

2½ pounds boiling hen
7 cups water
2 teaspoons salt
2 tablespoons minced parsley
½ cup sliced carrots
⅓ cup diced celery
½ cup minced onions
½ pound frozen peas
½ pound wide nooales

LENTIL STEW

Wash lentils and put into a large kettle, add water and soak overnight. Next day, bring water and lentils to a boil, add ham, celery and salt. Cover and boil gently for 3½ hours or until lentils are almost tender. Add potatoes, cover and cook for 45 minutes more, add salt to taste. ::: Makes 6 servings.

1½ cups dried lentils
8 cups water
1½ cups diced ham
¼ cup diced celery
2 teaspoons salt
1½ cups diced raw white potatoes

KARTOFFEL GERICHTE

KARTOFFELKLOESSE

2 Tassen gekochte Kartoffel
2 Essloeffel Mehl
1 Essloeffel fluessiges Fett
1 Ei
½ Teeloeffel Salz
¼ Teeloeffel Muskatnuss, gerieben

Die Kartoffel werden in der Schale am Tage vorher gargekocht und sofort durch die Fleischmaschine gepresst, dann ueber Nacht kaltgestellt. ::: Am naechsten Tag werden die Kartoffel mit den restlichen Zutaten zu einem Teig verarbeitet. Daraus formt man 6 Kloesse. Ein grosser Topf wird zuer Haelfte mit Wasser gefuellt und zum Kochen gebracht, dann gibt man die Kloesse hinein und laesst sie 13 Minuten schwach kochen. Wenn die Kloesse gar sind, Kommen sie zur Oberflaeche. ::: Das Rezept reicht fuer 3 Personen. Die Kartoffelkloesse werden zu Sauerbraten und schmackhaften Sossen gereicht.

STAMPFKARTOFFEL ODER KARTOFFELBREI

4 Pfund Kartoffel
2 Tassen Wasser
2 Teeloeffel Salz
½ Tasse Magarine
1 Tasse Milch
Salz und Pfeffer

Die gewaschenen und geschaelten Kartoffel werden in Viertel geschnitten und kommen in einen grossen Topf. Man gibt Salz und Wasser ueber die Kartoffel und laesst sie zugedeckt gar-kochen. ::: Das Wasser wird abgegossen. Man gibt Magarine zu den Kartoffeln und stampft sie klein. Die Milch gibt man teilweise hinzu und schlaegt die Kartoffeln mit einer Gabel oder Mixer. Sie werden mit Salz und Pfeffer abgeschmeckt. ::: Das Rezept reicht fuer 4 Personen.

POTATO DISHES

POTATO DUMPLINGS

Boil potatoes a day ahead, rice and refrigerate. ::: Next day combine potatoes with rest of ingredients. Shape into 6 balls. Put balls into a large saucepan of boiling water, lower heat and let simmer for 13 minutes. Dumplings will rise to the top, when done. ::: Serve with Sauerbraten or any rich brown gravy. Makes 3 servings.

2 cups cooked, riced potatoes
2 tablespoons flour
1 tablespoon melted shortening
1 egg beaten
½ teaspoon salt
¼ teaspoon nutmeg

MASHED POTATOES

Peel and wash potatoes, cut into quarters and put into a large sauce pan, add water and salt, cover and cook until tender. ::: Drain off water, add butter to potatoes and mash until fine, add milk a little at a time while beating with fork or mixer. Add salt and pepper to taste. ::: Makes 4 servings.

4 pounds white potatoes
2 cups water
2 teaspoons salt
½ cup margarine
1 cup milk
Salt and pepper

BRATKARTOFFEL

¼ *Tasse Magarine*
½ *Tasse gehackte Zwiebeln*
2 *Pfund kalte gekochte Kartoffel*
Salz und Pfeffer

Die Kartoffel koennen am Tage vorher gekocht werden. Sie werden von der Schale befreit und in duenne Scheiben geschnitten. Die Magarine wird in einer grossen Bratpfanne erhitzt und die Zwiebeln darin leicht gebraeunt. Man gibt Kartoffel Salz und Pfeffer hinzu und bratet die Kartoffel goldbraun. Sie werden oefters gewendet. ::: Das Rezept reicht fuer 4 Personen.

GEBRATENE KARTOFFELPLAETZCHEN

5 *Tassen kalte Stampfkartoffel*
2 *Eier*
⅔ *Tasse Mehl*
Salz und Pfeffer
Semmelmehl
⅓ *Tasse Magarine*

Die Kartoffel werden mit den Eiern, Mehl, Salz und Pfeffer zu einem Teig verarbeitet, man formt daraus kleine Plaetzchen von 2 inches Durchmesser, sie werden in Semmel gewendet. Dann in der heissen Magarine auf beiden Seiten goldbraun gebraten. ::: Das Rezept reicht fuer 6 Personen.

KARTOFFEL PUFFER

4 *Pfund rohe Kartoffel, geschaelt und gerieben*
2 *Eier*
¼ *Tasse geriebene Zwiebeln*
½ *Tasse Mehl*
1 *Teeloeffel Salz*
½–¾ *Tasse Schmalz*

Von den geriebenen Kartoffeln, giesst man etwas von der Fluessigkeit ab, gibt Eier, Zwiebel, Mehl und Salz hinzu und ruehrt es gut durch. ::: Ein Teil des Fettes wird in einer grossen Pfanne stark erhitzt, man gibt den Teig Essloeffelweise in die Pfanne und drueckt die Puffer etwas flach und braeunt sie auf beiden Seiten knusperig. ::: Das Rezept reicht fuer 4 Personen.

PETERSILIEN KARTOFFEL

3 *Pfund Kartoffel*
2 *Tassen Wasser*
2 *Teeloeffel Salz*
3 *Essloeffel gehackte Petersilie*
¼ *Tasse Magarine*

Die gewaschenen und geschaelten Kartoffel werden in Viertel geschnitten. Man legt sie in einen grossen Topf, gibt Wasser und Salz hinzu und laesst sie langsam weichkochen. ungefaehr 25 Minuten. Man schuettet das Wasser ab, gibt Petersilie und Magarine zu den Kartoffeln und ruehrt es vorsichtig darunter. ::: Das Rezept reicht fuer 4–6 Personen.

FRIED POTATOES

Potatoes can be boiled the day before. Cut into thin slices. In large skillet heat margarine, add onions and fry until golden brown. Add potatoes, salt and pepper and fry in open skillet until golden brown, turn often. Makes 4 servings.

¼ cup margarine
½ cup minced onions
2 pounds cold boiled white potatoes, peeled
Salt and pepper

FRIED POTATO CAKES

Mix mashed potatoes with eggs, flour, salt and pepper. Shape into small flat cakes. Roll in breadcrumbs. ::: Fry in hot margarine until golden brown on both sides. ::: Makes 6 servings.

5 cups leftover mashed potatoes
2 eggs
⅔ cup flour
Salt and pepper
Breadcrumbs
⅓ cup margarine

POTATO PANCAKES

In large bowl combine grated potatoes with eggs, onions, flour and salt. Stir well. ::: In large skillet heat some of the lard until very hot, add potato mixture by heaping tablespoons, shape into cakes and flatten with spoon. Fry 4 cakes at a time. Fry until golden brown on both sides, adding lard as needed. ::: Makes 4 servings.

4 pounds white potatoes, peeled and grated
2 eggs
¼ cup grated onion
½ cup flour
1 teaspoon salt
½–⅔ cup lard

PARSLEY BOILED POTATOES

Peel potatoes, wash and cut each into quarters. Put potatoes into large sauce pan, add water and salt and gently boil until done, about 25 minutes. Pour off water, add parsley and melted margarine to potatoes and toss lightly. ::: Makes 4–6 servings.

3 pounds white potatoes
2 cups water
2 teaspoons salt
3 tablespoons chopped parsley
¼ cup melted margarine

SALATE

KARTOFFELSALAT

4 Pfund Kartoffel
4 weichgekochte Eier, gehackt
¼ Tasse gehackte Zwiebel
⅓ Tasse gewuerfelte Gurken
½ Tasse Mayonese
⅛ Teeloeffel Pfeffer
½ Teeloeffel Salz
2 Teeloeffel Meerettich
2 Teeloeffel Senf
2 Teeloeffel Zitronensaft
2 Teeloeffel Zucker

Die Kartoffel werden gargekocht, gekuehlt und von der Schale befreit. Sie werden in duenne Scheiben geschnitten und mit den restlichen Zutaten vermengt. Der Kartoffelsalat wird auf eine Platte gehaeuft und mit Petersilie garniert. ::: Das Rezept reicht fuer 6 Personen.

HEISSER KARTOFFELSALAT

Die Kartoffel werden gargekocht und sofort von der Schale befreit und in duenne Scheiben geschnitten und mit den Rest der oben angegebenen Zutaten vermengt.

HUEHNER SALAT

2 Tassen gekochtes Huhn, in Wuerfel
1 Tasse Celery, gewuerfelt
1 Essloeffel Zwiebeln gehackt
½ Teeloeffel Salz
⅓ Tasse Mayonaise

Die obrigen Zutaten werden gut vermischt. Der Huehnersalat kann als Hauptgericht gereicht werden, oder zu belegten Broten verwendet werden. ::: Das Rezept reicht fuei 4 Personen.

SALADS

POTATO SALAD

Cook potatoes until done, cool. Peel and slice potatoes into a large bowl. Slice eggs and add with rest of ingredients, toss well. Heap on platter and garnish with parsley. ::: Makes 6 servings.

4 pounds white potatoes
4 soft boiled eggs
1/4 cup chopped onions
1/3 cup diced pickles
1/2 cup mayonnaise
1/2 teaspoon salt
2 teaspoons horseradish
2 teaspoons mustard
2 teaspoons lemon juice
2 teaspoons sugar
1/8 teaspoon pepper

HOT POTATO SALAD

Peel and slice potatoes while still hot and proceed as above.

CHICKEN SALAD

Combine all 5 ingredients, mix well. Serve as main dish, or use for sandwich filling. ::: Makes 4 servings.

2 cups cooked chicken, diced
1 cup celery, diced
1 tablespoon onions, minced
1/2 teaspoon salt
1/3 cup mayonnaise

FLEISCHWURST SALAT

2 Tassen Fleischwurst, in feine
Streifen geschnitten
¼ Tasse gehackte Zwiebeln
½ Tasse Gurken, gewuerfelt
Mayonaise

Die ersten 3 Zutaten werden mit etwas Mayonaise vermengt. Der Fleischwurst Salat kann als Hauptgericht gereicht werden, oder zu belegten Broten verwendet werden. ::: Das Rezept reicht fuer 4 Personen.

EIER SALAT

8 hartgekochte Eier
2 Essloeffel gehacktes Schnittlauch
⅓ Tasse feingehackte Gurken
2 Teeloeffel Senf
etwas Mayonaise

Die ersten 4 Zutaten werden mit Mayonaise vermengt. Der Eier Salat kann als Hauptgericht gereicht werden, oder zu belegten Broten verwendet werden. ::: Das Rezept reicht fuer 4 Personen.

GURKEN SALAT

2 Gurken, ungefaehr je 8 inches
lang
2 Essloeffel Salatoel
3 Essloeffel Zitronensaft
1 Teeloeffel Salz
¼ Teeloeffel Pfeffer
1 Essloeffel Zucker
2 Teeloeffel gehackter Schnittlauch

Die Gurken werden geschaelt, gewaschen und in feine Scheiben geschnitten. In einem kleinem Glas verruehrt man Salatoel, Zitronensaft, Salz und Pfeffer und schlaegt es kurz mit einer Gabel. Die Gurken werden mit dem Zucker und Schnittlauch bestreut und vermischt. Dann giesst man die bereitete Salatsosse darueber und vermischt den Salat gut. ::: Das Rezept reicht fuer 4 Personen.

TOMATEN SALAT

2 Pfund feste Tomaten
⅔ Tasse gruene Zwiebeln, samt den
Halmen, feingeschnitten
½ Teeloeffel Salz
⅛ Teeloeffel Pfeffer
1 Essloeffel Salatoel
2 Essloeffel Essig

Die gewaschnen Tomaten werden in duenne Scheiben geschnitten und werden mit den Zwiebeln vermischt. In einem kleinem Glas verruehrt man Salz, Pfeffer, Salatoel und Essig und schlaegt es kurz mit einer Gabel. Die fertige Salatsosse wird ueber die Tomaten gegossen und gut vermischt. ::: Das Rezept reicht fuer 4 Personen.

BOLOGNA SALAD

Combine first 3 ingredients, add only enough mayonnaise to moisten. Serve as main dish, or use for sandwich filling. ::: Makes 4 servings.

2 cups bologna, cut into strips
¼ cup minced onions
½ cup dill pickles, chopped
Mayonnaise

EGG SALAD

Combine first 4 ingredients, add only enough mayonnaise to moisten. Serve as main dish or use for sandwich filling. ::: Makes 4 servings.

8 hard-cooked eggs
2 tablespoons chopped chives
⅓ cup dill pickles, chopped
2 teaspoons mustard
Mayonnaise

CUCUMBER SALAD

Peel cucumbers, wash and slice very thin. ::: In a small jar combine salad oil, lemon juice, salt, pepper and shake well. Sprinkle cucumbers with sugar and chives. Pour prepared dressing over cucumbers, toss well. ::: Makes 4 servings.

2 large cucumbers
2 tablespoons salad oil
3 tablespoons lemon juice
1 teaspoon salt
¼ teaspoon pepper
1 tablespoon sugar
2 teaspoons finely cut chives

TOMATO SALAD

Wash and slice tomatoes very thin. Put into a bowl and add green onions. In a jar combine salt, pepper, salad oil and vinegar and shake well. Pour over tomatoes and toss well. ::: Makes 4 servings.

2 pounds tomatoes
⅔ cup green onions and stalks finely cut
½ teaspoon salt
⅛ teaspoon pepper
1 tablespoon salad oil
2 tablespoons vinegar

ENDIVIENSALAT MIT TOMATEN

1 grosser Kopf Endivien
½ Tasse gehackte Zwiebel
1 Tasse Tomaten, gewuerfelt
Salz und Pfeffer
2 Teeloeffel Zucker
2 Essloeffel Salatoel
3 Essloeffel Essig

Der gewaschene Endivien wird in lange duenne Streifen geschnitten. Man gibt Zwiebel, Tomaten, Salz und Pfeffer hinzu und mischt gut durch. Dann gibt man Zucker, Salatoel, und Essig darueber und mischt nochmals gut durch. ::: Das Rezept reicht fuer 4 Personen.

RADIESCHEN SALAT

1½ Pfund Radieschen
1 Teeloeffel Salz
1 Essloeffel Salatoel
2 Essloeffel Essig
1 Essloeffel gehackter Schnittlauch

Die gewaschenen Radieschen werden in feine Scheiben geschnitten und mit Salz bestreut. Man gibt Salatoel, Essig und Schnittlauch ueber die Radieschen und vermischt es gut. ::: Das Rezept reicht fuer 4 Personen.

GRUENER SALAT

1–1½ Pfund Iceberg oder Blattsalat
¾ Tasse Gurken, in Scheiben
¾ Tasse gruene Zwiebeln, samt Halmen, kleingeschnitten
2 Essloeffel gehackte Petersilie
3 Scheiben ausgebratener Speck—
⅓ Tasse
2 Essloeffel warmes fluessiges Fett
4 Essloeffel Essig oder Zitronensaft
1 Essloeffel Zucker
¾ Teeloeffel Salz
⅛ Teeloeffel Pfeffer

Der Salat wird in kleine Stuecke gebrochen, dazu gibt man Gurkenscheiben, Zwiebel und Petersilie und vermischt gut. Dann stellt man die Salatsosse her.

Essig, Zucker, Salz und Pfeffer werden etwas verschlagen, man gibt das Fett hinzu und schlaegt bis es dickfluessig ist. Es wird ueber den Salat gegossen, man gibt den Speck darueber und vermischt es gut. ::: Das Rezept reicht fuer 4 Personen.

ENDIVE AND TOMATO SALAD

Wash endive, shred or cut into thin long strips, add onion, tomatoes, salt and pepper and toss well. Add sugar, salad oil and vinegar, and toss again. ::: Makes 4 servings.

1 large head endive
½ cup chopped onions
1 cup diced tomatoes
Salt and pepper
2 teaspoons sugar
2 tablespoons salad oil
3 tablespoons vinegar

RADISH SALAD

Clean radishes and slice very thin. Sprinkle with salt, add salad oil, vinegar and chives and toss well. ::: Makes 4 servings.

1½ pounds radishes
1 teaspoon salt
1 tablespoon salad oil
2 tablespoons vinegar
1 tablespoon finely cut chives

GREEN SALAD

Break lettuce into small pieces, put into a large bowl, add cucumbers, onions, and parsley and toss well.

Dressing: Fry bacon until crisp, break into small pieces and add to salad. Mix bacon grease, vinegar, sugar, salt and pepper together and beat with a fork until mixture is creamy. Pour over salad and toss well. ::: Makes 4 servings.

1–1½ pounds iceberg or leaf lettuce
¾ cup thinly sliced cucumbers
¾ cup sliced green onions, including stalks
2 tablespoons chopped parsley
3 slices bacon, about ⅓ cup
2 tablespoons bacon grease
4 tablespoons vinegar or lemon juice
1 tablespoon sugar
¾ teaspoon salt
⅛ teaspoon pepper

GEMUESE

BLUMENKOHL MIT BUTTER

1 Kopf Blumenkohl, etwa 2 Pfund
3 Tassen Wasser
1½ Teeloeffel Salz
⅛ Teeloeffel geriebene Muskatnuss
¼ Tasse Butter oder Magarine

Der Blumenkohl wird in kleine Roeschen geteilt, gewaschen und kommt in einen Topf, wird mit Wasser und Salz bedeckt. Man laesst ihn zugedeckt 15–20 Minuten leicht kochen. Die Magarine wird gebraeunt. Man nimmt den Blumenkohl aus dem Wasser, legt ihn in eine Schuessel, bestreut ihn mit Muskatnuss und giesst die heisse Magarine darueber. ::: Das Blumenkohlwasser und einige der Roeschen, kann man aufheben und spaeter zu Blumenkohlsuppe verwenden. ::: Das Rezept reicht fuer 4 Personen.

GRUENE BUTTERBOHNEN

2 Pfund frische gruene Bohnen
2 Tassen Wasser
1 Teeloeffel Salz
⅓ Tasse Magarine

Die von den Faeden befreiten und gewaschenen Bohnen werden in einen grossen Topf gelegt, man giesst Wasser und Salz hinzu und laesst sie zugedeckt etwa 35 Minuten leicht kochen. Die Magarine wird gebraeunt. Das Wasser wird von den Bohnen gegossen. Die Bohnen werden in eine Schuessel gegeben und mit der heissen Magarine begossen. ::: Das Rezept reicht fuer 4 Personen.

VEGETABLES

BUTTERED CAULIFLOWER

Divide cauliflower into rosettes, wash and put into a large sauce pan, add water and salt, cover and gently boil for 15–20 minutes. Lift cauliflower from liquid and put into serving dish, sprinkle with nutmeg. Fry margarine until golden brown and pour over cauliflower. ::: Save liquid and a few rosettes for Cauliflower Soup. ::: Makes 4 servings.

2 pounds cauliflower
3 cups water
1½ teaspoons salt
⅛ teaspoon grated nutmeg
¼ cup margarine

BUTTERED GREEN BEANS

Remove strings and ends from beans. Wash and put into a large sauce pan, add water and salt, cover and gently boil for 35 minutes or until tender. Drain beans and put into serving dish. Fry margarine until golden brown, pour over beans and serve. ::: Makes 4 servings.

2 pounds fresh green beans
2 cups water
1 teaspoon salt
⅓ cup margarine

SPARGEL MIT BUTTER

1½ Pfund gefrorener Spargel
⅔ Tasse Butter

Der Spargel wird nach angegebenen Anweisungen gekocht und abgegossen. Die Butter wird gebraeunt und ueber den Spargel gegossen. ::: Das Rezept reicht fuer 4 Personen.

ROSENKOHL IN BUTTER

1½ Pfund gefrorener Rosenkohl
¼ Tasse gehackte Zwiebel
¼ Tasse Butter oder Magarine
Salz und Pfeffer

Der Rosenkohl wird nach angegebenen Anweisungen gekocht und das Wasser abgegossen. Die Zwiebeln werden in der Butter hellgelb gebraten. Man gibt Rosenkohl, Salz und Pfeffer zu den Zwiebeln und ruehrt es einige Male durch. ::: Das Rezept reicht fuer 4 Personen.

GEHACKTER SPINAT IN BUTTER

1½ Pfund gefrorener Spinat, gehackt
¼ Tasse Magarine
¼ Tasse gehackte Zwiebel
Salz und Pfeffer

Der Spinat wird nach angegebenen Anweisungen gekocht und das Wasser abgegossen. Die Zwiebeln werden in der Magarine hellgelb gebraten. Man gibt Spinat, Salz und Pfeffer zu den Zwiebeln und ruehrt es einige Male durch. ::: Das Rezept reicht fuer 4 Personen.

WEISSKOHL IN BUTTER

2 Pfund Weisskohl zerkleinert
¼ Tasse Butter oder Magarine
½ Tasse Zwiebel gehackt
1 Teeloeffel Kuemmel
Salz und Pfeffer
¼ Tasse Wasser

Die Magarine wird in einem grossen Topf erhitzt und die Zwiebeln darin hellgelb gebraten. Man gibt Kohl, ½ Teeloeffel Salz, Kuemmel und Wasser hinzu und laesst es zugedeckt 20 Minuten lang kochen. Man gibt etwas Pfeffer hinzu und ruehrt einige Male um. ::: Das Rezept reicht fuer 4 Personen.

BUTTERED ASPARAGUS

Cook asparagus according to label instructions. Drain. Fry butter until golden brown and pour over asparagus. ::: Makes 4 servings.

1½ pounds frozen asparagus
⅔ cup butter

BUTTERED BRUSSELS SPROUTS

Cook Brussels sprouts according to label instructions, drain. In medium sauce pan heat margarine, add onions and fry until golden brown, pour over brussel sprouts and stir well. ::: Makes 4 servings.

1½ pounds frozen Brussels sprouts
¼ cup minced onions
¼ cup butter or margarine
Salt and pepper

BUTTERED CHOPPED SPINACH

Cook spinach according to label instructions, drain. In medium sauce pan heat margarine, add onions and fry until golden brown. Pour over spinach and stir well, add salt and pepper to taste. ::: Makes 4 servings.

1½ pounds frozen chopped spinach
¼ cup margarine
¼ cup minced onions
Salt and pepper

BUTTERED CABBAGE

Wash cabbage and cut into wedges. In large saucepan heat margarine, add onions and fry until lightly browned. Add cabbage, ½ teaspoon salt, caraway seeds and water, stir, cover and simmer for 20 minutes. Add a speck of pepper, stir and serve. ::: Makes 4 servings.

2 pounds white cabbage
¼ cup butter or margarine
½ cup minced onions
1 teaspoon caraway seeds
Salt and pepper
¼ cup water

GEBRATENE EIERPFLANZE

1 Eierpflanze von etwa 1 Pfund
Salz und Pfeffer
½ Tasse Dosenmilch
1 Tasse Mehl
½ Tasse Oel

Die geschaelte Eierpflanze wird in ¼ inch dicke Scheiben geschnitten, mit Salz und Pfeffer bestreut und in die Milch getaucht, danach im Mehl oefters gewendet. ::: Ein Teil des Oels wird in einer Pfanne stark erhitzt und die Scheiben darin auf beiden Seiten braungebraten. Man gibt Oel nach Gebrauch hinzu. ::: Das Rezept reicht fuer 4 Personen.

ROTKOHL

2 Pfund Rotkohl, feingeschnitten
½ Tasse Schmalz
¾ Tasse gehackte Zwiebel
½ Tasse Backaepfel, feingeschnit-
ten
5 ganze Nelken
3 Essloeffel Weinessig
1½ Tassen Wasser
½ Teeloeffel Salz
1 Essloeffel Staerkemehl
3 Essloeffel Wasser
1 Essloeffel Zucker

Das Schmalz wird in einem grossen Topf erhitzt und die Zwiebeln darin leicht gebraeunt. Kohl, Aepfel, Nelken und Essig werden hinzugegeben und zugedeckt 10 Minuten leicht geduenstet. Dann gibt man Wasser und Salz zum Kohl und laesst ihn 2 Stunden duensten. ::: Die Staerke wird mit dem Wasser angeruehrt und in die kochende Fluessigkeit geruehrt, dann gibt man Zucker hinzu und ruehrt es durch. ::: Das Rezept reicht fuer 4–6 Personen.

ESSIGGURKEN

25 kleine Gurken, 4–5 inches lang
½ Tasse Salz
1½ Pfund Perlzwiebeln, geschaelt
4 Lorbeerblaetter
1 Teeloeffel weisse Pfefferkoerner
1½ Teeloeffel Senfkoerner
1 Essloeffel Dill
5 Tassen Wasser
4½ Tassen Weinessig
1 Essloeffel Salz
2 Tassen Zucker

Die Gurken werden am Tage vorher gewaschen und mit dem Salz bestreut. Man laesst sie ueber Nacht stehen. ::: Am naechsten Tag trocknet man die Gurken ab. Sie werden in einen Steinkrug schichtenweise mit den Zwiebeln und Gewuerzen gelegt. In einen grossen Topf gibt man Wasser, Zucker und Essig und bringt es zum Kochen. Die heisse Fluessigkeit wird ueber die Gurken gegossen. Man nimmt ½ Tasse Senfkoerner, bindet sie in ein Tuch und legt den Beutel auf die Gurken. Wenn die Fluessigkeit erkaltet ist, bedeckt man den Steinkrug mit mehreren Bogen Saran-Wrap und bindet ihn fest zu, damit keine Luft an die Gurken kommt. ::: Der Steinkrug wird an einem kuehlen Ort aufgehoben. Die Gurken muessen 2–4 Wochen gaeren.

FRIED EGGPLANT

Peel eggplant and cut into ¼ inch round slices. Sprinkle each with salt and pepper, dip in milk, then in flour until well coated. ::: In large skillet heat a little oil and fry egg plant slices until brown on both sides. Fry a few at a time, adding oil as needed. ::: Makes 4 servings.

1 egg plant, about 1 pound
Salt and pepper
½ cup canned milk
1 cup flour
½ cup salad oil

RED CABBAGE

Wash and shred cabbage. In large sauce pan heat lard, add onions and fry until lightly browned. Add cabbage, apples, cloves and vinegar, cover and simmer for 10 minutes, add water and salt and simmer for 2 hours. ::: Blend cornstarch with water and stir into boiling cabbage, add sugar, stir and serve. ::: Makes 4–6 servings.

2 pounds red cabbage
½ cup lard
¾ cup minced onions
½ cup cooking apples diced
5 whole cloves
3 tablespoons wine vinegar
1½ cups water
½ teaspoon salt
1 tablespoon cornstarch
3 tablespoons water
1 tablespoon sugar

VINEGAR PICKLES

The day before wash cucumbers well, put into a large bowl, sprinkle with ½ cup salt and let stand overnight. ::: Next day dry cucumbers. In a large crock arrange layers of cucumbers with layers of onions and spices. In a large kettle put water, sugar and vinegar and bring to a boil. Pour the hot liquid over cucumbers. ::: Tie ½ cup mustard seeds in cheese cloth. Place over cucumbers. When liquid has cooled, cover crock with several layers of Saran Wrap, tie a cord around it to make it airtight. ::: Store in a cool place. It takes from 2–4 weeks before pickles are ready for use.

25 small cucumbers, about 4″–5″ long
½ cup salt
1½ pounds very small onions, peeled
4 bay leaves
1 teaspoon white peppercorns
1½ teaspoons mustard seed
1 tablespoon dill
5 cups water
4½ cups wine vinegar
1 tablespoon salt
2 cups sugar

ALKOHOLISCHE GETRAENKE

KNICKEBEIN

2 ounces Kognak
⅛ Teeloeffel Vanille
1 Eigelb
2 ounces Milch
2 Essloeffel Fruchsaft, Trauben, Orangen oder Kirschsaft
2 ounces sodawasser

In einem 8 ounce Glase gibt man Kognak, Vanille und Eigelb und schlaegt es mit einer Gabel, gibt Milch, Fruchtsaft und Sodawasser hinzu und ruehrt es gut durch und serviert es. ::: Das Rezept reicht fuer 1 Person.

GLUEHWEIN

4 Tassen Rotwein
1 Tasse Zucker
8 Nelken
¼ Teeloeffel Zimt

Rotwein, Zucker, Nelken und Zimt werden zum Aufkochen gebracht und zugedeckt 15 Minuten schwach gekocht. Der Gluehwein wird heiss serviert. ::: Das Rezept reicht fuer 4–6 Personen.

ERDBEER BOWLE

1 Pfund frische Erdbeeren, zer-schnitten
1 Tasse feiner Zucker
8 Tassen Weisswein, gekuehlt
4 Tassen weisser Sekt, gekuehlt

In eine Bowlenterrine gibt man Erdbeeren, Zucker und 2 Tassen des Weissweins, ruehrt es etwas durch und laesst es 1½ Stunden ziehen. Dann giesst man den Rest des Weissweines und den Sekt hinzu, ruehrt kurz durch und serviert die Bowle. ::: Das Rezept reicht fuer 12–16 Personen.

HEISSER RUM

1½ ounces Rum
1 Teeloeffel feiner Zucker
1 kleines Stueckchen Zimtstange
2 Nelken
4 ounces oder ½ Tasse kochendes Wasser

Man gibt Rum, Zucker, Zimtstange und Nelken in ein 6 ounce Glas und gibt kochendes Wasser hinzu. Es wird gut verruehrt und serviert. ::: Das Rezept reicht fuer 1 Person.

ALCOHOLIC BEVERAGES

KNICKEBEIN

In an 8-ounce glass combine cognac, vanilla and egg yolk and beat with a fork, add milk, fruit juice and soda, stir well and serve. ::: Makes 1 serving.

2 ounces cognac
⅛ teaspoon vanilla
1 egg yolk
2 ounces milk
2 tablespoons fruit juice, grape, orange or cherry juice
2 ounces soda

MULLED RED WINE

In a large sauce pan combine, red wine with sugar, cloves and cinnamon. Bring to a boil, cover and simmer for 15 minutes. Serve hot. ::: Makes 4–6 servings.

4 cups dry red wine
1 cup sugar
8 whole cloves
¼ teaspoon cinnamon

STRAWBERRY PUNCH

In a large punch bowl combine strawberries, sugar and 2 cups white wine, stir and let soak for 1½ hours. Add rest of wine and champagne, stir and serve. ::: Makes 12–16 servings.

1 pound fresh strawberries, sliced
1 cup granulated sugar
8 cups dry white table wine, chilled
4 cups white champagne, chilled

HOT RUM

Put rum, sugar, cinnamon and cloves into a 6 ounce glass and fill with boiling water, stir well and serve. ::: Makes 1 serving.

1½ ounces rum
1 teaspoon granulated sugar
Small piece stick cinnamon
2 cloves
4 ounces or ½ cup boiling water

INHALTSVERZEICHNISS

INDEX

4TH EDITION
KEYBOARDING/TYPEWRITING
INTRODUCTORY

Charles H. Duncan
Professor of Business Education
Eastern Michigan University

S. ElVon Warner
Head, Department of Information Management
University of Northern Iowa

Thomas E. Langford
President, Bay State Junior College
Boston, Massachusetts

Susie H. VanHuss
Professor of Management
University of South Carolina

Copyright © 1986
By SOUTH-WESTERN PUBLISHING CO.
Cincinnati, Ohio

ISBN: 0-538-14540-4

1 2 3 4 5 6 7 8 9 10 11 12 13 14 H 2 1 0 9 8 7 6 5

Printed in U.S.A.

ADULT AND CONTINUING EDUCATION SERIES • SOUTH-WESTERN PUBLISHING CO.

Published by

N54 **SOUTH-WESTERN PUBLISHING CO.**

CINCINNATI   WEST CHICAGO, IL   DALLAS   PELHAM MANOR, NY   LIVERMORE, CA

CONTENTS

LABORATORY MATERIALS

PREFACE

Introductory Keyboarding/Typewriting, 4th edition, is the latest revision of a series of learning materials that were first designed specifically for college students over fifty years ago. Since 1930, the various editions of the book have established a reputation for providing students with those skills and knowledges required for efficient operation of keyboard-activated equipment. In keeping with this tradition, the 4th edition aims specifically at helping students achieve the following personal and professional goals:

1 to operate keyboard-activated equipment rapidly and accurately;

2 to improve their written communication skills;

3 to learn to format rapidly and accurately the kinds of documents most often used in business, professional, and government offices;

4 to become acquainted with terminology, equipment, and procedures of modern offices.

ORGANIZATION

Introductory Keyboarding/Typewriting is divided into two levels and eleven sections of learning structured to correspond with student skill-growth patterns. Introductory Keyboarding/Typewriting introduces students to keyboarding and formatting techniques, teaches them to proofread and make corrections, and develops basic keystroking and accuracy skills.

Level One focuses on keyboard learning, technique development, basic skill development, control of manipulative operations, and formatting simple documents such as personal letters.

Level Two focuses on further developing basic skills, proofreading and correcting errors, and formatting of basic communications including letters, memos, reports, tables, and outlines.

SPECIAL FEATURES

Content. The scientifically structured lessons in Introductory Keyboarding/Typewriting are built on the findings of scholars who have researched the areas of keyboarding learning and application.

The lessons, therefore, have a sound psychological as well as topical base that leads to practical achievement.

Goals. To orient and motivate students, learning goals are stated at the beginning of each section of lessons. Intermediate goals are stated periodically throughout the sections to identify purpose of practice, to indicate how to practice, and to identify expected outcomes.

Skill building. Supplemental skill-building sections are interspersed among the sections. Instructors may use these activities in the order of occurrence, group them for intensive emphasis, or select from them to tailor instruction to individual student needs.

Measurement. Portions of lessons that focus on measurement of achievement of basic skill and problem typing are included at the end of most of the sections. In addition, the last section focuses on measurement of achievement of basic and production skills.

Controlled copy. Basic skill-building and measurement paragraph copy is triple-controlled to insure uniformity of difficulty. Three factors—syllable intensity, average word length, and percentage of high-frequency words—are simultaneously controlled in each paragraph to assure valid and reliable measures of skill growth. Special keyboarding drills are controlled in other ways to assure "loading" of the factors to be emphasized. Even application problems are controlled so that they progress in length, in complexity, and in vocabulary.

Cycled learning. Each operational presentation (letters, reports, tables, and others) is repeated in cycles of emphasis that provide ample practice, assure longer and better retention, and maximize opportunities for transfer.

Communication skills. Periodic instruction and review to help students develop basic written communication skills are included in supplementary sections. In addition, selected document preparation jobs require students to apply the language skills they have developed. Further, this new edition includes the most up-to-date business terminology and gives specific attention to new procedures and equipment of electronic offices.

ACKNOWLEDGMENTS

The authors gratefully acknowledge the helpful contributions made by instructors who used prior editions of the text, especially those who responded to the national user survey made just prior to the preparation of this new edition. Special recognition is given, also, to Dr. D. D. Lessenberry, the original author of College Typewriting, who for over fifty years set the pattern and pace of typewriting instruction in the United States.

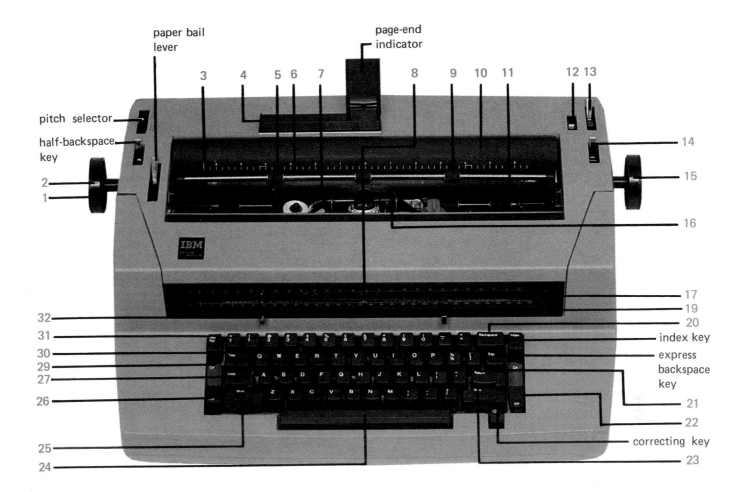

The diagram above shows the parts of an electric typewriter. Since typewriters have similar parts, you should be able to locate the parts of your machine from this diagram. However, if you have the instructional booklet that comes with your machine, use it to identify exact locations of these parts.

If you are learning on a non-electric (manual) typewriter, refer to page 3 for those machine parts and keys that differ in location from an electric machine.

Illustrated on page 2 is an array of data/word processing machines to which your keyboarding skills will transfer.

1 Left platen knob: used to activate variable line spacer

2 Variable line spacer: used to change writing line setting permanently

3 Paper guide scale: used to set paper edge guide at desired position

4 Paper edge guide: used to position paper for insertion

5/9 Paper bail rolls: used to hold paper against platen

6 Paper bail: used to hold paper against platen

7 Card/envelope holder: used to hold cards, labels, and envelopes against platen

8 Printing point indicator: used to position element carrier at desired point

9 (See 5)

10 Paper table: supports paper when it is in typewriter

11 Platen (cylinder): provides a hard surface against which type element strikes

12 Line–space selector: sets typewriter to advance the paper (using carrier return key) 1, 2, or (on some machines) 3 lines for single, double, or triple spacing

13 Paper release lever: used to allow paper to be removed or aligned

14 Automatic line finder: used to change line spacing temporarily, then refind the line

15 Right platen knob: used to turn platen as paper is being inserted

16 Aligning scale: used to align copy that has been reinserted

17 Line–of–writing (margin) scale: used when setting margins, tab stops, and in horizontal centering

18 Ribbon carrier: positions and controls ribbon at printing point (not shown—under the cover)

19 Right margin set: used to set right margin stop

20 Backspace key: used to move printing point to left one space at a time

21 Carrier return key: used to return element carrier to left margin and to advance paper up

22 ON/OFF control: used to turn electric typewriters on or off

23 Right shift key: used to type capitals of letter keys controlled by left hand

24 Space bar: used to move printing point to right one space at a time

25 Left shift key: used to type capitals of letter keys controlled by right hand

26 Tab set: used to set tab stops

27 Shift lock: used to lock shift mechanism so that all letters are capitalized

28 Ribbon control: used to select ribbon typing position (not shown—under cover)

29 Tab clear: used to clear tab stops

30 Tabulator: used to move element carrier to tab stops

31 Margin release key: used to move element carrier beyond margin stops

32 Left margin set: used to set left margin stop

On most electric and electronic machines, certain parts may be used for automatic repeat, such as:

20—backspace key
21—carrier return key
24—space bar

50c, continued

Problem 1

two-column table

half sheet (enter long side first)
Center and type SS the table in vertical and horizontal center; use a 10–space intercolumn.

LEADING AMERICAN MAGAZINES

In 1981

Magazine	Circulation	
Reader's Digest	17,926,542	20
TV Guide	17,670,543	24
National Geographic Magazine	10,861,186	32
Better Homes & Gardens	8,059,717	39
Family Circle	7,427,979	44
Modern Maturity	7,309,035	49
Woman's Day	7,004,367	53
McCall's	6,266,090	59
Ladies' Home Journal	5,527,071	65
Good Housekeeping	5,425,790	71

(words: 5, 7, 15)

Problem 2

three-column table

full sheet

Center and type DS the table in reading position; decide inter-column spacing.

EARLY AMERICAN COLLEGES

With Dates of Establishment

College	State	Year	
Brown	Rhode Island	1764	20
Columbia	New York	1754	25
Harvard	Massachusetts	1636	30
Moravian	Pennsylvania	1742	36
Pennsylvania	Pennsylvania	1740	42
Princeton	New Jersey	1746	47
Rutgers	New Jersey	1766	52
William and Mary	Virginia	1693	58
Yale	Connecticut	1701	62

(words: 5, 10, 15)

Problem 3

outline

full sheet

3″ top margin; 40–space line; add designation numerals and letters for each order; use correct capitalization and spacing

PLANTING LAWN GRASS

	words
clear the area	8
turn over and break up the soil	15
hand implements	19
power implements	23
remove old roots and stems	29
spread nutrients over area	36
prepare the seedbed	40
level high and low places	46
drag	48
light roller	52
rake to loosen lumps and clods	59
plant	61
sow seeds	64
add protective cover	69
straw	71
burlap	73
wet thoroughly to set seed	79

(PLANTING LAWN GRASS: 4)

50a ▶ 5
Preparatory practice

each line 3 times SS (work for smooth, continuous rhythm); DS between 3-line groups; repeat selected lines as time permits

alphabet 1 Meg was not packed to fly to Zanesville to inquire about her next job.

figures 2 Dial 649-4718 or 469-5709 to obtain your copy of this 32-page booklet.

long words 3 Buyers are ordinarily knowledgeable about performance characteristics.

easy 4 Due to the rigor of the quake, the city may dismantle the old chapels.

| 1 | 2 | 3 | 4 | 5 | 6 | 7 | 8 | 9 | 10 | 11 | 12 | 13 | 14 |

50b ▶ 11
Measure skill growth: rough-draft copy

a 3′ and a 5′ writing; determine *gwam*

Difficulty index

| all letters used | A | 1.5 si | 5.7 awl | 80% hfw |

	gwam 3′	5′
A lot of people (surprisingly,) measure job potential primarily no	4	3
the basis of the size of the pay check involved. it would be foolish	9	5
to argue that money should plan no essential part in job selection and	14	8
career planning, but money alone is not an accurate test to utilize use	18	11
when considering a possible career or looking for that first job.	23	14
There is a very subtle difference in philosophy between the person who	27	16
is "hunting for a job and another who is "beginning a career". These	32	19
position itself, however, is not pivotal central to this discussion. Rather	36	22
the divergence lays lies in the approach to the job by each applicant. One	41	25
is attracted by what the job bings; the other, by what it take.s	45	27
we must acknowledge that everybody, or almost everybody, is required	50	30
to work to purchase the necesities of life; money is used essential to that	55	33
extent. but when we calculate that we will spend each a third of our life-	60	36
times preforming that work, it follows that whatever we do ought to should be	64	39
enjoyable, allowing us to make a contribution, and help us grow.	68	41

50c ▶ 34
Measure skill application: tables and outlines

Time schedule

Assembling materials .... 3′
Timed production .... 25′
Final check; compute
   g-pram .... 6′

Materials needed

half sheet; 2 full sheets

When the signal to begin is given, insert the paper and begin typing Problem 1 as directed. Type the problems in sequence until the signal to stop is given.

Type Problem 1 again if you finish before time is called. Proofread all problems; circle errors. Compute *g-pram*.

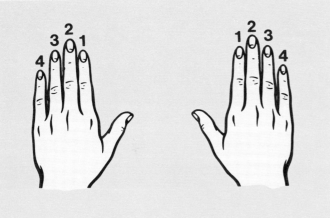

Finger Identification

If you are using a nonelectric (manual) typewriter to learn to keyboard, several of the reaches shown on subsequent pages may be different because of differences in location of the machine part on manual and electric machines. Refer to this page for help in locating these reaches.

Apostrophe

The ' (apostrophe) is the shift of 8. Shift with the left little (fourth) finger; then reach for ' with the right second finger.

k'k k'k k'k it's

Asterisk

The * (asterisk) is the shift of – (hyphen). Depress left shift; then strike * with the right fourth (;) finger.

;–; ;*; ;*; ;*;
*See page 190.

Backspacer

Reach to the backspace key with the appropriate little (fourth) finger. Depress the key firmly for each backspace desired.

Carriage return

Move the left hand, fingers bracing one another, to the carriage return lever.

Move the lever inward to take up the slack; then return the carriage with a quick inward flick–of–the–hand motion.

Drop the hand quickly to typing position without letting it follow the carriage across the page.

Carriage release

If your typewriter has a movable carriage, depress the right carriage release to move it freely. When you have finished keyboarding for the day, leave the carriage approximately centered.

Exclamation mark

On most manual typewriters (and some electrics), there is no exclamation mark key. To *make* an exclamation mark, strike ' (apostrophe); then backspace and strike . (period).

Oh!   I just won!

Quotation marks

The " (quotation mark) is the shift of 2. Shift with the right little (fourth) finger; then reach for " with the left third finger.

s"s s"s s"s "so"

Tabulator bar

Depress and hold down the tabulator bar with the right first finger until the carriage has stopped.

Tabulator key

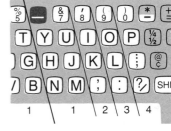

Depress and hold down the tabulator key with the nearest little (fourth) finger until the carriage has stopped.

Underline

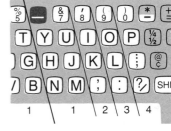

The — (underline) is the shift of 6. Shift with the left little (fourth) finger; then reach for — with the right first finger.

j j j To Yes

Special procedures for nonelectric typewriters

Format and type the prob-
lem as a 2–page report.
Center the heading; use a
1½" (pica) or 2" (elite) top
margin; 1" side and bot-
tom margins.

words

BUSINESSPEOPLE WITH A SENSE OF HUMOR? 8

Is there a place in the hurly-burly world of business for humor? Some 22
businesspeople--perhaps even some successful executives--seem to believe not. 38
Business is a very serious undertaking, they say; and there is not much time to 54
be lighthearted about it. Smiles are all right, but only on the way to the bank. 70

On the other hand, Businesspeople With a Sense of Humor--BWSH we 83
can call them--disagree. They say that the best recipe for business success 99
calls for equal parts of dedication and humor. 108

The BWSH know that business does not thrive on a devil-may-care 121
attitude; they know that it does not thrive on melancholy either. For them, a 137
sense of humor creates a "middle" attitude that tells them how to be con- 151
cerned and smile at the same time. 158

The BWSH are champions of the smile. They know that regardless of how 173
critical things become, a smile helps to ease pain and pressure. A millisecond of 189
life is lived only once, they say; and it can be relived only in retrospect. Nothing 206
will change those spent milliseconds, so the BWSH try to be as positive about 222
the disastrous milliseconds as they are about the more fortuitous ones. 236

A sense of humor is what gets BWSH through such calamities as the 250
last-minute Christmas rush, the over-order for 100 mechanized dolls, and the 265
front door that can't be unlocked on the day of the Big Sale. These problems 280
are truly not laughing matters, but how they are viewed determines how they 296
will be handled. With typical good humor, the BWSH keep business moving 310
positively ahead and on the right track. 319

The BWSH know also that a sense of humor helps build their ability 332
to communicate. To paraphrase a daily newspaper item, 343

If a business executive can speak to people with a little 355
warmth and humor, then those people will be more responsive 367
in listening. If they're paying attention to hear what the speaker 381
says next, he or she will have a better chance to communicate 393
effectively.[*] 396

Businesspeople With a Sense of Humor? Why not? Why not, indeed? 409
413

[*]Detroit Free Press, May 22, 1983, p. 3b. 421

① Adjust paper guide

Line up paper edge guide (4) with zero on the line-of-writing scale (17).

② Insert typing paper

Take a sheet of paper in your left hand and follow the directions and illustrations at the right and below.

1 Pull paper bail (6) forward (or up on some machines).

2 Place paper against paper edge guide (4), behind the platen (11).

3 Turn paper into machine, using right platen knob (15) or index key.

4 Stop when paper is about 1½ inches above aligning scale (16).

5 If paper is not straight, pull paper release lever (13) forward.

6 Straighten paper, then push paper release lever back.

7 Push paper bail back so that it holds paper against platen.

8 Slide paper bail rolls (5/9) into position, dividing paper into thirds.

9 Properly inserted paper.

③ Set line-space selector

Many machines offer 3 choices for line spacing—1, 1½, and 2 indicated by bars or numbers on the line-space selector (12).

Set the line-space selector on (—) or 1 to single-space (SS) or on (=) or on 2 to double-space (DS) as directed for lines in Level 1.

```
1  Lines 1 and 2 are single-spaced (SS).
2  A double space (DS) separates Lines 2 and 4.
3                        1 blank line space
4  A triple space (TS) separates Lines 4 and 7.
5
6                        2 blank line spaces
7  Set the selector on "1" for single spacing.
```

④ Determine type size

Most machines are equipped with pica (10 spaces to a horizontal inch) or elite (12 spaces to a horizontal inch) type size.

Marked intervals on the line-of-writing scale (17) match the spacing of letters on the machine. This scale reads from 0 to 110 or more for machines with elite type, from 0 to 90 or more for machines with pica type.

```
This is elite (12-pitch) type, 12 spaces to an inch.

This is pica (10-pitch) type, 10 spaces to an inch.
```

inches							
	1	2	3	4	5		

centimeters													
1	2	3	4	5	6	7	8	9	10	11	12	13	14

49a ▶ 5

Preparatory practice

each line 3 times SS (work for smooth, continuous rhythm); DS between 3-line groups; repeat selected lines as time permits

alphabet 1 Max queried Parker about having a jewel box for the many huge zircons.

figures 2 Are those last-minute reports on Bill 3657-84 due on October 19 or 20?

shift/lock 3 Ping-ying Fu typed the notations REGISTERED and CERTIFIED in ALL CAPS.

easy 4 The auditor may laugh, but the penalty for such chaotic work is rigid.

| 1 | 2 | 3 | 4 | 5 | 6 | 7 | 8 | 9 | 10 | 11 | 12 | 13 | 14 |

49b ▶ 11

Measure skill growth: statistical copy

a 3′ and a 5′ writing; determine *gwam*

Difficulty index

all letters used | A | 1.5 si | 5.7 awl | 80% hfw

gwam 3′ | 5′

According to a special report of NEWSWEEK (January 17, 1983), the · 4 · 3

makeup of the American work force is making some sharp adjustments. · 9 · 5

Extracting data from the 1980 census, NEWSWEEK says that the median age · 14 · 8

of workers dropped from 39 in 1970 to 34 in 1981. Quite a large number · 19 · 11

of women have entered the force--67 percent of women between the ages · 23 · 14

of 18 and 34 are working. In fact, a total of 46.8 million women--an · 28 · 17

amazing 52 percent of the female population--work. · 31 · 19

Fewer men are now working, explains the magazine. Consequently, · 36 · 21

their portion of the work force has come down since 1951 from 87.3 per- · 40 · 24

cent to just 77 percent, due perhaps to better disability benefits and · 45 · 27

early retirement. The departure of males begins at the age of 25 and · 50 · 30

speeds up at the age of 45. Of males 65 and older, the portion has de- · 55 · 33

clined from 44.6 percent in 1955 to 19.9 percent in 1981. · 58 · 35

The magazine also quotes some extraordinary figures about the · 62 · 37

situation of males and females who are 75 years old and older and who · 67 · 40

have continued to work. A total of 451,000 of them remained active in · 72 · 43

the 1981 labor force, and the unemployment rate was just 2.8 percent. · 77 · 46

gwam 3′ | 1 | 2 | 3 | 4 | 5 |
5′ | 1 | 2 | 3 |

49c ▶ 34

Measure skill application: reports

Time schedule

Assembling materials .... 3′
Timed production .... 25′
Final check; compute
    g–pram .... 6′

Materials needed

2 full sheets

When the signal to begin is given, insert paper and begin typing the problem on page 102, as directed. Type until the signal to stop is given. Begin the problem again if you finish before time is called. Proofread all problems; circle errors. Compute g–pram.

⑤ Plan margin settings

When 8½– by 11–inch paper is inserted into the typewriter (8½–inch end first) with left edge at 0 on the line–of–writing scale (17), center point is 51 (elite) or 42½ (pica). Use 42 for pica center.

To center typed lines, set left and right margin stops the same number of spaces left and right from center point. Diagrams at the right show margin settings for 50–, 60–, and 70–space lines. When you begin to use the warning bell, 5 or 6 spaces may be added to the right margin.

Elite center

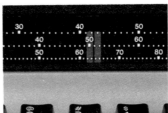

Pica center

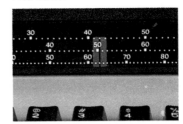

Elite (12-pitch)

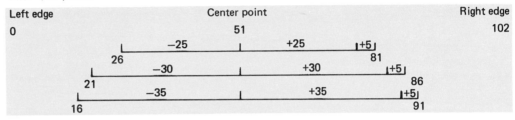

Left edge	Center point	Right edge
0	51	102

−25 +25 +5 |
26 81
−30 +30 +5 |
21 86
−35 +35 +5 |
16 91

Pica (10-pitch)

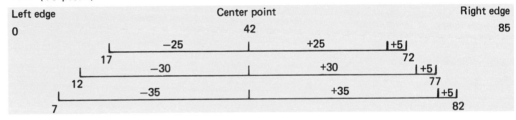

Left edge	Center point	Right edge
0	42	85

−25 +25 +5 |
17 72
−30 +30 +5 |
12 77
−35 +35 +5 |
7 82

⑥ Set margin stops

Type A
Push-button set
Adler, Olympia, Remington, Royal 700/870 manuals, Smith-Corona

1 Press down on the left margin set button.

2 Slide it to desired position on the line–of–writing (margin) scale.

3 Release the margin set button.

4 Using the right margin set button, set the right margin stop in the same way.

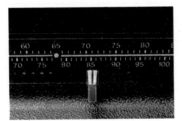

Type B
Push-lever set
Single element typewriters, such as Adler, Olivetti, Remington Rand, Royal, Selectric

1 Push in on the left margin set lever.

2 Slide it to desired position on the line–of–writing (margin) scale.

3 Release the margin set lever.

4 Using the right margin set lever, set the right margin stop in the same way.

Type C
Key set
IBM typebar, Olivetti electric

1 Move carriage to the left margin stop by depressing the return key.

2 Depress and hold down the margin set (IBM reset) key as you move carriage to desired left margin stop position.

3 Release the margin set (IBM reset) key.

4 Move carriage to the right margin stop.

5 Depress and hold down the margin set (IBM reset) key as you move carriage to desired right margin stop position.

6 Release the margin set (IBM reset) key.

Type D
Electronic set
To set margins on some electronic machines, such as Xerox and Silver–Reed, space to the desired margin position and strike the appropriate (left or right) margin key.

On other machines, such as IBM, space to the desired margin position and strike the CODE key and the appropriate (left or right) margin key *at the same time*.

> General information for setting margin stops is given here. If you have the manufacturer's booklet for your typewriter, however, use it; the procedure for your particular model may be slightly different.

48c ▶ 34
Measure skill application: letters

Time schedule

Assembling materials .... 3'
Timed production .... 25'
Final check; compute
  g-pram .... 6'

Materials needed

Letterheads and Monarch sheet [LM pp. 59-63]; copy sheet; carbon paper; large, small, and Monarch envelopes

Format and type as many problems as you can in 25'. Type Problem 1 again if you finish Problem 3 before time has been called. Proofread all problems; circle errors.

Problem 1
Business letter (letterhead)

block style, 1 carbon copy, large envelope; 60-space line; begin on Line 15

Problem 2
Business letter (letterhead)

modified-block style, small envelope; 60-space line; begin on Line 15

Problem 3
Personal letter (Monarch sheet)

modified-block style; Monarch envelope; 50-space line; begin on Line 15

June 9, 19-- | Ms. Debra V. Wynn | 80005 Grand Central Pkwy. | Jamaica, NY 11435-6071 | Dear Ms. Wynn — 14 / 19

(¶ 1) Word power! It's important to most people. It's absolutely indispensable to a businessperson like you. Word power commands recognition; it smooths the way to promotion and higher salary; and it brings much personal satisfaction. — 34 / 49 / 64 / 65

(¶ 2) Vocabulary is a good place to start, of course; but knowing how to choose words, pronounce and spell them, and fit them together to make meaningful sentences is the added knowledge that makes vocabulary work. This is word power. And it can take a lifetime to achieve it. — 80 / 95 / 110 / 120

(¶ 3) SPEAK OUT by Guy Hunter brings you a shortcut to word power. This 175-page book will help you to build your word power and give you confidence to put your thoughts and ideas to work for you. Your copy of SPEAK OUT is on our "save shelf." You can pick it up at your convenience. It's only $17.95. — 133 / 148 / 164 / 180

Sincerely | Cesar J. Strongbow | Manager | xx — 188/201

October 28, 19-- | Mrs. L. L. Sangtry, President | United Casings, Inc. | 1600 Kirby Street, W. | Shreveport, LA 71103-4923 | Dear Mrs. Sangtry — 14 / 27

(¶ 1) Last Tuesday afternoon, a shipment of rubber casings from your company arrived at our receiving dock. It had been rushed to us as requested, and we were grateful. — 41 / 57 / 60

(¶ 2) We were not so grateful when we discovered that the shipment was not complete, and I telephoned your sales staff to tell them so. The young lady who answered the telephone listened patiently while I exploded in her ear. Then she went to work. — 74 / 90 / 106 / 109

(¶ 3) She asked exactly what was missing and what was happening to our production schedule. She apologized for the mistake and promised to rush the missing casings to us. I bid her a very doubtful goodbye. — 123 / 138 / 150

(¶ 4) The parts arrived this morning, just 36 hours after I called. — 162

(¶ 5) Mrs. Sangtry, I am impressed with the way your firm handled this very serious problem. To have an error handled promptly and courteously was a pleasant surprise. We shall order from you again. — 176 / 191 / 201

Sincerely yours | Miss Phyllis E. Trerrett | Purchasing Director | xx — 214/234

---

543 El Caprice Avenue | Hollywood, CA 91605-7168 | August 19, 19-- | Miss Felicia Wymore | 278 Fryman Place | Hollywood, CA 91604-4811 | Dear Felicia — 15 / 28

(¶ 1) You asked me to write to you about the interviews and tests I took at the Brewer Publishing Company. I spent most of yesterday morning in the company's personnel office. The tests were intensive--mostly keyboarding, composing, editing, spelling, grammar, and vocabulary. — 42 / 57 / 72 / 83

(¶ 2) The interviewer asked about my in-school and out-of-school activities, what magazines I regularly read, and what books I had read recently. We also discussed current events. — 97 / 113 / 118

(¶ 3) Frankly, Felicia, I am excited about the prospects of working for Brewer. I'll let you know when I have more news. Thanks for your encouragement. — 133 / 148

Yours sincerely | Steve Merrewether — 151/176

LEVEL ONE
Learning to keyboard and to format copy

Your decision to learn to keyboard is a wise one. Just as the 1960's were the decade of the computer and data processing, the 1980's are the decade of microcomputers, text editors, and word or information processing. In business, industry, and the professions, the use of electronic input/output devices is growing at lightning speed. Whether you learn to keyboard on a typewriter or a microcomputer, your keyboarding skill will transfer directly to other data/word processing machines because all use the same standard arrangement of the letter and number keys. In addition, some machines have a 10-key numeric pad arrangement which is the same as that on electronic calculators.

Learning to keyboard with speed and accuracy is only the first step, however. To be able to *use* your skill productively, you must also learn the features of frequently prepared documents (such as letters, reports, and tables) and develop skill in arranging and typing them in their conventional formats.

The purpose of Level 1 (Lessons 1-29), therefore, is to help you develop keyboarding efficiency and to begin teaching you how to format and type documents for personal use. The textbook, like your keyboarding instrument, is only a partner in learning. For your textbook and your machine to help you effectively to learn, you as the third partner must *intend* to learn and must practice intensively to reach your goals.

Measurement goals

1 To demonstrate ability to type at acceptable levels average–difficulty writings in straight, rough–draft, and statistical copy for 3' and 5'.

2 To demonstrate ability to type letters, tables, and reports in proper format from semi–arranged copy, according to specific directions.

Machine adjustments

1 Check chair and desk adjustment and placement of copy for ease of reading.

2 Set ribbon control to type on upper half of ribbon.

3 Set paper guide at 0.

4 Set 70–space line.

Materials. Letterheads, full, half, Monarch, and copy sheets; large, small, and Monarch envelopes.

48a ▶ 5
Preparatory practice

each line 3 times SS (slowly, faster, slowly); DS between 3-line groups; repeat selected lines as time permits

alphabet	1	Jack is becoming acquainted with an expert on Venezuelan family names.
fig/sym	2	Our #38065 pens will cost Knox & Brady $12.97 each (less 4% discount).
direct reaches	3	June obtained unusual services from a number of celebrated decorators.
easy	4	It is a problem; she may sue the city for a title to the antique auto.

| 1 | 2 | 3 | 4 | 5 | 6 | 7 | 8 | 9 | 10 | 11 | 12 | 13 | 14 |

48b ▶ 11
Measure skill growth: straight copy

a 3' and a 5' writing; determine *gwam*

Difficulty index

all letters used | A | 1.5 si | 5.7 awl | 80% hfw

gwam 3' | 5'

Clothes do not "make the person." Agree? Still, clothes form an · 4 · 3
integral part of impressions we have of others. Whenever we first meet · 9 · 6
people, for example, we quickly look them over (and they us), and we · 14 · 8
mentally categorize each other. Inexpert as these conclusions may be, · 19 · 11
we all justify them in our own minds on the basis that clothing is the · 23 · 14
only evidence of personality we have. · 26 · 16

Clothes are, of course, quite practical; we need them for modesty · 30 · 18
purposes and to protect us from the hazards of extreme weather. Yet, · 35 · 21
clothes are also decorative; they should, beyond just looking nice, · 40 · 24
reflect a personality, a mood, and a natural coloring--but not a finan- · 44 · 27
cial status. Clothes should be part of a picture--a picture of a per- · 49 · 29
son--and the person should be the central part of the picture. · 53 · 32

Clothes do serve a purpose. They always make a direct statement · 57 · 34
about a person; so they should be suitable, and they should be fresh. · 62 · 37
High style (but not quality) is out for usual business occasions, as · 68 · 40
are excessive jewelry and tantalizing scents. A good mirror and a bit · 71 · 43
of common sense can indicate to a person what clothes are appropriate. · 76 · 46

gwam 3' | 1 | 2 | 3 | 4 | 5 |
5' | 1 | 2 | 3 |

Learning goals

1 To master alphabetic reaches.

2 To operate keyboard without looking at your fingers or the keys—"by touch."

3 To type easy paragraph copy.

4 To type or keyboard at a rate of 14 or more gross words a minute (*gwam*).

Machine adjustments

1 Set paper guide at 0.

2 Set ribbon control to type on upper half of ribbon.

3 Set left margin stop for a 50–space line (center − 25); set right margin stop at end of line–of–writing scale.

4 Set line–space selector for single spacing (SS).

1

Prepare for Lesson 1

1 Acquire a supply of 8½" by 11" typing paper of good quality.

2 If your chair is adjustable, raise or lower it to a height that is comfortable for you.

3 If your desk is adjustable, raise or lower it until your forearms parallel the slant of the keyboard when your fingers are placed over asdf jkl;.

4 Follow carefully all directions, both oral and written. Therein lies much of the secret for gaining keyboarding skill.

1a
Get ready to keyboard

1 Clear work area and chair of un–needed books and clothing.

2 Place textbook at right of machine, the top elevated for easy reading; stack paper supply at left of machine.

3 Refer briefly to page 1 of this book where typewriter parts are named, illustrated, and described. In these early lessons, frequent reference is made to these parts; you will need to refer to the illus–trated typewriter on page 1 at those times.

4 Locate on page 5 the type of margin sets that match those on your machine. Set the left margin stop for a 50–space line (center − 25); move the right stop to the ex–treme right end of the line–of–writing scale.

5 Study pages 4 and 5 carefully. If necessary, adjust the paper edge guide (at 0) on your machine. In–sert paper as illustrated.

6 Set line–space selector for single spacing (SS) as directed on page 4.

**Compose at the
keyboard**

Make all decisions
about format.

1 Assume that you have
agreed to run for president of
the student body at your col–
lege. Compose a four– or
five–line paragraph in which
you set forth some of the
changes you would attempt to
inaugurate.

2 Proofread the ¶; make
changes with proofreader's
marks.

3 Type a final copy. Center the
title **MY PLATFORM**.

47c ▶ 10
Review tables

Make all decisions about format.

			words
CALUMINEX			2
19-- Representatives of the Year			9
Region	*Representatives*	*Sales*	20
Eastern	*Polly Murger*	*$ 357,214*	26
Southern	*Brent Ortega*	*542,168*	32
Midwestern	*Rick Hyatt*	*497,135*	38
Western	*Mika Shibasaki*	*568,900*	44

47d ▶ 22
**Measure skill
application: tables**

Time schedule

Assembling materials .... 2′
Timed production .... 15′
Final check; proofread;
  compute *g–pram* .... 5′

Problem 1

half sheet (enter long side first);
SS; exact center; decide intercolumn spacing

FAMOUS AMERICAN PAINTINGS			5
Painter	Title	Size	12
Mary Cassatt	After the Bath	26″ × 39″	20
Willem de Kooning	Woman I	76″ × 58″	27
Winslow Homer	The Gulf Stream	28″ × 49″	35
Jackson Pollock	Number 27	11′ × 24′	42
Robert Rauschenberg	Tracer	84″ × 60″	50
John Singer Sargent	Madame X	82″ × 43″	57
Grant Wood	American Gothic	30″ × 25″	65
Andrew Wyeth	Christina's World	32″ × 48″	73

Problem 2

half sheet; make all decisions for
placement of copy

THE UNITED NATIONS			4
Small-Nation Members			8
Country	Admitted	Est. Pop.	18
Belize	1981	146,000	22
Dominica	1978	80,000	26
Grenada	1974	108,000	31
Maldives	1965	150,000	35
St. Lucia	1979	124,000	40
St. Vincent and the Grenadines	1980	120,000	48
Sao Tome and Principe	1975	90,000	55
Seychelles	1976	70,000	60
Vanutu	1981	112,700	64

1b
Take keyboarding position

1 Sit back in chair, body erect.

2 Place both feet on floor to maintain proper balance.

3 Let your hands hang relaxed at your sides. Your fingers will relax in curved position.

4 From this position, raise the left hand and lightly place the fingertips of your left hand on **a s d f** (home keys). Study the location of these keys.

5 Similarly, lightly place the fingertips of your right hand on **j k l ;** (home keys). Study the location of these keys.

6 Your fingers should be curved and upright; wrists should be low, but they should not touch the frame of the machine.

1 Keep fingers curved and upright, wrists low.

2 Keep forearms parallel to slant of keyboard.

3 Keep eyes on copy.

4 Sit back in chair, body erect.

5 Place textbook at right of machine, top raised for easy reading.

6 Keep table free of unneeded books.

7 Keep feet on floor for balance.

1c
Strike home keys, space bar, and return

1 Strike each key with a quick, sharp finger stroke; snap the fingertip toward the palm as the stroke is made.

Type (keyboard):

ffjjffjjfj

2 Strike the space bar with a down–and–in motion of the right thumb.

Type (on same line):

dd kk dd kk dk

space once

3 Keep the fingers well–curved. Concentrate on proper finger action as you keyboard.

Type (on same line):

ss ll ss ll aa ; ;

space once

4 Reach with the little finger of the right hand to the return key and tap it. Then quickly return the little finger to its home position. *Refer to page 3 if your machine is nonelectric.*

Problem 1

full sheet; reading position; DS; decide intercolumn spacing

PRINCIPAL WORLD LANGUAGES		words
		5
Language	Millions	12
Arabic	155	14
English	397	17
French	107	19
German	119	21
Hindi	254	23
Japanese	119	26
Mandarin Chinese	726	30
Portuguese	151	33
Russian	274	35
Spanish	258	37

Problem 2

half sheet (insert long side first); exact center; SS; decide inter-column spacing

THE SPRINGARN MEDAL		words
		4
Selected Winners		7
Recipient	Year	13
Martin Luther King, Jr.	1956	19
Edward (Duke) Ellington	1958	25
Leontyne Price	1964	29
Sammy Davis, Jr.	1967	33
Henry Aaron	1974	36
Andrew Young	1977	40
Coleman Young	1980	44

Problem 3

Make all decisions about place-ment of copy.

Notes:

For Column 3, set the tab for the longest number in the column; then backspace one space to type the dollar sign. Align figures at the decimal.

Many electronic typewriters and microcomputers have a decimal tab which automatically aligns copy at the decimal.

THE ALGONQUIN CLUB			words
			4
Operating Budget, 19--			8
Committee	Chairperson	Budget	19
Business Affairs	C. Villeneuve	$310.50	27
Conservation	D. Treece	95.00	33
Finance	A. Perez	8.50	37
International Relations	F. Heckman	85.00	46
Program	I. Breece	375.00	51

47a ▶ 6

Preparatory practice

each line 3 times SS (work for fewer than 2 errors per group); DS between 3-line groups; repeat selected lines as time permits

alphabet	1	May the judge quiz the clerks from Iowa about extensive profit-taking?
figures	2	Flight 374 will leave at 10:46 a.m. and arrive in Buffalo at 9:58 p.m.
double letters	3	The school committee will do well to pass on all the Tennessee offers.
easy	4	It is a duty of the civic auditor to aid a city firm to make a profit.

| 1 | 2 | 3 | 4 | 5 | 6 | 7 | 8 | 9 | 10 | 11 | 12 | 13 | 14 |

47

1d
Learn the home row

1 Strike the return key twice more to leave extra space between the line you have just typed and the lines you will now type.

2 Practice once each line shown at the right. Strike the return key once to single–space (SS) be–tween the two lines of a pair.

3 Strike the return key twice to double–space (DS) between pairs of lines.

4 Strike the return key 3 times to triple–space (TS) after completing Line 6.

5 Repeat the drill.

> **Technique hint:**
> Keep fingers well curved; keep wrists low, but do not allow them to touch the typewriter.

Fingers curved

Fingers upright

```
1 fj fj fj dk dk dk sl sl sl a; a; a; fj dk sl a; a;
2 jf kd ls ;a al ak aj sl sk sj dl dk dj fj fk fl f;
```
Return twice to double–space (DS)

```
3 as as ask ask sad sad jak jak fad fad lad lad lass
4 ad ad ads ads jak jak dad dad all all add add fall
```
DS

```
5 a lad; a lass; a jak; all ads; all fall; ask a lad
6 ask dad; all ads; a jak ad; a sad lad; a jak falls
```
Return 3 times to triple–space (TS)

1e
Learn new keyreach: E

1 Find new key on illustrated keyboard; then find it on your keyboard.

2 Study carefully the "Reach technique for **e**."

3 Watch your finger make the *reach* to **e** and back to **d** a few times *without striking the keys.* Keep your fingers curved.

4 Practice the lines once as shown. Keep your eyes on the copy as you keyboard; look only when you "feel lost."

5 If time permits, repeat the drill.

Reach technique for **e**

Reach *up* with *left second* finger.

Left Fingers 4 3 2 1   1 2 3 4 Right Fingers

all reaches learned
```
1 e ed ed led led lea lea ale ale elk elf eke els ed
2 ed fed fed fled fled kale kale self self lake lake
```
Return twice to double–space (DS)

```
3 e elk ekes leek leak sale dale kale lake fake self
4 sell fell jell sale sake jade sled seek leal deal;
```
DS

```
5 a sled sale; a fake jade; see a lake; a kale leaf;
6 sell a safe; a leaf fell; see a leaf; sell a desk;
```

1f
End the lesson

(standard procedure for all lessons)

1 Raise the paper bail (6) or pull it toward you. Pull the paper release lever (13) toward you.

2 Remove paper with your left hand. Push paper release lever back to its normal position.

3 Turn off the power on an electric or electronic machine. See page 3 if you have a movable carriage typewriter.

46a ▶ 6
Preparatory practice

each line 3 times SS (work for fewer than 2 errors per group); DS between 3-line groups; repeat selected lines as time permits

alphabet 1 Julie began to study the six chapters on vitamins for her weekly quiz.

figures 2 I will send 2,795 of the 4,680 sets now and the remainder on the 13th.

one hand 3 I refereed only a few cases; I regarded waste water as a greater case.

easy 4 May I also fix the shape of the right hand and elbow of the clay form?

| 1 | 2 | 3 | 4 | 5 | 6 | 7 | 8 | 9 | 10 | 11 | 12 | 13 | 14 |

46b ▶ 10
Preapplication drill: center column headings

half sheet; DS; 10 spaces between columns

1 Read the information about centering column headings.

2 Type the drill below; center headings over the columns. Underline the headings.

Guides for centering columnar headings

• A column heading is typed a double space above a column centered over the longest item in the column.

a To determine the center point of the longest item in a column, space forward from the starting point of the column *once* for every *two* strokes or spaces in the longest item. Disregard a leftover stroke.

b The point where the forward spacing stops is the center point of the column. Backspace *once* for each *two* strokes in the heading; disregard a leftover stroke. Starting at the place where backspacing ended, type the heading.

• You may prefer to type column headings after you type the columns. After typing the table headings, space down to the approximate position for the first line of the table, leaving the column heading line vacant. After the columns have been typed, you may enter the column headings.

• If the column heading is longer than its column, use the heading as the longest item in the column for horizontal placement purposes. Then, center the column under the column heading.

Book	Author
Jane Eyre	Bronte
Oliver Twist	Dickens
The Great Gatsby	Fitzgerald
Showboat	Ferber

Key |*The Great Gatsby* | 10 | *Fitzgerald* |

46c ▶ 34
Format/type tables with column headings

Read the information at the right; then format and type the tables on page 97.

Guidelines for formatting a table

To format a table attractively, certain questions must be answered appropriately; as:

• Single or double spacing? Double spacing is more attractive and easier to read, but it may require more space than you have available.

• Full or half sheet? Consider how the table will be used and how much space is available. If more than 20 lines are required, use a full sheet.

• Reading position or exact center? Reading position is recommended for a full sheet, exact center for a half sheet.

• Number of intercolumn spaces? Backspace for columns. Then backspace once for each two spaces to be left between columns (leave an even number of spaces between columns). Be sure the body of the table will be wider than the table heading.

2a
Prepare to keyboard

Reread procedures described in
1b, 1c, and 1d, pages 8 and 9.

2b
Preparatory practice

each line twice SS
(slowly, then faster);
DS between 2-line groups

home row 1 `ff jj ff jj dd kk dd kk ss ll ss ll aa ;; aa ;; a;`

e 2 `e el els led ale lea eke lee elf elk eel lake kale`

all reaches
learned 3 `as all ask; a jak ad; ask a lad; a fall fad; a fee`
TS

2c
Learn new keyreaches: T and O

Use the standard procedure at the
right to learn each new keyreach
in this lesson and in lessons that
follow.

Standard procedure for learning new keyreaches

1 Find new key on illustrated keyboard; then find it on your keyboard.

2 Study carefully the reach technique illustrated for the key.

3 Watch your finger make the reach to the new key a few times. Keep other fingers curved on home keys. Straighten the finger slightly for an upward reach; curve it a bit more for a downward reach.

4 Practice twice SS the two lines in which the new reach is emphasized. Keep your eyes on the book copy as you keyboard.

5 DS; then learn and practice the next new keyreach according to Steps 1-4.

6 Finally, DS; then practice Lines 5-8 once as shown. If time permits, repeat them. Work for continuity. Avoid pauses.

Reach technique for t

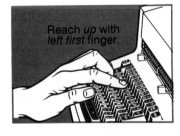

Reach *up* with
left first finger.

Left Fingers   4 \ 3 \ 2 \ 1 \   \ 1 \ 2 \ 3 \ 4   Right Fingers

Reach technique for o

Reach *up* with
right third finger.

t
1 `t tf tf aft aft tall tall talk talk tale tale task`
2 `tf at at aft jet let take tell felt flat slat salt`
DS

o
3 `o ol ol sol sol sold sold of of off off fold folds`
4 `ol old sold sole dole do doe does lo loll sol solo`

t/o
5 `to tot tote told dolt toe toes load toad foal soak`
6 `to too toot lot slot do dot oft loft soft jot jolt`

all letters
learned
7 `to do | to do a lot | take a jet | to let a | to do a task`
8 `so to | so to do | to take a | to tell a joke | left off a`
TS

45c ▶ 28
Format/type tables with main and secondary headings

Problem 1

full sheet; DS; reading position; 20–space intercolumn

A TS usually separates a main heading from a table; when a secondary heading is used, DS after the main heading and TS after the secondary heading.

For columns with dollar signs, use the dollar sign only with the top figure and the total (when one is shown). Keystroke $ one space to the left of horizontal beginning point of the longest line in the column. It should be typed again in the same position when a *total line* appears in the table.

		words
CALUMINEX		2
Branch Office Sales for March DS		8
TS		
Albuquerque	$ 32,791	12
Allentown	47,781	16
Birmingham	60,898	19
Denver	4,558	22
Honolulu	8,432	25
New Haven	104,932	28
St. Louis	13,166	32
San Diego	89,005	35
San Juan	113,364	39
Seattle	21,539	43
	DS	
	$496,466	45

Problem 2

full sheet; DS; reading position; 16–space intercolumn

		words
SOUTH AMERICAN COUNTRIES		5
Approximate Area in Square Miles		12
Argentina	1,072,067	16
Bolivia	424,162	19
Brazil	3,286,470	22
Chile	292,256	25
Colombia	439,512	28
Ecuador	105,685	31
Peru	496,222	34
Uruguay	72,172	37
Venezuela	352,143	40

Problem 3

1 Read the guidelines for deciding intercolumn spacing.

2 Repeat Problem 1. Use a half sheet; exact center; SS. Set a new width for the intercolumn.

Guides for deciding intercolumn spacing

These guidelines will help you decide on the number of spaces to use for intercolumns.

• The body of a table should be wider than its main and secondary headings.

• To center a table, backspace for columns first, intercolumns last.

• Backspace for intercolumns until an appropriate place for setting the left margin has been reached. Set the margin stop; space forward as usual.

2d
Practice keystroking technique

each line twice SS; DS between 2-line groups

home row 1 as ask asks ad ads add jak jaks all fall lass dads

e 2 led lead fee feel ell ells elk elks fee fees leads

t 3 at kat sat tall talk last fast salt slat task tall

o 4 so sol old do ado odd sod of off oaf oak loaf load

all letters learned 5 of a | to do | do so | a joke | to lead | odd leaf | ask a lad

TS

2e
Practice words/phrases

1 Practice the Level 1 lines once SS at an easy pace.

2 DS; then practice the Level 2 lines in the same way.

3 DS; then practice the Level 2 lines again at a faster pace.

4 If time permits, practice the Level 3 lines once, trying to keep the carrier (carriage) moving steadily.

Note: The 3 sets of lines progress gradually in diffi-culty.

Goal: *At least* 1 line per minute (10 *gwam*).

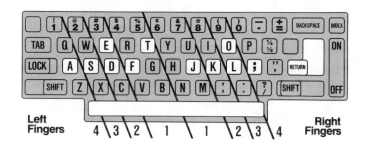

all reaches learned

Level 1
1 a as ask to too foe doe jot jet jak so do sod does
2 ale ask ode old oak let led ade a at kat take told
3 to see; to a set; ask a lad; lot of tea; ate a jak

Level 2
4 ale oak jet lot all jak doe too off oft odd dot to
5 led doe eat let sol ask add eel sad eke see old of
6 do a loaf; a leaf fell; tell a joke; a lot of talk

Level 3
7 elf self ask asks jet jets lot lots led lead takes
8 elk elks add adds joke jokes feel feels talk talks
9 to a lake; eat a salad; ask a lass; sell oak desks

2f
End the lesson

(See page 9 if necessary.)

Remove paper

Turn electric off

44c, continued

Problem 2

Format and type Problem 1 again; use the same directions, but change SS to DS.

Problem 3

Format/type the problem at the right on a half sheet (insert long side first); SS; exact center; 14–space intercolumn.

CALUMINEX BRANCH MANAGERS

words: 5

TS

		words
Gertrude F. Schuyler	Albuquerque	12
Albert C. Chung	Allentown	17
Dale T. O'Hargran	Birmingham	23
F. Janice Montgomery	Denver	28
Rose B. Shikamuru	Honolulu	34
Carla E. Bragg	New Haven	39
Margret G. Bredeweg	St. Louis	45

Key | *Gertrude F. Schuyler* | *14* | *Albuquerque* |

45

45a ▶ 6
Preparatory practice

each line 3 times SS (work for fewer than 2 errors per group); DS between 3-line groups; repeat selected lines as time permits

alphabet 1 The king and queen brought dozens of expensive jewels from the colony.

fig/sym 2 Check #4690 for $1,375, dated February 28, was sent to O'Neill & Sons.

adjacent reaches 3 As Louise Liu said, few questioned the points asserted by the porters.

easy 4 He may fish for a quantity of smelt; he may wish for aid to land them.

| 1 | 2 | 3 | 4 | 5 | 6 | 7 | 8 | 9 | 10 | 11 | 12 | 13 | 14 |

45b ▶ 16
Preapplication drills: realigning/aligning items

Drill 1

twice as shown DS; 14-space intercolumn

> **Realigning items at the left**
>
> After setting the left margin as usual, adjust it to the right (in this instance 3 spaces) to accommodate the most common line setting. Use the margin release and backspacer for longer lines.
>
> **Aligning items at the right**
>
> Since spacing forward and backward will be needed to align items at the right, adjust the tab setting for the item length that requires the least forward and backward spacing.

District 9   tab
Reset margin ——▶ Almont   27
                 Belden   Backspace once ——▶ 150
District 10
                 Erie   85
                 Lamberg   Space forward once ——▶ 9
District 11
                 Orville   46
                 Racine   9

Key | *District 10* | *14* | *150* |

Drill 2

half sheet (enter long side first); DS; exact center; 12–space inter-column

To align a column of words at the right (as in the second column), backspace as usual to set left margin. When spacing forward, set the tab at the end of the second column rather than at the beginning; backspace once for each character in the second column to position for keyboarding.

PROPOSED BANQUET AGENDA

Tab stop ↓

Preliminary remarks	Ellen Prater
Introductions	Grant Dubin
Speaker	Rosalyn Booth
Commentary	Drake Eppingham
Closing remarks	Ellen Prater

Key | *Preliminary remarks* | *12* | *Drake Eppingham* |

3a
Prepare-to-keyboard checklist

Before you begin to keyboard, check your readiness to begin the lesson.

- ✔ Work area cleared of unneeded clothing and books
- ✔ Book elevated at right of machine
- ✔ Left margin set for 50–space line (center − 25)
- ✔ Right margin set at extreme right end of scale
- ✔ Ribbon control set to type on upper half of ribbon
- ✔ Paper edge guide on correct setting
- ✔ Paper inserted expertly, straightened if necessary

3b
Preparatory practice

each line 3 times SS (slowly, faster, still faster); DS between 3-line groups

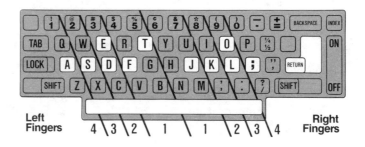

home row 1 a; sl dk fj a;sl dkfj all lad as ask fall lass add

o/o/t 2 ol old sold ed fed led ft oft at dot doe let of to

all reaches learned 3 to fold; take a loaf; a lot of; as a joke; at last
TS

3c
Check position and techniques

As you complete the remainder of the lesson, observe the points of good keyboarding position and techniques listed at the right.

- ✔ Seated erect in chair
- ✔ Both feet on floor
- ✔ Fingers relaxed, curved, upright
- ✔ Fingertips touching home keys
- ✔ Wrists low but not touching the machine
- ✔ Slant of forearms parallel to slant of the keyboard
- ✔ Each key struck with a quick stroke of the fingertip
- ✔ Space bar struck with inward motion of the thumb

3d
Practice keystroking technique

each pair of lines SS as shown; DS between 2-line groups; repeat if time permits

Technique hint: Strike keys at a smoo... avoid pauses.

home row 1 a jak; ask dad; as a lad; as a lass; add a fall ad
2 a fad; as a dad; a fall ad; as all ask; a sad fall

e 3 a doe; led a doe; a sea eel; see a lake; jade sale
4 a sea; a joke; tell tales; a doe fled; seal a deal

to do so; odd load; lot of old; sold a sofa
old oak; jot off a; does a lot; a soft sofa

to talk; tall tale; eat a lot; told a tale
to salt; at a late; take a lot; took a seat
TS

Rinko

44c ▶ 35
Center tables

3 half sheets

Center the tables verti-
cally and horizontally.

Problem 1

Study the information at
the right and the illus-
trations below.

Format and type the illustrated problem on a half
sheet (insert long side
first); SS; exact center;
10–space intercolumn.

Guidelines for centering columns horizontally

1 Take preparatory steps

a Move margin stops to ends
of scale. Clear all tabulator
stops.

b Move carrier (carriage) to
center point.

c If spacing is not given, estimate spacing for intercolumns
(the area between columns)—
preferably an even number
of spaces (4, 6, 8, 10, or 12,
for example).

2 To set left margin stop

Check the longest item in each
column. Then from the center
point, backspace *once* for
each 2 characters and spaces
in the longest items in each
column then for each 2 spaces
to be allowed for the intercolumns. Set the left margin
stop at this point.

If the longest item in one
column has an extra character,
combine the extra character
with the first letter in the
next column. If one stroke
is left over after back-
spacing for all columnar
items, disregard it.

Study the illustration below
used to center two items and a
10-space intercolumn for the
first table.

3 To set tabulator stops

After setting the left margin
stop, space forward once for
each character in the longest
item in the first column, then
for each space to be allowed
for the first intercolumn. Set
tab stop at this point. Follow
this procedure for each subsequent column and inter-
column.

backspace once
for each two
characters ⟶
| 1 | 1 | 1 | 1 | 1 | 1 | 1 | 1 | 1 | 1 | 1 | 1 | 1 | 1 | 1 | 1 | 1 | 1 | 1 | 1 | 1 |
Ca | ro | ly | n | Ly | nn | C | ar | ve | re | Vi | ce | P | re | si | de | nt | 1-2 | 3-4 | 5-6 | 7-8 | 9-10 |

```
 1
 2
 3
 4
 5
 6
 7
 8
 9
10
11
12                                                                    words
13            CALUMINEX  BOARD  OF  DIRECTORS                            6
                                          TS
14   Margin stop                   Tab stop
15        ↓                          ↓
16        Muriel E. Bouhm          President                           11
17        R. Grady Atgood          Vice President                      17
18        Alonzo J. Cruz, Sr.      Secretary                           23
19        Carolyn Lynn Carvere     Treasurer                           29
20        Myron A. Moilion         Member                              34
21        Sara Harley Beck         Member                              39
22   Key │Carolyn Lynn Carvere │  10  │Vice President│
23
```

3e
Practice special reach combinations

each line twice SS;
DS between 2-line groups

> **Technique hint:**
> Do not push for speed; work for smooth, fluid keystroking.

as/sa 1 `as ask task fast last lass asks sad salt sale sake`

lo/ol 2 `lo lot lots lode load loaf old fold sold told sole`

ed/de 3 `led fed deed seed sled fled ode lode ade deal desk`

el/le 4 `el els sell felt jell self let leak dale dole lest`
TS

3f
Practice phrases

1 Practice the Level 1 lines once SS at an easy pace.

2 DS; then practice the Level 2 lines in the same way.

3 DS; then practice the Level 2 lines again at a faster pace.

4 If time permits, practice the Level 3 lines once, trying to keep the carrier (carriage) moving steadily.

Note: The 3 sets of lines progress gradually in diffi–culty.

Goal: *At least* 1 line per minute (10 *gwam*).

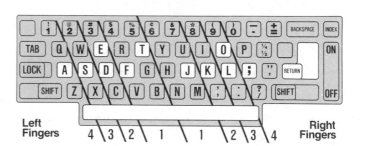

Left Fingers 4 3 2 1 / 1 2 3 4 Right Fingers

all reaches learned

```
        1 to let; to set; a jak; to do all of; to a sad lad;
Level 1 2 to set; to do a; fed a doe; ask a fee; ask a lass;
        3 ask a lad; a sad ode; to see a foe; a sad old oak;
```
DS

```
        4 to last a; take a jet; tell a tale; take a lot of;
Level 2 5 fall ad; as a set; take a deed; to sell a loaf of;
        6 old jade; to see a; of a sad doll; to seek a deal;
```

```
        7 of a flake; to take a salad; to lose a sales deal;
Level 3 8 too stale; to float a; add a total; of a sad tale;
        9 to a; told jokes; soaks a lot; see a lot of lakes;
```

3g
End the lesson

(See page 9 if necessary.)

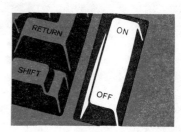

Learning goals

1 To type tables in exact center and in reading position.
2 To type main, secondary, and column headings.
3 To align figures, decimals, and dollar signs in columns.
4 To center announcements horizontally and vertically.

Machine adjustments

1 Set paper guide at 0; remove tab stops.
2 Set ribbon control to type on upper half of ribbon.
3 Use a 70–space line.
4 SS drills; DS paragraphs.

44a ▶ 6
Preparatory practice

each line 3 times SS (work for fewer than 2 errors per group); DS between 3-line groups; repeat selected lines as time permits

alphabet 1 Jack may provide a few extra quiz questions or problems for the group.

figures 2 We can try to add these fractions: 2/3, 3/4, 4/5, 5/6, 7/8, and 9/10.

shift/lock 3 THE LAKES TODAY, published in Dayton, Ohio, is issued in June or July.

easy 4 Enrique may fish for cod by the city docks, but he may risk a penalty.

| 1 | 2 | 3 | 4 | 5 | 6 | 7 | 8 | 9 | 10 | 11 | 12 | 13 | 14 |

44b ▶ 9
Format/type centered announcement

half sheet

Review centering procedures shown at the right.

Use a half sheet (insert long side first). Center the problem verti–cally; center each line horizon–tally; DS.

Vertical centering

1 Count the lines to be centered.
2 Subtract counted lines from total lines available (66 for a full sheet and 33 for a half sheet).
3 Divide the remaining lines by 2 and distribute these lines as top and bottom margins. Ignore fractions.
4 Space down from the top edge of the paper 1 more line than the number of lines figured for the top margin.

Horizontal centering

1 Move margin stops to ends of the scale.
2 Clear all tab stops.
3 From the center point, backspace *once* for each 2 letters, figures, spaces, or punctuation marks in the line to be centered. Do not backspace for a leftover stroke at the end of a line.
4 Begin to keyboard where you complete the backspacing. If all lines are of the same length, set a margin stop; if not, repeat Steps 3 and 4 for each subsequent line.

	words
ARS MUSICA	2
under the direction of Serge Chomentikov	10
will present its	14
Annual Spring Concert	18
Friday evening, April 24, at eight o'clock	27
Taer Recital Hall	30

4a
Prepare-to-keyboard checklist

Check your readiness to begin
Lesson 4.

✔ Work area cleared of unneeded
clothing and books
✔ Book elevated at right of
machine
✔ Left margin set for 50–space line
(center − 25)
✔ Right margin set at extreme right
end of scale

✔ Ribbon control set to type on
upper half of ribbon
✔ Paper edge guide on correct
setting
✔ Paper inserted expertly,
straightened if necessary

4b
Preparatory practice

each line twice SS
(slowly, then faster); DS
between 2-line groups

home row 1 `fj dk sl a; jk fd kl ds l; sa as all fad jak dads;`

e/o/t 2 `ed ol tf led old oft ode dot toe doe foe jets fold`

space bar 3 `to do | do so | a foe | to add | a lot | as a joke | to do so;`

all reaches
learned 4 `a jak fell; tell a tale; sold a desk; to a sole ad`
TS

4c
Learn new keyreaches:
C and H

Reach technique for c

Follow the "Standard procedure
for learning new keyreaches" on
page 10 (Lines 1–4 twice; Lines
5–8 once; repeat 5–8 if time
permits).

Technique hint:
Strike the space bar with a
down–and–in motion of the
thumb.

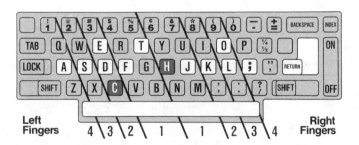

Reach technique for h

Reach to *left* with
right first finger.

c 1 `c cd cd cod cod cot cot call call code codes tacks`
2 `cold clod clad coal cola lack lock dock cool cakes`
DS

h 3 `h hj hj he he she she ah ah ha ha lash dash flash;`
4 `oh ho aha the has had hoe that josh shad hall halt`

c/h 5 `ache echo each cash chat chef hack hock tech check`
6 `a chef; a chat; the ache; all cash; check the hack`

all letters
learned 7 `had a look | took the jet | josh the chef | cash a check`
8 `to teach | had the jack | he took half | a cache of food`
TS

Period and question mark

1 Make decisions about place–ment of the copy. A full sheet and a 1½" top margin are suggested.
2 Proofread carefully; correct errors.
3 Note your comments about your placement decisions at the bottom of the page.
4 Study the rules and examples from your copy.

THE PERIOD AND THE QUESTION MARK

1. Use a period after a complete sentence; follow the period with two blank spaces.

Examples: Buy the books. She will use them later.
I know Don. He is a member of our club.

2. Use a period after an abbreviation. Space once after periods used after abbreviations unless the abbreviation is made up of letters that are combined to represent more than one word; in that case, space only after the final period.

Examples: Mr. Ogden will be graduated with a Ph.D.
Mrs. Sipe arrived at 6 a.m. last Monday.

3. Use periods to form an ellipsis. Ellipsis periods, commonly three in number, represent the omission of words from quoted data. Use four periods when an ellipsis ends a sentence. Space once between ellipsis periods.

Examples: The economy . . . has not yet responded.
We agree the general won the war . . . .

4. Use a question mark after a direct question--not after an indirect question. Space twice after a question mark that is used to terminate a question.

Examples: Where is he? I wonder if he had dinner.
Did she go? I asked if she had tickets.

5. A request that is phrased as a question is usually terminated with a period.

Examples: Will you please bring me a glass of tea.
Will you kindly mail that letter for me.

6. Use a question mark after each of a series of short questions that are related to a single thought. Capitalize the first word of each of the questions only if it is a complete sentence. Space once after all but the final question mark.

Examples: Was it birds? squirrels? rabbits? ducks?
Who wrote this? Was it Lee? Was it Dale?

Compose at the keyboard

Make all format decisions.
1 Read the ¶ thoughtfully.
2 Compose a second ¶ of five or six lines in which you express your ideas about success. Begin with the word **Personally**.
3 Proofread your ¶.
4 Type a final copy of both ¶s. Center a title over the ¶s.

Each of us is building a road that is to lead to some ultimate place known as "success." We construct our highway in stages, passing from one objective to another, expecting in time to reach our goal--to be successful. But how shall we recognize success when we reach it? What is success? When is a person successful?

Personally, (Compose the remainder of the second paragraph.)

4d
Learn new keyreaches:
R and Right Shift

Reach technique for r

Reach *up* with *left first* finger.

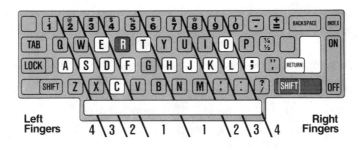

Left Fingers 4 \ 3 \ 2 \ 1 \ 1 \ 2 \ 3 \ 4 Right Fingers

Control of right shift key

Reach *down* with *right little* finger; shift, type, release.

Follow the "Standard procedure for learning new keyreaches" on page 10 (Lines 1–4 twice; Lines 5–8 once; repeat 5–8 if time permits).

r

1 r rf rf or or for for fro fro ore ore her her ford
2 roe for oar are fork role tore oral soar rode fort
DS

right shift

3 A; A; Al Al Alf Alf Flo Flo Ed Ed Ted Ted Del Del;
4 Flo Dole; Chad Alte; Alf Slak; Ella Todd; Sol Ekas

r/right shift

5 Alf Roe; Elke or Rolf Dorr; Rose Salk or Dora Ford
6 Sol Ross asked for Ella; Carl Alda rode for Rhoda;

all reaches learned

7 Rose Ford told Cora the joke Ross had told to her;
8 Dot Roe has the oar here; Al left the oar for her;
TS

4e
Practice words/phrases

1 Practice the Level 1 lines once SS at an easy pace.

2 DS; then practice the Level 2 lines in the same way.

3 DS; then practice the Level 2 lines again at a faster pace.

4 If time permits, practice the Level 3 lines once, trying to keep the carrier (carriage) moving steadily.

Note: The 3 sets of lines progress gradually in diffi-culty.

Goal: *At least* 1 line per minute (10 *gwam*).

all reaches learned

Level 1
1 or to do so of he for the she roe toe cod cot coal
2 jak jet hat hot lot jar her car ask lad lass chose
3 Cal had a jar; Rod has a cat; Della has a red hat;

Level 2
4 cod code jet jets for fore ash cash old hold holds
5 are hare ere here car card ale kale rod rode check
6 Al left; Theo has roe; Flo ate cake; Doc had half;

Level 3
7 elf self shelf led sled sleds fed feed feeds chose
8 old fold folds she shed sheds hot shot shots jokes
9 Rolf added a cash ad; Flora called here for Chloe;

Measure straight-copy skill

two 3' writings; proofread; determine *gwam*; circle errors

Difficulty index

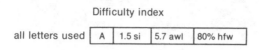

all letters used | A | 1.5 si | 5.7 awl | 80% hfw

gwam 1' | 3'

Just recently an acquaintance of mine was complaining about how   13   4 | 50

quickly papers accumulated on her desk; she never seemed able to reduce   27   9 | 54

the load down to ground zero. There appeared to be some law working,   41   14 | 59

she explained, that continued to increase the stack each day by exactly   56   19 | 64

the amount she had reduced it the day before.   65   22 | 67

My friend ought to be better organized. She should schedule activi-   14   26 | 72

ties so that work is attended to daily. Any paper that requires only a   28   31 | 76

glance, a decision, and swift, final action should get just that. Any   42   36 | 81

paper that must for some reason get closer attention should be subject   56   40 | 86

to a fixed schedule for completion. Self-discipline is the key to order.   71   45 | 91

gwam 1' | 1 | 2 | 3 | 4 | 5 | 6 | 7 | 8 | 9 | 10 | 11 | 12 | 13 | 14 |
      3' | 1 | 2 | 3 | 4 | 5 |

Measure skill growth

Take one 3' and one 5' writing; determine *gwam*; proofread and circle errors.

Difficulty index

all letters used | A | 1.5 si | 5.7 awl | 80% hfw

gwam 3' | 5'

Usually, writing a report does not seem quite so difficult if the   4 | 3

writer breaks the task down into smaller jobs. Before even starting to   9 | 5

write, for example, a writer must know exactly what is to be written,   13 | 8

for whom, and why; and a request for a report ought to have specific   18 | 11

directions with it. The next step is to build a working outline that   23 | 13

summarizes the report. The outline can later be changed to a skeleton   28 | 17

report with statements of purpose and main headings, subheadings, and   32 | 19

paragraph headings that will in time grow into a completed report.   37 | 22

Solutions to the problem under study must be found and analyzed;   41 | 25

and supporting data can be found, among other sources, by observation,   46 | 28

by experimentation, in books, with a questionnaire, with interviews,   50 | 30

and by examining all kinds of records. Each bit of data can be jotted   55 | 33

on a file card, along with a complete citation of its source. As a   60 | 36

last step, these data are added to the skeleton report; the citations   65 | 39

are the footnotes. Then all that is needed are the final touches that   69 | 41

produce a report that is usable, complete, to the point, and readable.   74 | 44

gwam 3' | 1 | 2 | 3 | 4 | 5 |
      5' | 1 | 2 | 3 |

5a
Prepare-to-keyboard checklist

Are you ready to keyboard? Check the items listed at the right before you begin. Review 4a, page 14, if you are unsure about any of the items.

✔ Work area
✔ Book placement
✔ Margin stops
✔ Ribbon control
✔ Paper guide
✔ Paper insertion

5b
Preparatory practice

each line twice SS
(slowly, then faster);
DS between 2-line
groups

home row 1 a; as all lad ask add ash fad jak sad has had lash

c/r 2 or ore core jar jars ark lark rock cord lack cross

h/t 3 a hat ate hate the that oath heat halt sloth loath

all reaches learned 4 Ro has a fake jade; ask Cal to let her do the lot;
TS

5c
Learn new keyreaches: W and U

Reach technique for w

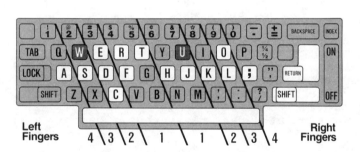

Left Fingers 4 \ 3 \ 2 \ 1 \ 1 \ 2 \ 3 \ 4 Right Fingers

Reach technique for u

Follow the "Standard procedure for learning new keyreaches" on page 10 (Lines 1–4 twice; Lines 5–8 once; repeat 5–8 if time permits).

w 1 w ws ws was was sow sows law laws jaw jaws wow wow
   2 ow how owl owe woes cow cows row rows sow sows low
DS

u 3 u uj uj jut jut cut cut us us use use due due fuse
   4 cue sue hue rut rude just jute sure lure loud cute

w/u 5 how we do; just a duck; we work out our four cues;
     6 we row; use a wok; our used fuse; Sue wore a tutu;

all reaches learned 7 two or four; the cut hurt Wu; a hut for us to use;
                     8 cut two; Duke had a cake; we just saw Dale at two;
TS

Introducing

SALLY ANN DUPOIS
123 Poinciana Road
Memphis, Tennessee 38117-4121
(901-365-2275)
                                   TS

Present Career Objective

Eager to accept part-time position that provides opportunities for
additional training and potential for full-time employment.
                                                TS

Personal Qualifications

Cheerful, outgoing personality; dependable, cooperative worker
Very interested in retailing work; find it challenging
Excellent health; participate in golf, racquetball, and tennis

Experience

1985--present	The Toggery, 100 Madison Avenue, Memphis, TN 38103-
	4219; Assistant Manager
1984 (summer)	Chobie's, 1700 Poplar Avenue, Memphis, TN 38104-
	2176; Inventory Clerk and Cashier
1983 (summer)	Todds, 1450 Union Avenue, Memphis, TN 38104-5417;
	Clerk and Assistant to the Buyer
1982 (summer)	Chobie's, 1700 Poplar Avenue, Memphis, TN 38104-
	2176; Salesperson and Utility Helper

117
122
135
141
154
161
174
181

Education

Junior, Marketing, Memphis State University, Memphis, Tennessee
AA degree (associate degree/advertising; honors), State Technical
Institute, Memphis, Tennessee
Graduate (honor student), East High School, Memphis, Tennessee

References

Mrs. Evelyn J. Quinell	Professor Aldo R. MacKenzie
Manager, Chobie's	Department of Marketing Management
1700 Poplar Avenue	Memphis State University
Memphis, TN 38104-2176	Memphis, TN 38114-3285
Ms. Lanya Roover	Mr. Robert E. Tindall, Jr.
The Toggery	Attorney-at-Law
100 Madison Avenue	1045 Quinn Avenue
Memphis, TN 38103-4219	Memphis, TN 38106-4792

244
255
263
273
282
287
294
304

5d
Learn new keyreaches:
Left Shift and . (period)

Control of left shift key

Reach *down* with *left little* finger; shift, type, release.

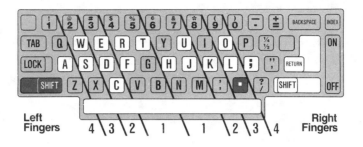

Left Fingers   4   3   2   1   1   2   3   4   Right Fingers

Reach technique for . (period)

Reach *down* with *right third* finger; space twice after . at end of sentence.

Follow the "Standard procedure for learning new keyreaches" on page 10 (Lines 1–4 twice; Lines 5–8 once; repeat 5–8 if time permits).

> **Period:** Space once after a period that fol-lows an abbreviation or an initial, twice after a period that ends a sentence. Do not, however, space after a period at the end of a line.

left shift	1 L La La Lars Lake Ladd Jae Jake Karl Kate Hal Harl
	2 Jae or Jake Kale or Lara Karl or Lars Hart or Ladd
	DS
. (period)	3 . .l .l l.l fl. fl. Dr. E. F. Roe asked for a lot.
	4 Dale has left for Soho. Dr. Sorel saw her at two.
left shift and .	5 Hal saw us. He also saw Joe. He was at the lake.
	6 J. J. does work for us; he used to work for Laura.
all reaches learned	7 Kae used to read to Joe; she works for the Roe Co.
	8 Sr. Jude left for Tulsa; her car was full of food.
	TS

5e
Practice words/sentences

1 Practice the Level 1 lines once SS at an easy pace.

2 DS; then practice the Level 2 lines in the same way.

3 DS; then practice the Level 2 lines again at a faster pace.

4 If time permits, practice the Level 3 lines once, trying to keep the carrier (carriage) moving steadily.

Note: The 3 sets of lines progress gradually in diffi-culty.

Goal: *At least* 1 line per minute (10 *gwam*).

all reaches learned

	1 rf or of uj us sue use ws ow sow cow ol lo low old
Level 1	2 ed led eke tf to lot dot cd cod doc hj hut hue wok
	3 Jeff used the old wok to cook; Lu added the sauce.
	4 we woe awl cow sow led low for fur let cut our hut
Level 2	5 for fat law saw how use jet jut the work chew fake
	6 Aldo took the saw; Ed has to cut the old jak tree.
	7 we our was wore were just jade josh take sake hour
Level 3	8 that lurk wash four keel chew walk crow talk would
	9 Suella saw the letter that Cora wrote at the lake.

43a ▶ 6
Preparatory practice

each line 3 times SS (work for fewer than 3 errors per group); DS between 3-line groups; repeat selected lines as time permits

alphabet	1	Wilma thinks freezing prices at fixed levels for July is questionable.
fig/sym	2	A grant of $12,367.50 won't fund 10% of the studies; it is $948 short.
direct reaches	3	No doubt my brother Cecil served as an umpire on that bright June day.
easy	4	A fox lay in an island lair; a girl dug a quantity of pale lake worms.

| 1 | 2 | 3 | 4 | 5 | 6 | 7 | 8 | 9 | 10 | 11 | 12 | 13 | 14 |

43b ▶ 14
Format/type a bibliography

full sheet; use standard unbound report format; 1½" top margin recommended

1 Read the guides at the right; study the illustrated bibliography.

2 Keyboard the bibliography; make one carbon copy.

Guidelines for preparing a bibliography

A bibliography is a list of works cited or used in some way in the preparation of a report. Bibliographical entries are distinctive from footnotes, as can be noted in the following items:

● A bibliography is the final part of a report.

● The first surname of an entry is identified first, allowing the list to be arranged in alphabetic order.

● The first line of an entry is placed flush left; all succeeding lines of the entry are indented five spaces.

● Reference characters are not used.

● Items are made more incisive with the elimination of most parentheses and commas.

● Specific page numbers used in a footnote may be omitted.

BIBLIOGRAPHY

pica type

Langford, Floyd. "Systems Concept." The Changing Office Environ-
    ment. Reston: National Business Education Association.
    Yearbook No. 18, 1980.

Lesikar, Raymond V. Business Communication: Theory and Applica-
    tion. 4th ed. Homewood: Richard D. Irwin, Inc., 1980.

Will, Mimi, and Donette Dake. Concepts in Word Processing: The
    Challenge of Change. Boston: Allyn and Bacon, Inc., 1981.

43c ▶ 30
Format/type a personal data sheet

full sheet; 1" top and side margins; set tab stop at center point

1 Read the information about data sheets at the right.

2 Keyboard a copy of the data sheet on page 89.

Developing personal data sheets

A personal data sheet is a summary of pertinent, personal facts, organized for quick reading. Data can be categorized in a number of ways, and the writer should use a form that will best display her or his qualifications. Note the following suggestions:

● The data sheet is accompanied by a well-worded letter of application.

● The appearance of the data sheet is as important as what it says.

● Complete sentences are rarely used.

● The data sheet should stress capabilities, not just aspirations.

● The data sheet should be as brief as possible but as long as necessary. Try not to exceed one page.

6a
Prepare-to-keyboard checklist

Are you ready? Check the list at the right.

- ✔ Desk and chair
- ✔ Work area
- ✔ Book placement
- ✔ Paper guide
- ✔ Line–space selector (SS)
- ✔ Margin stops

6b
Preparatory practice

each line twice SS (slowly, then faster); DS between 2-line groups

home row	1	a jak lad as ash ad had add has all fall hash dash
e/o/t/c	2	ed ol tf cd led old cot toe eke due lot colt docks
w/h/r/u	3	ws hj rf uj we raw hut war who haul hawk rule what
all reaches learned	4	Rosela had to cut her rate; Jeff took a weak lead.

TS

6c
Check keystroking technique

each set of lines twice SS; DS between 3-line groups

Technique hint:
Check the list of techniques at the right; use them as you do the drill lines.

- ✔ Seated erect in chair
- ✔ Both feet on floor
- ✔ Fingertips lightly touching home keys
- ✔ Wrists low, but not touching the machine
- ✔ Slant of forearms parallel to slant of keyboard
- ✔ Each key struck with a quick stroke of the fingertip
- ✔ Space bar struck with inward motion of the thumb

all reaches learned

words	1	or do he so of cl la ow to she for the fur due row
	2	cue jak foe sod cut doe sow sue all too wood would
	3	alto also hall fall tall rust dust lark dark jowls
phrases	4	to do so | he or she | to do the | of all our | as the doe
	5	had to do | ask the lad | ate the jak | has the fur coat
	6	do the work | saw the show | just as she | take the test
sen-tences	7	Drew saw the late show. She had to cut law class.
	8	Walt was at Olde Lake at two; Joel also was there.
	9	Kate was at the dock at four to see all of us off.

TS

6d
Check spacing/shifting technique

each set of lines twice SS; DS between 3-line groups

- ✔ Space with down–and–in motion of the thumb
- ✔ Shift with quick, 1–2–3/ shift–type–release motions
- ✔ Quiet hands; no pauses before or after spacing or shifting
- ✔ Space once after abbreviation period
- ✔ Space twice after a sentence period
- ✔ Space once after a semicolon

Technique hint:
Check the techniques above right; use them as you do the drill.

all reaches learned

spacing	1	ah so he do la of el us to ha for she due cot work
	2	to do of us do so a jak the fur for the of all the
	3	Ask the lad for the oak. He cut the wood at work.
shifting	4	Ask for Dr. Lor. She took a call. Jae heard her.
	5	Todd has to work. Talk to Jewel; she has the ads.
	6	Laura left for Duluth. She took the jet at three.

---

words

2   314

<u>Reference characters</u>. To keystroke a superior figure,   329

turn the platen back half a line and type the figure. Aster-   341

isks and other refrence symbols requires no such adjustment.   353

Keyboards equipped with special symbol keys for report writing are also   367

available for regular use.   369

<u>Page</u> endings. A few very simple guides become important when-   383

ever a report has more than one page. For example, never end a   396

page with a hyphenated word. Further, do not leave a single   408

line a of paragraph at the bottom of a page or at the top of a   420

page (unless the paragraph has only one line, of course.)   432

<u>Footnote content</u>. Underline titles of <u>complete</u> publica-   446
tions; use quotation marks with <u>parts</u> of publications. Thus,   460
DS the name of a magazine will be underlined, but the title of an   472
article within the magazine will be placed in quotation marks.   485
Months and locationla words, such as <u>volume</u> and <u>number</u>, may be   500
abbreviated.   503

<u>Penciled guides</u>. A light pencil mark can be helpful to   517

mark approximate page endings, planned placement of page numbers,   530

and potential foot note locations. When the report has been   542

finished, of course, erase any visable pencil marks.   553

TS

Conclusion   557

With patience and skill, the keyboard operator can give a   569

well-written report the porfessional appearance it desrev deserves. Says   582

Lesikar,   584

    Even with the best typewriter available, the fin-   594
ished work is no better than the efforts of the typist.   605
But this statement does not imply that only the most   616
skilled typist can turn out good work. Even the the   626
inexperienced typist can produce acceptable manuscripts   637
simply by exercising care.   642

  646

2 Raymond V. Lesikar, <u>Basic Business Communcation</u> (Homwood: 657
Richard D. Irwin, Inc., 1979), p. 364.   665

7a ▶ 8
Preparatory practice

each line twice SS
(slowly, then faster);
DS between 2-line groups

Note: Beginning with Lesson 7, each lesson part will include in its headings a suggested number of minutes for practicing that activity.

all letters learned 1 Doc took just four hours to row to the south lake.
c/u/r 2 Lou cut the rate cost of our letters to the coast.
w/h 3 Ask Walt Howe to heat the water to wash the shelf.
all reaches learned 4 We saw Jack a lot later; he worked for four hours. TS

7b ▶ 6
Develop keyboarding fluency

two 30″ writings on each line
Goal: To complete each line in 30″ (14 *gwam*).

all letters learned

1 Do the oak shelf for the lake dock.
2 She cut half the fuel for the auto.
3 Throw the kale to the cow for Jake.
4 The autos do the work of the world. TS

7c ▶ 12
Learn new keyreaches: X and I

Reach technique for x

Left Fingers   4 3 2   1   1 2 3 4   Right Fingers

Reach technique for i

Follow the "Standard procedure for learning new keyreaches" on page 10 (Lines 1–4 twice; Lines 5–8 once; repeat 5–8 if time permits).

x 1 x xs xs ox ox axe axe sox sox fox fox hex hex axle
  2 xs ax ox tux lox lax sax flex flax flux crux taxed

i 3 i ik ik if if is is it it did did kid kid aid aids
  4 ik kit sit fit wit sir lid its side cite kick wick

x/i 5 Felix fixed the six tax rules I asked Exie to fix.
    6 I will fix tea for Dixie if she will wax the taxi.

all reaches learned 7 Sid Cox said it was a lax law; Roxie also said so.
                    8 Jackie will fix the cut foot of the old fox I saw. TS

words

preparing REPORTS: THE PROFESSIONAL TOUCH ‹ TS   9

Both the writer and keyboard operator, or compositor, share   21

a mutual concern for the preparation and for the ultimate suc-   30

cess of a report, but usually the writer must accept final   42

accountability. The compositors contribution, however, is an   54

extremely vital one; and she or he should por/ceed with great   62

caution. For example, even before they start ing to prepare a   73

final copy of a report, the compositor should proceed with   82

determine   84

1. the specified purpose of the report and whether some par-   96
ticular format is required;   102

2. the number, kind, and grade of cpies required; and   113

3. deadliens for completion.   119

Thekeyboard operator should be prepared to word from the   130

script, rough-draft, or printed copy and yet give the report a   143

final presentation that is as professional as it is functional.   156

‹ TS before a side heading
"Tricks of the Trade"   164

Those with experience in preparing reports have found that   176

there are special procedures they can use to simplify their   188

tasks. The following paragraphs contain samples of some pro-   200

cedures that can be especially ehlpful to a person who has not   212

prefiously keyboarded reports. (Anyone who palns to prepare   224

more that a few reports, however, should read several good books on the subject.)   241

Right margins. Attractive right margins result result when   254

good judgment is exercised used. Using the warning bell judiciously   267

ensures right margins that approxiimate left margins in width.   279

SS   283

[1]For further information see The Chicago Manual of Style,   300

13ˆth ed. (Chicago: The Universiyt of chicago Press, 1982),   312

p. 40.   314

(continued on page 87)

7d ▶ 12
Learn new keyreaches:
G and N

Reach technique for g

Reach to *right* with *left first* finger.

Left Fingers   4 \ 3 \ 2 \ 1 \   / 1 / 2 / 3 / 4   Right Fingers

Reach technique for n

Reach *down* with *right first* finger.

Follow the "Standard procedure for learning new keyreaches" on page 10 (Lines 1–4 twice; Lines 5–8 once; repeat 5–8 if time permits).

g
1 g gf gf go go fog fog got got rug rug dog dog frog
2 gf log dug fig wig dig lag tog leg keg jig cog got
DS

n
3 n nj nj an an and and end end hen hen ran ran lend
4 nj on won wan den tan ten can land want rent sends

g/n
5 Gwen longs to sing a grand song she knew in Genoa.
6 Gig noted that one swan wing was green with algae.

all reaches learned
7 Leonor left the show to take a cruise to Calcutta.
8 Just set a fair goal; then work hard to extend it.
TS

7e ▶ 12
Build keyboarding continuity

1 Practice the Level 1 lines once SS at an easy pace.

2 DS; then practice the Level 2 lines in the same way.

3 DS; then practice the Level 2 lines again at a faster pace.

4 If time permits, practice the Level 3 lines once, trying to keep the carrier (carriage) moving steadily.

Note: The 3 sets of lines progress gradually in difficulty.

Goal: *At least* 1 line per minute (10 *gwam*).

Count typewritten words:

Five characters and spaces are counted as one standard typewritten word. The figures in the scale under the copy show the word–by–word count (5 strokes a word) for each line.

all reaches learned

Level 1
1 I will need four to six weeks to work out the act.
2 Janet can ask six of the girls to guide the tours.
3 Ask Nellie to sing one alto aria in our next show.

Level 2
4 He will fix a snack; he will also fix fruit juice.
5 The four girls will use their auto or hire a taxi.
6 Gil has asked six girls to a light lunch in Akron.

Level 3
7 Luann wore a ring and long necklace of green jade.
8 Dixie will send her tax check to the local office.
9 Lex is an officer of high rank in Jackson Tool Co.

| 1 | 2 | 3 | 4 | 5 | 6 | 7 | 8 | 9 | 10 |

To determine words-a-minute rate:

1 List the figure 10 for each line completed during a writing.

2 For a partial line, note from the scale the figure directly below the point at which you stopped.

3 Add these figures to determine the total gross words typed (the same as *gwam* for a 1' writing).

42a ▶ 6
Preparatory practice

each line 3 times SS (work for fewer than 3 errors per group); DS between 3-line groups; repeat selected lines if time permits

alphabet	1	We have printed just sixty dozen meal tickets for the banquet meeting.
fig/sym	2	Room #476 is $39 a day, but call 615-2890 (before 2 p.m.) for 7% less.
hyphen/ dash	3	Hyphenate a multiword modifier preceding a noun--a hard-and-fast rule.
easy	4	The town may wish to blame us for the auditory problems in the chapel.

| 1 | 2 | 3 | 4 | 5 | 6 | 7 | 8 | 9 | 10 | 11 | 12 | 13 | 14 |

42b ▶ 9
Improve concentration

1 Keyboard a copy of the ¶ DS. Where a blank space occurs, insert either the word **they** or **that**.

2 Using your corrected copy, take as many 1' writings as time permits.

Difficulty index

all letters used | A | 1.5 si | 5.7 awl | 80% hfw

gwam 1'

Typically, women and men who are successful give the best _____ can 13

give. _____ do not do this just because _____ have the personality makeup 28

_____ demands it; _____ do so because _____ are seemingly oriented to be 42

achievers. Quite simply, _____ expect to succeed; and _____ refuse to 56

recognize any effort, including theirs, _____ is not top rated. 68

gwam 1' | 1 | 2 | 3 | 4 | 5 | 6 | 7 | 8 | 9 | 10 | 11 | 12 | 13 | 14 |

42c ▶ 35
Format/type a two-page report with footnotes

2 full sheets; standard unbound report format; SS and indent enumerated items 5 spaces from each margin; number second page in upper right corner

1 Review unbound report format on page 80 and the illustrations at the right. Do not type from the illustrations.

2 Format and type the report on pages 86 and 87 as an unbound report.

3 Proofread; correct errors.

1½" pica (Line 10)

Main heading

PREPARING REPORTS: THE PROFESSIONAL TOUCH
TS
Both the writer and keyboard operator, or compositor, share concern for the preparation and ultimate success of a report, but usually the writer must accept final accountability. The compositor's contribution, however, is a vital one; and she or he should proceed cautiously. For example, before starting to prepare a final copy of a report, the compositor should determine:

1. the specified purpose of the report and whether some particular format is required;

2. the number, kind, and grade of copies required;[1] and

3. deadlines for completion.

The keyboard operator should be prepared to work from script, rough-draft, or printed copy and yet give the report a final presentation that is as professional as it is functional.
TS
Side heading
DS
"Tricks of the Trade"
Those with experience in preparing reports have found that there are special procedures they can use to simplify their tasks. The following paragraphs contain samples of some procedures that can be especially helpful to a person who has not previously keyboarded reports. (Anyone who plans to prepare more than a few reports, however, should read several good books on the subject.)

¶ heading
DS
Right margins. Attractive right margins result when good judgment is exercised. Using the warning bell judiciously ensures right margins that approximate left margins in width.

[1]For further information see The Chicago Manual of Style, 13th ed. (Chicago: The University of Chicago Press, 1982), p. 40.

Pica pitch

2" elite (Line 13)

Main heading

PREPARING REPORTS: THE PROFESSIONAL TOUCH
TS
Both the writer and keyboard operator, or compositor, share concern for the preparation and ultimate success of a report, but usually the writer must accept final accountability. The compositor's contribution, however, is a vital one; and she or he should proceed cautiously. For example, before starting to prepare a final copy of a report, the compositor should determine:

1. the specified purpose of the report and whether some particular format is required;

2. the number, kind, and grade of copies required;[1] and

3. deadlines for completion.

The keyboard operator should be prepared to work from script, rough-draft, or printed copy and yet give the report a final presentation that is as professional as it is functional.
TS
Side heading
"Tricks of the Trade"
DS
Those with experience in preparing reports have found that there are special procedures they can use to simplify their tasks. The following paragraphs contain samples of some procedures that can be especially helpful to a person who has not previously keyboarded reports. (Anyone who plans to prepare more than a few reports, however, should read several good books on the subject.)

¶ heading
DS
Right margins. Attractive right margins result when good judgment is exercised. Using the warning bell judiciously ensures right margins that approximate left margins in width.

[1]For further information see The Chicago Manual of Style, 13th ed. (Chicago: The University of Chicago Press, 1982), p. 40.

Elite pitch

8a ▶ 8
Preparatory practice

each line twice SS
(slowly, then faster);
DS between 2-line
groups

all letters learned — 1 Alexi Garcia had gone to San Juan for three weeks.

x/i — 2 I next fixed the axle; then I waxed the six taxis.

g/n — 3 Ginger is going to England to sing for Jonah King.

all reaches learned — 4 Lex and Rolf saw Luan Ling; Jack had not seen her.

Recall: TS between lesson parts.

| 1 | 2 | 3 | 4 | 5 | 6 | 7 | 8 | 9 | 10 |

8b ▶ 8
Improve keyboarding technique

each line once as shown; if time permits, repeat the drill

all reaches learned

keystroking and spacing
1 ws ik ed ol nj rf uj tf cd .l xs gf hj ec un rg tf
2 if so is do it of an go he el ha ox ah or eh to us
3 as to | we go | at an | we do | as he | see us | get it | ate an

spacing and shifting
4 Ken can win if he will set a goal and work for it.
5 Dorn is now in Rio; Janice is to go there in June.
6 Ann and J. D. Fox had seen Lt. Green at the dance.

| 1 | 2 | 3 | 4 | 5 | 6 | 7 | 8 | 9 | 10 |

8c ▶ 12
Learn new keyreaches: V and , (comma)

Reach technique for v

Reach *down* with *left first* finger.

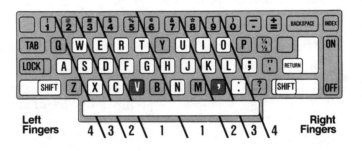

Left Fingers 4 3 2 1 | 1 2 3 4 Right Fingers

Reach technique for , (comma)

Reach *down* with *right second* finger; space once after , used as punctuation.

Follow the "Standard procedure for learning new keyreaches" on page 10 (Lines 1–4 twice; Lines 5–8 once; repeat 5–8 if time permits).

v
1 v vf vf vie vie vow vow van van via via five fives
2 vf vf live have dive love vane vain vile view viva
DS

,
3 , ,k ,k kit, kit, Dick, Jane, Nate, and I read it.
4 a rug, a jig, a ski, an igloo, the ring, two songs

Comma: Space once after a comma.

v/,
5 Vic, Iva, and Viv dived over and over to save Van.
6 Val, Reva, and Vi voted for Eva; even so, Iva won.

all reaches learned
7 Kevin Nix was a judge at the garden show in Flint.
8 Joan, not Vi, took the jet; Vic also tried for it.

| 1 | 2 | 3 | 4 | 5 | 6 | 7 | 8 | 9 | 10 |

Lesson **8** | Section **1** | Learning letter keyreaches

41a ▶ 6
Preparatory practice

each line 3 times SS
(work for fewer than
3 errors per group);
DS between 3-line
groups; repeat
selected lines as
time permits

alphabet 1 Jenny Saxon left my squad a week after giving back the disputed prize.

fig/sym 2 I paid $1.95 for 2% milk and $3.87 for 60 rolls at J & D's on June 14.

long words 3 A probability study is particularly helpful for effective forecasting.

easy 4 At a signal, he may sign a name and title at the end of the amendment.

| 1 | 2 | 3 | 4 | 5 | 6 | 7 | 8 | 9 | 10 | 11 | 12 | 13 | 14 |

41b ▶ 44
Format/type reports: second page; two footnotes

Problem 1

full sheet

1 Type copy as the *second* page of a report.
2 Refer to pages 80, 81, and 83 for format direc–tions if necessary.

Problem 2

full sheet

1 Type copy as the *first* page of a report. Use the heading: TECHNOLOGICAL CHANGE
2 Omit the last paragraph before the footnotes.
3 Refer to pages 80, 81, and 83 for format direc–tions if necessary.

words

line 4 **2** 0

line 7 Today, much of the movement for technological change involves the 14
search for efficiency; that is, shortcutting time and energy, especially as they 30
touch upon the flow of information. Langford says, "Society today is an infor- 45
mation society. Information is what office operations produce." [1] In today's 61
highly competitive business world, accurate information must be readily avail- 76
able; and it is this need, of course, that has given us word processing. 91

Sociologists say that society does not adopt new technology until con- 105
ditions, always changing, make it ready to do so; then it assimilates change very 121
rapidly. The automobile, for example, was invented years before its acceptance 137
as a popular method of transportation. It seems, therefore, that as technology 153
becomes available, society needs pioneers with foresight who will work for its 169
acceptance. Speaking of word processing, Will and Dake say, 181

> In order to keep up with technological change and at the same 194
> time address human factors, those involved in setting up and run- 206
> ning word processing systems must be change agents. Change 218
> agents know where to find information on the constant changes in 231
> the industry and how to utilize it advantageously.[2] 242

Other "agents of change" must function to prepare a consuming society 256
to trust change; to support it financially; and, above all, to use it. Perhaps the 273
greatest challenge involving technology is not to create change, but to learn to 289
live with it. 292

_____ 296

[1] Floyd Langford, "Systems Concept," The Changing Office Environ- 314
ment (Reston: National Business Education Association, Yearbook No. 18, 329
1980), p. 31. 332

[2] Mimi Will and Donette Dake, Concepts in Word Processing: The Chal- 353
lenge of Change (Boston: Allyn and Bacon, Inc., 1981), p. v. 368

8d ▶ 12
Learn new keyreaches: Q and Y

Reach technique for q

Reach *up* with *left little* finger.

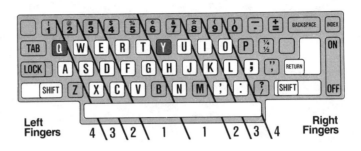

Left Fingers 4 \ 3 \ 2 \ 1 \ 1 \ 2 \ 3 \ 4 Right Fingers

Reach technique for y

Reach *up* with *right first* finger.

Follow the "Standard procedure for learning new keyreaches" on page 10 (Lines 1–4 twice; Lines 5–8 once; repeat 5–8 if time permits).

q
1 q qa qa qu qu quo quo quit quits quad quads quotes
2 qa qu quo quit quad quick quite equal quilt quarts
DS

y
3 y yj yj jay jay you you yet yet day day yell yells
4 yj eye yes rye dye sky cry sly try joy soy yen toy

q/y
5 Jay says Quay is quite young; he is quiet and shy.
6 Troy, Quent, and I are quite glad that Quinn quit.

all reaches learned
7 Frank Cage enjoyed the novel; Jo can read it next.
8 Next, Jacky Quire will leave; she can go in a day.

| 1 | 2 | 3 | 4 | 5 | 6 | 7 | 8 | 9 | 10 |

8e ▶ 10
Build sustained keyboarding power

1 Practice Paragraph (¶) 1 once SS.
2 DS and practice ¶ 2 in the same way.

Technique hints:

1 Keep your eyes on the book copy as you keyboard.
2 Do not pause or look up as you return the carrier or carriage (or cursor on a personal computer).

all reaches learned

¶ 1 We often need to choose, and yet it is never easy to know which of two roads to take. One can look exactly like another, yet we are never quite sure what is involved with each journey or each choice.

¶ 2 However, we do have to choose; and, since we will not know where the unchosen road would have taken us, we have to trust that we chose the right road.

| 1 | 2 | 3 | 4 | 5 | 6 | 7 | 8 | 9 | 10 |

40d ▶ 15
Preapplication drill: format/type source footnotes

1 Study carefully the guides and models for preparing footnotes.

2 Using the appropriate model (pica or elite) below, type the final lines of a page and its source footnotes. Use 1″ side margins. (Note: Since 19 typed and blank lines are needed to complete the 66–line page, begin typing on Line 48.)

3 Compare the appearance and content of your finished product with the model in the textbook.

Format/type source footnotes

Preparing footnotes correctly takes skill, knowledge, and careful planning. The guidelines below will help you to plan and type the footnotes in Section 9.

• Footnotes should be placed at the foot of the page on which reference to them is made.

• Use a superior figure (raised a half line) in the text as reference to the footnote; repeat the superior figure with the footnote.

• Separate footnotes from the body of the report with a single underline 1½″ (18 elite or 15 pica spaces); SS before the line and DS after it.

• SS footnotes; DS between them if more than one occurs on a page.

• When one or more footnotes must appear at the foot of a page, allowances must be made for a 1″ (6 lines) bottom margin, 3 or 4 lines for each footnote, and 2 lines for the dividing line. As can be seen, it is important to know when to stop keyboarding and when to begin the footnotes.

---

pica | formats as discussed by Guffey and Erickson[1] (business reports) | 48
| | 49
and Hashimoto, Kroll, and Schafer[2] (academic reports). | 50

SS _____ | 51

DS [1]Mary Ellen Guffey and Lawrence W. Erickson, <u>Business Office</u> | 52
<u>Practices Involving the Typewriter with Implications for Business</u> | 53
<u>Education Curricula</u>, Monograph 136 (Cincinnati: South-Western | 54
Publishing Co., 1981), pp. 17, 27, and 28. | 55
| | 56

DS [2]Irvin Y. Hashimoto, Barry M. Kroll, and John C. Schafer, | 57
<u>Strategies of Academic Writing: A Guide for College Students</u> | 58
(Ann Arbor: The University of Michigan Press, 1982), p. 1. | 59
| | 60

1″ (6 lines) | 61
bottom margin | 62
| | 63
| | 64
| | 65
| | 66

---

elite | formats as discussed by Guffey and Erickson[1] (business reports) and Hashimoto, | 48
| | 49
Kroll, and Schafer[2] (academic reports). | 50

SS _____ | 51

DS | 52
[1]Mary Ellen Guffey and Lawrence W. Erickson, <u>Business Office Practices</u> | 53
<u>Involving the Typewriter with Implications for Business Education Curricula</u>, | 54
Monograph 136 (Cincinnati: South-Western Publishing Co., 1981), pp. 17, 27, | 55
and 28. | 56

DS | 57
[2]Irvin Y. Hashimoto, Barry M. Kroll, and John C. Schafer, <u>Strategies of</u> | 58
<u>Academic Writing: A Guide for College Students</u> (Ann Arbor: The University of | 59
Michigan Press, 1982), p. 1. | 60

1″ (6 lines) | 61
bottom margin | 62
| | 63
| | 64
| | 65
| | 66

9a ▶ 8

Preparatory practice

each line twice SS
(slowly, then faster);
DS between 2-line
groups

all letters learned 1 Work quickly, and we can fix the van Janet got us.

v/q/,/y 2 Standing on the quay, Dave, too, felt very queasy.

space bar 3 if it | to do | or he | an ox | for us | to do the | a yen for

easy 4 The city got a quantity of fish for the town lake.

| 1 | 2 | 3 | 4 | 5 | 6 | 7 | 8 | 9 | 10 |

Recall: TS between
lesson parts.

9b ▶ 14

Practice keyreaches

1 Practice each line twice SS;
DS between 2–line groups.
2 Repeat lines that seem most troublesome.

x 1 Lex next sent six yards of flax to Roxy in a taxi.

g 2 Gwen sang a song as George raised the ragged flag.

y 3 I say Ayn is shy; yet I did enjoy her story a lot.

n 4 For Nana, France was a land of sun, sand, and tan.

v 5 Van ran to visit the levee to view the vast river.

q 6 Quay quickly quoted Queen Arqua.   Quent was quiet.

| 1 | 2 | 3 | 4 | 5 | 6 | 7 | 8 | 9 | 10 |

9c ▶ 14

Develop machine parts control

twice as shown; repeat
as time permits

Lines 1-4: Practice each
short line and return without
pausing or looking up.
Lines 5-7: Use space bar ef–
ficiently and maintain typing
fluency.
Lines 8-10: Shift smoothly
and rhythmically.

1 Finish final stroke in the line.

return 2 Reach quickly to the return key.

3 Hold your eyes down on the text.

4 Return; start next line at once.

5 an key fox van vie own hay can jay coy lay rug any

space bar 6 Vote for Gin; Lu is not a good choice. Tell Quin.

7 Lex, not Tay, has a wagon; he will hang the signs.

8 Owen Hays and Lil Young will see Neil in New York.

shift keys 9 Cyd, Rod, Susi, and Don will go on to Vienna soon.

10 J. C. Wert will see Nel Foyt at the Old City Hall.

| 1 | 2 | 3 | 4 | 5 | 6 | 7 | 8 | 9 | 10 |

9d ▶ 14

Build sustained keyboarding power

1 Practice Paragraph (¶) 1 once.
2 DS and practice ¶ 2 in the
same way.

> **Technique hint:**
> Keystroke smoothly, con–
> tinuously; avoid pauses.

all reaches learned

¶ 1 There are certain things that each of us wants to own, and we know there are ways to acquire things we want.   However, there is a flaw in this design.

¶ 2 As soon as we get the thing we want, it loses its value; so we exchange one want for another.   Then we find that just having does not satisfy wanting.

| 1 | 2 | 3 | 4 | 5 | 6 | 7 | 8 | 9 | 10 |

40a ▶ 6
Preparatory practice

each line 3 times SS
(work for fewer than 3
errors per group); DS
between 3-line
groups

alphabet	1	The objective of the tax quiz was clarified by checking samples of it.
fig/sym	2	Ship the $567 order for 29 1/3 grams of X8-D40 (8% solution) tomorrow.
shift	3	Will Pamela Forsman be quite happy visiting Kansas and Alaska in July?
easy	4	In the land of enchantment, the fox and the lamb sit down by the bush.

| 1 | 2 | 3 | 4 | 5 | 6 | 7 | 8 | 9 | 10 | 11 | 12 | 13 | 14 |

40b ▶ 4
Keystroke the * (asterisk)

The * (asterisk) may be used to
refer to a footnote. Find the location of the * on your machine;
type the drill line twice.

* ** * I may use * and ** to indicate the first and second footnotes.

40c ▶ 25
Format/type a report with a footnote

full sheet; refer to pages
80 and 81 for format
guidelines if necessary

words

FOOTNOTES
TS

4

Formal reports are usually written to put forward some point of view, to 18
convince readers, and/or to convey information in such a way that it will be 34
relied upon, accepted, or believed. To substantiate the contents of a report and 50
to give it greater weight of authority, a writer often cites evidence that other 66
people support his or her conclusions. Sources for such support are then shown 82
as footnotes at appropriate places within the report. 93

Citations for all such opinions or statements of fact spoken or written by 108
someone other than the writer should be documented. This procedure is simply 124
a matter of fair play, of "giving credit where credit is due." Whenever a writer 140
paraphrases or quotes directly from the work of someone else, credit should be 156
given. 158

Footnotes are also frequently used to clarify points, provide additional 172
information, or add other forms of editorial comment that the writer may wish 188
to make. For whatever reason a footnote is included, it must be done with the 204
idea of assisting a reader. 209

Footnotes may be placed at the end of a report, or they may be placed at the 224
foot of the page on which reference to them is made.* In either case, the 239
footnotes are typed in sequential order and numbered consecutively throughout 255
the report. Footnotes on a partially filled page may immediately follow the last 271
line of the text, or they may be placed to end one inch from the bottom of the 287
page. 288

1½" underline ——————— SS ———————
DS 291

* Footnotes at the foot of the page are usually preferred for academic 305
writing. 307

10a ▶ 8
Preparatory practice
each line twice SS
(slowly, then faster);
DS between 2-line
groups

all reaches learned 1 Yes, Clive took a few quarts; Jan had six gallons.

shift keys 2 The Fortune Five will sing at our Lake Youth Hall.

v/y 3 Every year, I have given Yves five heavy old keys.

easy 4 Diane owns the oak shanty; she also owns the land.

Recall: TS between lesson parts.

| 1 | 2 | 3 | 4 | 5 | 6 | 7 | 8 | 9 | 10 |

10b ▶ 8
Reach for new goals
1 Take a 30–second (30″) writing on Line 4 of 10a above; determine *gwam* (total words typed × 2).
2 From the sentences at the right, choose one that will cause you to aim for 2–3 *gwam* more than your rate in Step 1. (30″ *gwam* for each sentence is shown in Column 2 at the right.)

3 Take two 30″ guided writings on the chosen sentence; try to reach the end of the line each time "Return" is called.
4 If you reach your goal in both 30″ writings, take two 30″ writings on the next sentence. (A total of eight 30″ writings will be given.)

5 Take another 30″ writing on Line 4 of 10a above; determine *gwam* (total words typed × 2).

Goal: An increase of *at least* 2 *gwam* from Step 1 to Step 5.

	words in line	gwam 30″	gwam 20″
1 Nan lent the auto to the girl.	6	12	18
2 Iris did throw a rock at the signs.	7	14	21
3 He did work with vigor to land the fish.	8	16	24
4 Hang the keys to the shanty on the oak chair.	9	18	27
5 The girls wish to visit the city to fix the signs.	10	20	30

| 1 | 2 | 3 | 4 | 5 | 6 | 7 | 8 | 9 | 10 |

10c ▶ 12
Learn new keyreaches: Z and M

Reach technique for z

Left Fingers 4 3 2 1 1 2 3 4 Right Fingers

Reach technique for m

Follow the "Standard procedure for learning new keyreaches" on page 10 (Lines 1–4 twice; Lines 5–8 once; repeat 5–8 if time permits).

z 1 z za za az az zoo zoo zed zed jazz jazz lazy crazy
2 za za haze doze zone cozy zany zing zinc size raze

m 3 m mj mj jam jam ham ham may may yam yam make makes
4 mj am me ma man men made must fame dome fume major

z/m 5 Zack was amazed when Mazie came home from the zoo.
6 Lazy Mr. Zym dozed at home in the dim haze of May.

all reaches learned 7 Craving quiet, Jeff mildly dozed; he awoke at six.
8 Zed will move as quickly next June; why, I forget.

| 1 | 2 | 3 | 4 | 5 | 6 | 7 | 8 | 9 | 10 |

39c ▶ 34

Format/type reports/ spread headings

Problem 1

full sheet; DS; 1" side margins: 5–space ¶ indention.

1 Read carefully the guides for preparing reports.

2 Follow these guidelines as you keyboard.

Preparing reports

Before you prepare any report, determine whether or not there are specific instructions for its format. In the absence of such instructions, the guides given here are generally accepted for reports that are not to be bound. Follow these guidelines for the reports in Section 9.

• Use a 1½" top margin (pica) or 2" (elite) for the first page; otherwise, use 1" margins for all four sides.

• Use double spacing.

• Do not number the first page.

• Number the second and all subsequent pages in the upper right corner, ½" (Line 4) from the top of the page.

• Enclose short quotations in quotation marks. Indent longer quotations 5 spaces from each margin; omit quotation marks, and use single spacing.

---

	words
SIMPLE REPORT FORMAT	4
TS	

It is important that students who prepare term papers, themes, and other forms of academic writing know the procedures for typing reports. — 19, 32

In the previous sections, your typed work has been set to a stated line length of 50, 60, or 70 spaces, regardless of whether your machine was equipped with pica- or elite-size type. Here in Section 9 you will be asked to prepare formal reports that require placement in accordance to the number of inches in top, bottom, and side margins rather than to the number of spaces in the writing line. — 46, 62, 79, 95, 110, 111

Because of the difference in type size, pica and elite solutions will differ somewhat. When 1-inch side margins are used, a pica line will contain 65 spaces; an elite line will contain 78 spaces. Both sizes of type, of course, will accommodate 6 line spaces to a vertical inch. — 127, 141, 158, 167

When side margins of 1 inch are used, 10 pica spaces should be allowed in each margin; on the other hand, users of elite type should allow 12 spaces. — 182, 197

Problem 2

half sheet; 2" top margin; center each heading at the far right as a spread heading, as shown in the first heading.

Center spread headings

1 To center a spread heading, backspace from the center point once for each letter, character, and space except for the last letter or character in the heading.

2 From this point, type the heading, spacing once after each letter or character and 3 times between words.

	words
S P R E A D H E A D I N G S	6
SIMPLE REPORT FORMAT	10
SOURCE FOOTNOTES	14
PREPARING AN OUTLINE	18

Problem 3

full sheet

Repeat the report in Problem 1.
Use a spread heading.

10d ▶ 12
Learn new keyreaches:
B and P

Reach technique for b

Reach *down* with *left first* finger.

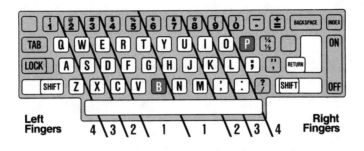

Left Fingers 4 3 2 1   1 2 3 4 Right Fingers

Reach technique for p

Reach *up* with *right little* finger.

Follow the "Standard procedure for learning new keyreaches" on page 10 (Lines 1–4 twice; Lines 5–8 once; repeat 5–8 if time permits).

b
1 b bf bf by by fib fib fob fob bit bit jib jib buff
2 bf by fib fob but rub job rib rob buy tub bid boff
DS

p
3 ; p; p; pa pa pan pan pen pen pad pad pep pep paid
4 up up; cup cup; sip sip; nap nap; map map; ape ape

b/p
5 Pepe bobbed for an apple; Bo jumped rope; I boxed.
6 Pablo Paz paid Barb to probe deeply for old bulbs.

all reaches learned
7 Caleb sipped a cup of pink juice at the Boise Zoo.
8 Five quiet zebus walk up; yet, Drex Marsh jogs on.

| 1 | 2 | 3 | 4 | 5 | 6 | 7 | 8 | 9 | 10 |

10e ▶ 10
Review keyboarding techniques

each line once SS; repeat as time permits

Lines 1-3: Keep wrists low; do not rest palms on machine.

Lines 4-6: Keep unused fingers in home–row position.

Lines 7-9: Move quickly and smoothly from letter to letter and word to word (no pauses).

Spacing review: Strike the space bar with a down–and–in motion of the thumb.

all letters
1 Alice is to speak for the group at the next forum.
2 Dan joined the squad for spring drills last month.
3 Denzyl took a short, fast hike; Bev went with him.
DS

spacing and shifting
4 If it were up to me, I would go for the top prize.
5 Vi, Don, and Jo have yet to win a set in the meet.
6 Ask Dr. Su. She knows O. J.; she once taught him.

easy sentences
7 It is the duty of the firm to fix the eight signs.
8 This land is held by the city to make into a park.
9 If you wish to make a big profit, work with vigor.

| 1 | 2 | 3 | 4 | 5 | 6 | 7 | 8 | 9 | 10 |

**Format/type
an outline**

full sheet; 1½" top mar-
gin; 70-space line;
center heading

words

UNBOUND REPORTS
TS

3

    I. MARGINS   6

      A. Top Margins   9

        1. First page: pica, 1 1/2"; elite, 2"   17

        2. Other pages: 1"   21

      B. Side and Bottom Margins   27

        1. Left and right margins: 1"   33

        2. Bottom margin: 1"   38

   II. SPACING   40

      A. Body of Manuscript: Double   47

      B. Paragraph Indentions: 5 or 10 Spaces Uniformly   57

      C. Quoted Paragraphs   62

        1. Four or more lines   66

          a. Single-spaced   70

          b. Indented 5 spaces from each margin   78

          c. Quotation marks not required   84

        2. Fewer than 4 lines   89

          a. Quotation marks used   94

          b. Not separated from text or indented from text margins   105

  III. PAGINATION   109

      A. Page 1: Usually Not Numbered, but Number May Be Centered 1/2"   122
          from Bottom Edge   125

      B. Other Pages: Number Typed at Right Margin, 1/2" from Top Edge   139
          of Paper Followed by a Triple Space   146

39

39a ▶ 6

**Preparatory
practice**

each line 3 times SS;
(concentrate on
copy); DS between
3-line groups; repeat
selected lines if time
permits

alphabet 1   Our unexpected freezing weather quickly killed Joann's massive shrubs.

figures 2   Invoices 625, 740, and 318 were dated June 5, 1984; and all were paid.

br 3   Brad's brother, Bruce, broke my bronze brooches and brass bric-a-brac.

easy 4   Did the roan foal buck, and did it cut the right elbow of the cowhand?

| 1 | 2 | 3 | 4 | 5 | 6 | 7 | 8 | 9 | 10 | 11 | 12 | 13 | 14 |

39b ▶ 10

Compose at the keyboard

2 full sheets; decide top
margin and spacing

1 Read the questions at the right.

2 Compose an answer for each
question in one or two sentences.
Join the sentences into paragraphs to make a short essay.
Center the title **MY CAREER** over
the paragraphs.

3 Proofread; mark errors. If time
permits, retype the copy in final
form.

1   What is your career goal as you now see it?

2   What led you to make this career choice?

3   In what part of the world do you think you would like to live
and work?

4   Why do you want to live and work there?

5   Do you see yourself following any other career path in the
years ahead?

11a ▶ 8
Preparatory practice
each line twice SS
(slowly, then faster);
DS between 2-line
groups

Recall: TS between
lesson parts.

all letters 1 Have Jeff Pim quickly walk the bridge zone at six.

z/p 2 Pat puzzled Zora; he played a happy piece of jazz.

m/b 3 Bob may remember he was a member of my brass band.

easy 4 The big map firm may make the usual profit for us.

| 1 | 2 | 3 | 4 | 5 | 6 | 7 | 8 | 9 | 10 |

11b ▶ 10
Practice difficult
reaches

1 Practice each line once. Place a
check mark on your paper next to
lines that seem difficult for you.
2 Practice at least twice each line
that you checkmarked.

q 1 Quay made a quiet quip to quell a quarrel quickly.

x 2 Knox can relax; Alex gets a box of flax next week.

y 3 Ty Clay may envy you for any zany plays you write.

v 4 Eve and Vera drive the heavy vans every five days.

n 5 Nan danced many a dance, often with Nick and Donn.

| 1 | 2 | 3 | 4 | 5 | 6 | 7 | 6 | 7 | 8 | 9 | 10 |

11c ▶ 12
Learn new keyreaches:
: (colon) and ? (question mark)

Reach technique for : (colon)

Reach technique
for ? (question)

Left shift and strike ; key;
space twice after : used
as punctuation.

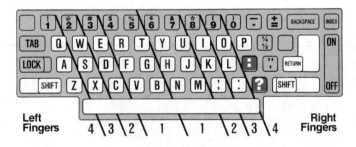

Left shift; reach *down* with
right little finger;
space twice after ? at
end of sentence.

Follow the "Standard procedure
for learning new keyreaches" on
page 10 (Lines 1–4 twice; Lines
5–9 once; repeat 5–9 if time
permits).

: 1 ; :; :; : : To wit: Date: Name: Address: From:
2 Space twice after a colon, thus: To: No.: Time:
DS

? 3 ; ?; ?; ? ? Who? When? Where? Who is? Why not?
4 Did he go? Is she ill? Do I see it? Is it here?

Colon, Question mark:

Hold the left shift key down as
you strike ? and : keys. Except in
rare instances, they are followed
by 2 blank spaces.

:/? 5 Who is here? I see the following: Joe, Lee, Ray.
6 Have you a pen? Copy these two words: tier, rye.

7 When you are puzzled, ask yourself some questions;

all
letters 8 for example: Do I have facts? Can I judge? What

9 options do I have? Who else may be of help to me?

| 1 | 2 | 3 | 4 | 5 | 6 | 7 | 8 | 9 | 10 |

Learning goals

1 To prepare topical outlines.
2 To prepare unbound reports.
3 To prepare a data sheet.
4 To keyboard spread headings.
5 To develop greater awareness of copy content.
6 To improve ability to think and compose at the keyboard.

Machine adjustments

1 Set paper guide at 0; remove all tab stops.
2 Set ribbon control to type on upper half of ribbon.
3 Use a 70–space line unless otherwise directed.

38a ▶ 6
Preparatory practice

each line 3 times SS (concentrate on copy); DS between 3-line groups; repeat selected lines if time permits

alphabet	1	Dixie Vaughn acquired the prize job with a large firm just like yours.
figures	2	The ad said to call 964-5781 before 3 p.m. to order 20 sheets on sale.
shift	3	Rosa and Lazaro spent April in Connecticut and May and June in Hawaii.
easy	4	The eight auto firms may pay for a formal field audit of their profit.

| 1 | 2 | 3 | 4 | 5 | 6 | 7 | 8 | 9 | 10 | 11 | 12 | 13 | 14 |

38b ▶ 14
Align at the right

half sheet; 40-space line; exact vertical center; SS

1 Space forward from left margin 20 spaces; set tab; space forward 20 more spaces; set second tab.

2 Keyboard first column at left margin; use the margin release and backspacer to type "10." Backspace from tab stops to type second and third columns.

			words
1.	I.	one	2
2.	II.	two	4
3.	III.	three	7
4.	IV.	four	9
5.	V.	five	12
6.	VI.	six	14
7.	VII.	seven	17
8.	VIII.	eight	20
9.	IX.	nine	22
10.	X.	ten	24

38c ▶ 14
Preapplication drill: format/type an outline

1 Study the information and the sample outline at the right.

2 Because the lines of the outline are short, set for a 40–space line (center point −20/center point +20); SS; 4–space indentions; 1½" top margin; full sheet.

3 Use **PREPARING OUTLINES** as a main heading; TS; prepare a copy of the outline.

Preparing outlines

It is important that students and others interested in organizing data be able to use a standard form of outline. As you study and keyboard the example at right, note:

● that 4-space indentions separate divisions and subdivisions of various orders.

● that first-order divisions are typed in all capitals; second-order divisions have main words capitalized; third- and subsequent-order divisions have only the first word capitalized.

● that single spacing is used except above and below first-order divisions.

● that there must be at least two parts to any division.

● that the left margin is set for II. Space forward once for single-digit numerals; use the margin release and backspacer for Roman numerals longer than two digits.

● that the line length used must accommodate the longest line in the outline but not exceed a 70–space line.

I. FIRST-ORDER DIVISION
DS
  A. Second-Order Division
  B. Second-Order Division
    1. Third-order division
    2. Third-order division
  C. Second-Order Division
DS
II. FIRST-ORDER DIVISION

  A. Second-Order Division
    1. Third-order division
    2. Third-order division
      a. Fourth-order division
      b. Fourth-order division
    3. Third-order division
  B. Second-Order Division

11d ▶ 10
Learn to operate the tabulator mechanism

1 **Clear all tab stops**

1 Move carrier to extreme right (or carriage to extreme left).
2 Depress tab clear (29) and hold it down as you return carrier to extreme left (or move carriage to extreme right).

2 **Set tab stops**

Move the carrier (or carriage) to the desired position; then depress the tab set (26). Repeat this proce– dure for each stop needed.

3 **Tabulate (tab)***

Tap lightly the tab key (30), using the nearer little finger; or bar, using the right index finger, and return the finger to home position at once.

* If you are using a nonelectric typewriter, refer to page 3 for tabulating technique.

1 Clear all tab stops as directed.
2 Beginning at the left margin, set 3 tab stops at 5–space intervals from the margin stop.
3 Practice the drill once DS as shown. Begin Line 1 at left mar– gin; tab once for Line 2; twice for Line 3; 3 times for Line 4.

1 It is now time for me to learn to use the tab key.

2 $\underset{\text{once}}{\text{tab}}$→Every tab stop now set must first be cleared.

3 $\underset{\text{twice}}{\text{tab}}$→After that, I set tab stops that I need.

4 $\underset{\text{three times}}{\text{tab}}$→Then I touch the tab key to indent.

11e ▶ 10
Check keyboarding skill

1 Practice the two ¶s once DS. Try to type without looking up, especially at the end of lines.
2 Take two 1' writings on each ¶; determine *gwam*.

Goal: At least 14 *gwam*.

Difficulty index

| all letters | E | 1.2 si | 5.1 awl | 90% hfw |

gwam 1'

¶ 1   Some people like their music fast; some of us   9

do not.   Some people have a taste for certain food   19

that others abhor.   Some like flying; some do not.   29

¶ 2   Just why we differ should be quite clear.   We   9

set our own example.   We try a thing, then we make   19

a choice.   Decisions others make need not faze us.   29

| . | 2 | 3 | 4 | 5 | 6 | 7 | 8 | 9 | 10 |

Key to difficulty index of timed writings

E = easy
LA = low average difficulty
A = average difficulty
si = syllable intensity
awl = average word length
hfw = high–frequency words

To determine words-a-minute rate

1 Note the figure at the end of the last line of the writing that you completed.

2 For a partial line, note the figure on the scale directly below the point at which you stopped keyboarding.

3 Add these two figures to deter– mine the total gross words a minute (*gwam*) you typed.

Number usage

Follow directions given on page 77.

Key: 1b. 43 2c. One 3b. 18 4d. 9 4e. 23d 5b. correct 6b. ⅛

review 1a. The Treaty of Ghent is covered in Chapter 9 of the history text.
apply b. Cesar went to Room forty-three and delivered his application.

review 2a. Pick up the parcel at One Elm Way and take it to 4729 Fifth Avenue.
review b. The new address of the Museum of Modern Art is 2647--56th Street.
apply c. The taxi stopped at 1 Sixth Street and 234--42d Street.

review 3a. At 8 a.m. the chef simmered the 3 lbs. of beef in the kettle.
apply b. Their carton (14 in. × 14 in. × eighteen in.) was mailed.

review 4a. She will arrive in Boston between the 2d and the 4th of January.
review b. On May 13 we shall attend the opening of the art exhibit in Richmond.
review c. I shall arrive on the 15th. He will leave Mexico on the 12th.
apply d. Victoria arrived on the 12th of April, and she left on June 9th.
apply e. The cast had a rehearsal on the twenty-third.

review 5a. Maxine earned $68 last week for her work at the local garden store.
apply b. This antique vase, which is made of porcelain, is valued at $400.

review 6a. What is the sum of 1/2, 3/4, and 4 2/3?
apply b. The tailor cut 2 2/3, 1 1/4, one-eighth, and 4 5/8 yards of fabric.

Proofread/revise as you keyboard

half sheet; 74-space line; 1″ top margin; DS

1 Cover the answer key at the bottom of the column. When you have finished keyboarding, check your answers.

2 Keyboard the guide number (with period), space twice, and type the sentence.

3 As you keyboard each line, decide if the sentence is correct according to the guides for number usage. If the sentence is not correct, make the appropriate correction as you keyboard.

Key: 1. 2 **2.** seven **3** cents **4.** three, eight **5.** $25 million **6.** forty--six, 3d **7.** 9 **8.** One, 231--18th **9.** correct **10.** ¼, ½

1. A recipe containing two lbs. of veal won Al the 20th annual contest.

2. About 7 20-ounce containers of milk were on the counter yesterday.

3. He gave the clerk $5 and waited for the 25¢ change.

4. Yoko stacked 3 books and 8 magazines on the shelf.

5. Nearly two thirds of the $25,000,000 was spent on medical research.

6. Six hundred forty six graduates receive diplomas on the third of June.

7. Julio read Rule nine and then applied the principle to the problem.

8. We sent the gifts to 1 Laurel Avenue and 231 18th Street.

9. The company increased productivity by approximately 20 percent in May.

10. What is the sum of 2 1/8, one fourth, and one half?

12a ▶ 8
Preparatory practice
each line twice SS
(slowly, then faster);
DS between 2-line
groups

Recall: TS between
lesson parts.

alphabet	1	Biff was to give the major prize quickly to Dixon.
space bar	2	is it me of he an by do go to us if or so am ah el
shift keys	3	Pam was in Spain in May; Roy Bo met her in Madrid.
easy	4	He may sign the form with the name of the auditor.

| 1 | 2 | 3 | 4 | 5 | 6 | 7 | 8 | 9 | 10 |

12b ▶ 15
Develop keystroking technique

1 Practice each line 3
times SS; DS between
3-line groups; place a
check mark on your
paper next to each line
that was difficult for
you.
2 If time permits, repeat each line that was
difficult.

home row	1	Dallas sadly had a salad as Hal had a large steak.
bottom row	2	Can my cook, Mrs. Zockman, carve the big ox roast?
third row	3	The purple quilt is quite pretty where you put it.
1st/2d fingers	4	I took the main route by the river for five miles.
3d/4th fingers	5	Pam saw Roz wax an aqua auto as Lex sipped a cola.
double letters	6	Ann took some apples to school; Dee, a cherry pie.

| 1 | 2 | 3 | 4 | 5 | 6 | 7 | 8 | 9 | 10 |

12c ▶ 15
Reach for new goals

1 Take a 1' writing on Line 4
of 12a above; determine
gwam (total words typed).
2 From the second column
at the right (*gwam* 30"),
choose a goal that will cause
you to aim for 2–3 *gwam*
more than your rate in Step 1.
Note the sentence that accompanies that goal.
3 Take two 1' writings on
the chosen sentence; try
to reach the end of the
line each time "Return" is
called (each 30").

4 If you reach your goal on both 1'
writings, take two 1' writings on
the next sentence. (A total of eight
1' writings will be given.)

5 Take another 1' writing on Line 4
of 12a above; determine *gwam*
(total words typed).

Goals:
12–14 *gwam*, acceptable
15–17 *gwam*, good
18–20 *gwam*, very good
21+ *gwam*, excellent

		words in line	gwam 30"	gwam 20"
1	I paid for six bushels of rye.	6	12	18
2	Risk a penalty; this is a big down.	7	14	21
3	Did their form entitle them to the land?	8	16	24
4	Did the men in the field signal for us to go?	9	18	27
5	Did she enamel a sign on the auto body with a pen?	10	20	30
6	The ivory emblem is on a shelf in the town chapel.	10	20	30

| 1 | 2 | 3 | 4 | 5 | 6 | 7 | 8 | 9 | 10 |

12d ▶ 12
Check/develop keyboarding continuity

1 Clear tab stops; set a tab for
5-space ¶ indention.
2 Practice ¶1 once DS for orientation.
3 Take two 1' writings on ¶1; determine *gwam* on each writing.
4 Use ¶2 as directed in Steps 2
and 3.

Goal: *At least* 14 *gwam*.

Difficulty index

all letters | E | 1.2 si | 5.1 awl | 90% hfw |

gwam 1'

¶ 1   What is time? Time is the standard needed to   9
fix in sequence each event that makes up the whole   19
fabric of this effort that we like to call living.   29

¶ 2   Time, we realize, means constant pressure for   9
each of us; it must be used. Our minutes are just   19
tiny sums in a book of account. We are the total.   29

| 1 | 2 | 3 | 4 | 5 | 6 | 7 | 8 | 9 | 10 |

Number usage

half sheet; 74-space line; 1″ top margin; SS sentences; DS between groups

1 Cover the answer key at the bottom of the column. When you have finished keyboarding, check your answers.

2 Study guides for number usage.

3 Keyboard guide number 1a. (with period), space twice, and keyboard review sentence(s), noting guide applications.

4 Keyboard apply sentence(s), correcting errors in number usage as you prepare the copy.

Key: 1b. Eight 2c. three, seven 2d. 7 3b. four, 20, two, four 4b. forty, two thirds 5b. Eighty–five 5c. thirty–one

Express as words

1. A number which begins a sentence even if figures are used later in the sentence.
2. Numbers ten and lower unless they are used in close proximity to numbers higher than ten, which are expressed as figures.
3. One of two adjacent numbers. Preferably the smaller number should be spelled for efficiency.
4. Isolated fractions and indefinite numbers.
5. Use a hyphen to separate compound numbers between twenty-one and ninety-nine that are spelled out, whether they stand alone or as a part of a number over one hundred.

review 1a. Six players were cut from the 37-member team.
apply b. 8 altos and 21 sopranos filled the front row of the stage.

review 2a. We saw five or six wild ducks swim away; three were mallards.
review b. All but 5 of the 15 lamps were turned on.
apply c. Andrew took 3 sweaters and 7 shirts to the cleaning service.
apply d. The librarian repaired the loose bindings on seven of the 25 books.

review 3a. The six 200-gallon drums are in the truck.
apply b. Cora bought 4 twenty-cent stamps; she used only 2 of the 4 stamps.

review 4a. About fifty women registered, but only one half stayed for the meal.
apply b. Close to 40 attended the meeting; 2/3 offered to help.

review 5a. Seventy-two of the four hundred fifty-eight pages were about Brahms.
apply b. Eighty five of the one hundred forty-six entry forms were submitted.
apply c. Out of the one hundred thirty one varieties, sixty-two were hybrids.

Number usage

Follow directions given above.

Key: 1b. Forty percent, 86 percent 1c. 37 percent, 5 percent 2c. 75 cents

Express as figures

1. Percentages; spell out the word *percent*. Use the % symbol in tables, technical writing, and some statistical copy.
2. Large round numbers in the millions or higher with their word modifiers, such as 25 *million* or 63 *billion*; use with or without a dollar sign. Use the word *cents* after figure amounts of less than one dollar.

Note

To avoid confusion or error, businesses commonly use figures for all numbers except those which begin a sentence.

review 1a. Attendance was 97 percent; however, 10 percent of the men left early.
apply b. 40% of the 86% increase came from annual donations.
apply c. The firm reinvested 37% of last year's five percent profit.

review 2a. They budgeted $12 million for highways and $10 million for parks.
review b. She took $25 from her savings account; now she has only 14 cents.
apply c. The group collected $1 million; some donations were only 75¢.

Learning goals

1 To achieve smoother keystrok–ing.
2 To improve use of special machine parts.
3 To develop a relaxed, confident attitude.
4 To increase keystroking speed.

Machine adjustments

1 Set paper guide at 0.
2 Set ribbon control to type on upper half of ribbon.
3 Set left margin for a 50–space line (center point – 25); move right stop to end of scale.
4 Single–space (SS) drills; double–space (DS) paragraphs (¶).

13a ▶ 8
Preparatory practice

each line twice SS (slowly, then faster); DS between 2-line groups

Recall: TS between lesson parts.

alphabet	1	Jacques Lopez might fix the wrecked navy tugboats.
z	2	Liz drove hazardous, zigzag Zaire roads with zeal.
y	3	Kay said you should stay with Mary for sixty days.
easy	4	Their form may entitle a visitor to fish the lake.

| 1 | 2 | 3 | 4 | 5 | 6 | 7 | 8 | 9 | 10 |

13b ▶ 12
Develop keyboarding technique

once as shown; repeat if time permits

Lines 1-2: Reach with fingers; keep hand movement to a mini–mum.

Lines 3-4: Curve fingers over home row.

Lines 5-6: Reach fingers to third–row keys without moving hands.

bottom row	1	Did Cam, the cabby, have extra puzzles? Yes, one.
	2	Do they, Mr. Zack, expect a number of brave women?
home row	3	Gayla Halls had a sale; Jake had a sale last fall.
	4	Gladys had half a flask of soda; Josh had a salad.
third row	5	There were two or three quiet people at our party.
	6	Trudy Perry quietly sewed the four pretty dresses.

| 1 | 2 | 3 | 4 | 5 | 6 | 7 | 8 | 9 | 10 |

13c ▶ 8
Practice difficult reaches

1 Each line once; checkmark any line that you do not keystroke fluently.

2 Repeat each checkmarked line as time permits.

> **Technique hint:**
> Work for smoothness and continuity.

v	1	Eva visited every vivid event for twelve evenings.
m	2	A drummer drummed for a moment, and Mimi came out.
p	3	Pat appears happy to pay for any supper I prepare.
x	4	Tex Cox waxed the next box for Xenia and Rex Knox.
b	5	My rubber boat bobbed about in the bubbling brook.

| 1 | 2 | 3 | 4 | 5 | 6 | 7 | 8 | 9 | 10 |

Supplemental skill-building practice

Improve keystroking control

each line twice SS; proofread and circle errors before typing the next line; DS between 2-line groups; repeat selected lines as time permits

direct reaches	1 My brother, Mervyn, has my army carbines; Bernice has my breechloader.
adjacent reaches	2 Three guides loped in a column as we stalked over trails after a lion.
double letters	3 Lynn will see that Jill accepts an assignment in the office next week.
long words	4 Governmental departments encourage associations to photocopy booklets.
1st/ fingers	5 Those 456 heavy black jugs have nothing in them. Fill them by June 7.
2d/ fingers	6 Mike Deak, who was 38 in December, likes a piece of ice in cold cider.
3d & 4th/ fingers	7 Zone 12 was impassable; we quickly roped it off. Did you wax Zone 90?
fig/sym	8 General T & T (common stock) had sales of 5,936,067 shares at 142 5/8.

Measure skill growth: straight copy

a 3' and a 5' writing; determine gwam; proofread and circle errors

Difficulty index

all letters used	A	1.5 si	5.7 awl	80% hfw

gwam 3' | 5'

Diogenes, quaint little light in hand, journeyed out night after — 4 | 3

night looking for an honest man. We don't know exactly how Diogenes — 9 | 5

intended to recognize honesty, but he was very serious about his effort. — 14 | 8

He really thought he would know such a person when he met one. — 18 | 11

Just as a matter of conjecture, do you wonder whether Diogenes, if — 22 | 13

he were living today, might look for an educated person? If he were — 27 | 16

to undertake such a search, would an educated person be recognizable? — 32 | 19

If so, how? What qualities might you expect an educated person to have? — 37 | 22

The idea poses interesting questions. Just what is education? Is — 41 | 25

it a mental thing? Can it be recognized in the actions or reactions of — 46 | 28

a person? Is it backed up by a diploma? Or is it more? Does it perhaps — 51 | 30

include such unscholarly elements as experience and observation? — 55 | 33

gwam 3' | 1 | 2 | 3 | 4 | 5 |
5' | 1 | 2 | 3 |

Measure skill growth: statistical copy

1 Keyboard the ¶ once for orientation. Be especially aware of number usage as you prepare the copy.
2 Take two 3' writings; determine *gwam*.
Goal: at least 19 *gwam*.

Difficulty index

all letters/figures used	LA	1.4 si	5.4 awl	85% hfw

gwam 3'

We started to manufacture Dixie Real Tractors in the back of a small — 5

plant at 3720 First Avenue in Quantico, Virginia; and in that first year — 9

of 1968, we actually completed only five or six of these small-size 9 hp. — 14

machines. Today, in our big, modern factory at One 45th Avenue, we find — 19

it hard to realize that we turn out about seventy of our machines in just — 24

one day and that our profit for last year was over $1 million. — 28

gwam 3' | 1 | 2 | 3 | 4 | 5 |

13d ▶ 10
Control machine parts

once as shown; repeat if time permits

Lines 1-3: From left margin, set two tab stops at 20–space intervals; tab for second and third sentences in each line.

Lines 4-6: Use space bar with down–and–in motion; space correctly after punctuation marks.

Lines 7-8: Use shift–type–release motions.

tab/return	1	Why not us?	Did she ask?	Is it not?
	2	Who was it?	Will he bid?	Why is it?
	3	Can he see?	Is she well?	Was it he?

space bar
4 an any many am ham them by buy bouy ha ah bah bath
5 to buy | for any | the man | did both | by them | the theory
6 I went; Bo did, too. Is it true? To: Ms. Dudley

shift keys
7 Sofie Lamas visits Al and Mae in Denver, Colorado.
8 Tony lives on Elm Court; he works for K. L. Hains.

| 1 | 2 | 3 | 4 | 5 | 6 | 7 | 8 | 9 | 10 |

13e ▶ 12
Develop keyboarding continuity

1 Clear tab stops; set tab stop for 5–space indention.

2 Practice each ¶ once as shown for orientation.

3 Take three 1' writings on each ¶.

Goal: At least 16 *gwam*.

Technique hint:
Work for smooth, continuous typing, not for high speed.

Difficulty index

all letters used	E	1.2 si	5.1 awl	90% hfw

gwam 1'

¶ 1   If we exert great efforts to do something, it   9

could be true that our effort will bring us higher   19

quality returns to match the work that we put out.   29

¶ 2   Is zeal worth the cost? Some people say that   9

maximum efforts will pay off in real results; even   19

others say the joy of hard work is its own reward.   29

| 1 | 2 | 3 | 4 | 5 | 6 | 7 | 8 | 9 | 10 |

14

14a ▶ 8
Preparatory practice

each line twice SS (slowly, then faster); DS between 2-line groups

alphabet 1 Kim Janby gave six prizes to qualified white cats.
shift keys 2 Jay Nadler, a Rotary Club member, wrote Mr. Coles.
y 3 Why do you say that today, Thursday, is my payday?
easy 4 Did the girl also fix the cowl of the formal gown?

| 1 | 2 | 3 | 4 | 5 | 6 | 7 | 8 | 9 | 10 |

**Measure skill
application:
business correspondence**

Time schedule:

Assembling materials .... 2'
Timed production .... 15'
Final check; proofread;
  compute *g–pram* .... 5'

Materials needed:

2 letterheads and envelopes, 1
half–page memorandum [LM pp.
43–47], or plain paper
Letters: 60–space line, Line 16.
Memo: 1" side margins, Line 7.

When the signal to begin is given,
insert paper and begin typing
Problem 1. Keyboard the problems
in sequence until the signal to
stop is given. Prepare a large en–
velope for each letter. Proofread

all problems; circle errors.
Calculate *g–pram*.

$$g\text{–}pram = \frac{\text{total words typed}}{\text{time (15')}}$$

words

	Prob. 1	Prob. 3

Problem 1

block style

(Current date) | Mr. Lonny L. Johnson, Director | The House by the Side of the — 15
Road | 679 Truman Street | Abilene, TX 79601-5739 | Dear Mr. Johnson — 28

(¶) The Executive Board of The House by the Side of the Road has instructed me — 43 | 28
to express to you how deeply it regrets your resignation as House Director. — 58 | 43
(¶) The Board recognizes that you have served as Director for 18 years. Your — 73 | 58
leadership, loyalty, and perseverance will be missed; and finding your replace- — 89 | 74
ment will not be easy. — 93 | 78
(¶) We shall begin a search for a new Director; but, in the meantime, please — 108 | 93
let us know of any assistance we can provide. — 117 | 102
Sincerely yours | Dale L. Berger | Secretary | xx — 126/147 | 102

Problem 2

modified block style

(Current date) | Mr. Byung Chung, Manager | Nikki's Paris Shop | 1890 San Luis — 15
Street | Las Vegas, NV 89110-7241 | Dear Mr. Chung — 24

(¶) This letter introduces Gale Senter, our Nevada representative for Cleo — 38
Sportswear. Gale will stop at your shop in a day or two to show you samples of — 54
our new spring line. — 59
(¶) One of the features you should look for in Cleo clothes--and stress to your — 74
customers--is the basic, uncluttered look of each style. Our designers fashion — 90
clothes that do not have faddish elements that outdate them after one or two — 105
seasons. — 107
(¶) Also, examine carefully the fine cloth used to make our Cleo line. All our — 122
fabrics are washable and do not need ironing. — 132
(¶) Gale will be happy to discuss availability and terms of purchase with you. — 147
You'll be glad she called. — 152
Sincerely yours | Miss Celia Murtagh | Sales Manager | xx — 162/180

Problem 3

Retype Problem 1 as a
memorandum but ad–
dress it as shown at
the right. No envelope.

TO:	Lonny Johnson	3
FROM:	Dale Berger	5
DATE:	(Current date)	8
SUBJECT:	Appreciation of Service	13

(Word count for body of memo is listed in the second column in Problem 1.)

14b ▶ 9
Improve response patterns

once as shown; then repeat

Lines 1-2: *Say* and type each word as a unit.

Lines 3-4: Spell each word as you type it; work at a steady pace.

Lines 5-6: *Say* and type short, easy words as units; spell and type longer words letter by letter.

word response
1 he of to if ah or by do so am is go us it an me ox
2 The corps may pay for the land when they visit us.

stroke response
3 was pop saw ink art oil gas kin are hip read lymph
4 Sara erected extra seats; Jimmy sat in only a few.

combination response
5 is best | an area | to pump | to join | an acre | he read it
6 My act forms a base for a tax case with the state.

| 1 | 2 | 3 | 4 | 5 | 6 | 7 | 8 | 9 | 10 |

14c ▶ 9
Control machine parts

once as shown; repeat if time permits

Lines 1-4: Clear tabs; set tab at center point. Tab where indicated.

Line 5: Use correct spacing after each punctuation mark.

Line 6: Depress shift key firmly; avoid pauses.

tab and return
1 ——————tab——————▶Can you work the parts of
2 your machine?————tab——▶Can you work them without
3 looking at them?——tab—▶Do you trust your fingers
4 to do the work you have taught them to do?

space bar
5 We did.   Was it here?   I saw it; Lois saw it, too.

shift keys
6 Jena visited Washington, D.C., to see Kay and Pat.

| 1 | 2 | 3 | 4 | 5 | 6 | 7 | 8 | 9 | 10 |

14d ▶ 10
Improve keyboarding technique

1 Once as shown; checkmark each line that you do not keystroke fluently.

2 Repeat any line that caused you difficulty.

adjacent reaches
1 Bert read where she could stop to buy gas and oil.
2 We three are a trio to join the Yun Oil operation.

direct reaches
3 My uncle and my brother have run many great races.
4 Grace Nurva hunted my canyon for unique specimens.

double letters
5 Jeanne took a day off to see a book show in Hobbs.
6 Jerry has planned a small party for all the troop.

| 1 | 2 | 3 | 4 | 5 | 6 | 7 | 8 | 9 | 10 |

14e ▶ 14
Reach for new goals

1 Take a 1' writing on Line 2 of 14b above; determine *gwam* (total words typed).

2 From the second column at the right (*gwam* 30"), choose a goal that will cause you to aim for 2–3 *gwam* more than your rate in Step 1. Note the sentence that accompanies that goal.

3 Take two 1' writings on the chosen sentence; try to reach the end of the line each time "Return" is called (each 30").

4 If you reach your goal on either 1' writing, take two 1' writings on the next sentence. (A total of eight 1' writings will be given.)

5 Take another 1' writing on Line 2 of 14b above; determine *gwam* (total words typed).

Goals:
13–15 *gwam*, acceptable
16–18 *gwam*, good
19–21 *gwam*, very good
22+   *gwam*, excellent

	words in line	gwam 30"	gwam 20"
1 The six girls work with vigor.	6	12	18
2 He got the right title to the land.	7	14	21
3 He works a field of corn and rye for us.	8	16	24
4 Row to the big island at the end of the lake.	9	18	27
5 They do their duty when they turn the dials right.	10	20	30

| 1 | 2 | 3 | 4 | .5 | 6 | 7 | 8 | 9 | 10 |

37a ▶ 6
Preparatory practice

each line 3 times SS (slowly, faster, still faster); repeat if time permits

alphabet 1 Gwendolyn Post lives in a quiet area just six blocks from the old zoo.

figures 2 The 1983 edition of this book had 5 parts, 40 chapters, and 672 pages.

hyphen 3 Here is an up-to-date reference for those out-of-this-world questions.

easy 4 The rich man paid half of the endowment, and this firm also paid half.

| 1 | 2 | 3 | 4 | 5 | 6 | 7 | 8 | 9 | 10 | 11 | 12 | 13 | 14 |

37b ▶ 12
Keyboard letter parts

Lines 1-3: Take two 1′ writings on each line. Try to finish each line at least once in the time alloted.

Lines 4-5: Take two 45″ writings on Lines 4–5, arranging them in 3–line address format.

Goal: To complete each address in Lines 4–5 in 45″.

Technique hint:
Type at a controlled, but constant rate. Do not pause before typing figures.

1 123 Brandy Street; 459 Reynolds Drive; 650 River Road; 78 Osage Avenue

2 Erie, PA 16511-4478; Brooklyn, NY 11227-2785; Dayton, OH 45410-3367

3 April 29, 19--; May 18, 19--; June 27, 19--; July 26, 19--; January 17

4 Ms. Deirdre Ann Beebe | 262 Orient Boulevard | Wichita, KS 67213-4976

5 Mrs. Rosetta Hayman | 595 Singingwood Drive | Torrance, CA 90505-3047

| 1 | 2 | 3 | 4 | 5 | 6 | 7 | 8 | 9 | 10 | 11 | 12 | 13 | 14 |

37c ▶ 10
Review memorandums

Half-page memorandum [LM p. 43]

Format and type the memorandum at the right. Review the format on page 73 if necessary.

1″ side margins; proofread; circle errors.

words

TO: All Employees — 3

FROM: Bessie Arthur, Personnel Department — 10

DATE: June 30, 19-- — 13

SUBJECT: Booklet on Fringe Benefits — 18

Included with your next payroll check will be a booklet developed by 32 our staff that outlines employee benefits. Of particular importance 46 is the section relating to the changes taking place in the Social 59 Security law and how you can make an inquiry to be sure your de- 72 ductions and our contributions are being properly credited to your 85 account. 87

Please call me should you have any questions regarding your fringe 100 benefits or the information contained in the booklet. 111

xx 112

15a ▶ 8
Preparatory practice
each line twice SS (slowly, then faster); DS between 2-line groups

alphabet	1	Max Jewel picked up five history quizzes to begin.
space bar	2	Did she say she may copy the form in a day or two?
z	3	Liz Zahl saw Zoe feed the zebra in an Arizona zoo.
easy	4	They risk a penalty if he signs their usual forms.

| 1 | 2 | 3 | 4 | 5 | 6 | 7 | 8 | 9 | 10 |

15b ▶ 14
Improve response patterns

1 Once as shown; checkmark three most difficult lines.

2 Repeat the lines you checked as difficult.

3 Take a 1' writing on Line 2, next on Line 4, and then on Line 6. Determine *gwam* on each writing.

word response	1	with they them make than when also work such right
	2	Diana did key work for the city dock for half pay.
stroke response	3	were only date upon ever join fact milk care nylon
	4	Milo acted on only a few tax rebate cases in July.
combination response	5	with were they only them upon than ever when plump
	6	Julio paid the tax on six acres of rich lake land.

| 1 | 2 | 3 | 4 | 5 | 6 | 7 | 8 | 9 | 10 |

15c ▶ 14
Reach for new goals

1 Using your best rate in 15b as a base, choose from the sentences at the right one that will raise your goal by 2–3 *gwam*.

2 Beginning with that sentence, take a series of 1' writings as directed in 14e, page 31.

Goals:

13–15 *gwam*, acceptable
16–18 *gwam*, good
19–21 *gwam*, very good
22+ *gwam*, excellent

		words in line	gwam 30"	gwam 20"
1	This is an authentic ivory antique.	7	14	21
2	Did the cowhand dismantle the worn auto?	8	16	24
3	Is the body of the ancient dirigible visible?	9	18	27
4	If they wish, she may make the form for the disks.	10	20	30
5	Did they mend the torn right half of their ensign?	10	20	30

| 1 | 2 | 3 | 4 | 5 | 6 | 7 | 8 | 9 | 10 |

15d ▶ 14
Check/develop keyboarding continuity

1 Clear tab stops; set a tab for 5–space ¶ indention.

2 Practice ¶ 1 once DS for orientation.

3 Take two 1' writings on ¶ 1; determine *gwam* on each writing.

4 Use ¶ 2 as directed in Steps 2 and 3.

Goal: At least 15 *gwam*.

Technique hints:

Keep the carrier moving at a fairly steady pace. Avoid looking up, especially at line endings.

Difficulty index

all letters used | E | 1.2 si | 5.1 awl | 90% hfw

gwam 1'

¶ 1   To learn to keyboard requires that you simply   9
allow the skill to form day by day. You may often   19
be concerned as a result of doubt that the fingers   29
will do just what you have been told they will do.   39

¶ 2   So the secret is revealed. Typing is not the   9
hard job it once may have seemed. Now you realize   19
that what you must do is simply relax and read the   29
copy carefully; your hands should do all the rest.   39

| 1 | 2 | 3 | 4 | 5 | 6 | 7 | 8 | 9 | 10 |

Prepare memorandums

Full-page memorandum
[LM p. 41]

1 Read the information in the memorandum below.

2 Format and type the memo.

3 Address a COMPANY MAIL envelope to:

**Mr. Edward Davis, Director
Information Processing
Center**

Note: Memorandums are often prepared on printed forms. If a printed form is not available, follow the half–page illustration at the right. Begin the heading on Line 7 for a half-page memo and on Line 10 for a full–page memo. Set 1″ side margins.

		words
TO:	All Information Processors	5
FROM:	Cathy Carapezzi, Director	10
DATE:	December 21, 19--	13
SUBJECT:	Interoffice Correspondence	18

Correspondence within a company is frequently formatted on in- 30
teroffice forms, either half or full sheets, depending on the length of 44
the message. The following points describe the features of a 56
memorandum prepared on a printed form. 64

1. Space twice after the colon in the first line of the printed heading 79
   and set the left margin. The heading items and the body of the 92
   memo will begin at this point. Set the right margin stop an equal 105
   distance from the right edge. These margin adjustments will 117
   usually give you side margins of 1″. 124

2. Full addresses, the salutation, the complimentary close, and the 138
   signature are omitted. 143

3. Personal titles are usually omitted from the memo heading. They 157
   are included on the envelope, however. 164

4. TS between the last item in the heading and the body of the mes- 178
   sage. SS the paragraphs, but DS between them. DS above and 190
   below a table or a numbered list when one is included in the mes- 203
   sage. Space twice after the number in a numbered list; align the 216
   whole paragraph under the first line. 221

5. Reference initials, enclosure notations, and copy notations are 234
   included. 236

Special colored envelopes usually are used for memorandums. Type 249
the addressee's name, personal title, and business title or name of 263
department for the address. Type COMPANY MAIL (in ALL CAPS) in 276
the postage location. 280

xx   281/292

Learning goals

1 To learn figure keyreaches.
2 To proofread/revise copy.
3 To type statistical copy.
4 To type handwritten copy.
5 To improve stroking continuity.

Machine adjustments

1 Set paper edge guide at 0.
2 Set ribbon control to type on upper half of ribbon.
3 Set left margin for a 50–space line (center point − 25); move right stop to end of scale.
4 SS drills; DS paragraphs.

16

16a ▶ 7

Preparatory practice

each line twice SS (slowly, then faster); DS between 2-line groups; repeat selected lines if time permits

alphabet	1	We got six quaint bronze cups from heavy old junk.
q/?	2	Did Marq Quin go? Did Quent Quin go? Did Quincy?
z/:	3	To: Zane Mozel, Tempe, AZ From: Ezra A. Lazzaro
easy	4	She may do the work when she signs the right form.

| 1 | 2 | 3 | 4 | 5 | 6 | 7 | 8 | 9 | 10 |

16b ▶ 16

Learn new keyreaches: 3 7 1

Follow the "Standard procedure for learning new keyreaches" on page 10 (Lines 1–6 twice; Lines 7–10 once; repeat 7–10 if time permits).

Under certain circumstances, the small letter l can be used to type the figure 1. Your instructor will tell you which reach to use for daily work.

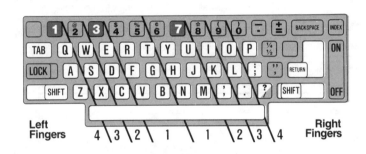

Left Fingers 4 3 2 1 1 2 3 4 Right Fingers

Reach technique for 3

Reach *up* with *left second* finger.

Reach technique for 7

Reach *up* with *right first* finger.

Reach technique for 1

Reach *up* with *left little* finger.

NOTES ON ABBREVIATIONS

Space once after a period (.) following an initial. Abbreviations such as M.D., B.C., Ph.D., U.S., N.Y., C.O.D., a.m., and p.m. may be typed solid (without internal spacing).

Abbreviations such as mph, rpm, and mg are usually expressed without caps, periods, or internal spacing.

Abbreviations such as ERA, AMA, and TVA are typed in ALL CAPS (without internal spacing).

3	1	d 3d 3d 3 3; 3 did, 3 days, 3 deals, 3 dozen, 3 33
	2	The 33 girls and 3 boys met at 3 p.m. near Gate 3.
7	3	j 7j 7j 7 7; 7 jobs, 7 jets, 7 jacks, 7 jeeps, 7 7
	4	She wrote 7, 7, 7, not 777. She wrote it 7 times.
1	5	a la la l l lla; l arm, l aide, l awl, ll ayes, ll
	6	He bought 11 tons of No. 1 coal on May 1 at 1 p.m.
3/7/1	7	Page 371 of Volume 31 states the date as 1737 B.C.
	8	Flight 173, a 737 jet, left on May 31 at 1:31 p.m.
all figures learned	9	Only 3 of the 7 cars clock 71 to 73 mph or better.
	10	Read pages 7, 17, and 37; copy Lines 3, 7, and 31.

| 1 | 2 | 3 | 4 | 5 | 6 | 7 | 8 | 9 | 10 |

36a ▶ 6
Preparatory practice

each line 3 times SS (slowly, faster, still faster); DS between 3-line groups; repeat if time permits

alphabet 1 Jim Bond quickly realized that we could fix the pretty girl's vehicle.

fig/sym 2 Serial #815-47 was stamped on the engine; Model #209(36) was below it.

combina-
tion 3 Look for the fastest racer to get a big treat at the end of the races.

easy 4 Both of the towns bid for the giant quantity of coal down by the dock.

| 1 | 2 | 3 | 4 | 5 | 6 | 7 | 8 | 9 | 10 | 11 | 12 | 13 | 14 |

36b ▶ 10
Align copy in columns

half sheet, long side up; 50-space line; begin on Line 14; DS

1 Set tab stops according to both the key at the bottom of the table and the guides above the table. Tabs should be set to require the least forward and backward spacing.

2 Format and type the drill; repeat it if time permits.

margin	tab	tab	tab	words
answer	592.79	I	TO:	3
brochure	24.83	I I	FROM:	7
follows	6.02	I I I	DATE:	11
technical	57.42	IV	SUBJECT:	16

key | 9 | 8 | 6 | 8 | 3 | 8 | 8 |

36c ▶ 12
Review modified block letter style

1 letterhead and envelope [LM p. 39]; 60-space line; begin on Line 15

Prepare the letter; proofread and correct your copy before removing it from the machine.

words

(Current date) | Mrs. Lynn Martinez | 431 Poplar Lane | Annapolis, MD 21403-2261 | Dear Mrs. Martinez | 15 / 19

(¶) Our Credit Department informs me that you recently returned to us for credit a Wilcox Model 24 toaster. It appears from the report that some question was raised about the condition of the toaster when it was returned and that you objected to certain statements made at the credit counter. 33 / 49 / 65 / 77

(¶) I apologize if in any way the routine return of this toaster was questioned. As you know if you are a longtime shopper in our store, we guarantee our merchandise to be satisfactory in every way. If you, the customer, are not satisfied, then we, the store, are not satisfied either. 93 / 108 / 125 / 134

(¶) I assure you, Mrs. Martinez, that we have properly adjusted your account to reflect credit for the return. If you have any further questions about this matter, please contact me personally. 150 / 166 / 173

Sincerely yours | Myles J. Longano, Head | Customer Relations | xx 185/197

16c ▶ 12
Reach for new goals

Follow the directions given for 12c on page 28. Use Line 4 of 16a to determine beginning and ending *gwam*.

Goals:

12–14 *gwam*, acceptable
15–17 *gwam*, good
18–19 *gwam*, very good
20+ *gwam*, excellent

all figures learned

		words in line	gwam 30"	gwam 20"
1	Did the girl hang the 37 maps?	6	12	18
2	She paid Jane to turn the 71 dials.	7	14	21
3	I got 73 burlap panels to make the form.	8	16	24
4	Kent kept 17 worn keys to work the 17 panels.	9	18	27
5	Did they augment the 371 bushels of corn with rye?	10	20	30
6	I did visit a neighbor at 1737 Iris Lane on May 7.	10	20	30
7	Dismantle the 37 chairs in the shanty at 173 Palm.	10	20	30

| 1 | 2 | 3 | 4 | 5 | 6 | 7 | 8 | 9 | 10 |

16d ▶ 7
Improve figure response patterns

each line once DS; repeat Lines 2, 4, and 6

Technique hint:

Control your reading speed. Read only slightly ahead of what you are typing.

all figures learned

1 Flight 371 left Miami at 3:17 on Monday, March 31.

2 *Bill 731 was for 71 boxes of No. 33 bailing brads.*

3 Rico counted 3,711 cartons containing 7,317 tools.

4 *Send Nan 731 No. 3 nails for her home at 771 Anne.*

5 On May 31, Eva drove 373 miles to Denver in Van 7.

6 *Max put 71 extra boxes in the annex at 3731 Parks.*

16e ▶ 8
Improve keystroking technique

once as shown; repeat if time permits

all letters used

1st finger
1 Bob Mugho hunted for five minutes for your number.
2 Juan hit the bright green turf with his five iron.

2d finger
3 Kind, decent acts can decidedly reduce skepticism.
4 Kim, not Mickey, had rice with chicken for dinner.

3d/4th fingers
5 You will write quickly: Zeus, Apollo, and Xerxes.
6 Who saw Polly? Max Voe saw her; she is quiet now.

| 1 | 2 | 3 | 4 | 5 | 6 | 7 | 8 | 9 | 10 |

17

17a ▶ 7
Preparatory practice

each line twice SS (slowly, then faster); DS between 2-line groups; repeat selected lines if time permits

alphabet 1 Roz Groves just now packed my box with five quail.

b 2 Barb, not Bob, will buy the new bonds at the bank.

figures 3 Try Model 3717 with 7 panels or Model 1733 with 3.

easy 4 Their problems may end when they audit the profit.

| 1 | 2 | 3 | 4 | 5 | 6 | 7 | 8 | 9 | 10 |

Communications Design Associates

348 INDIANA AVENUE
WASHINGTON, DC 20001-1438
Tel: 1-800-432-5739

Tabulate to center to type
date and closing lines

Dateline   Line 15 November 28, 19--   4

Operate return 4 times

Letter   Mr. Otto B. Bates, President   9
address   Third Bank and Trust Company   15
9080 Reservoir Avenue   20
New Brunswick, NJ 08901-4476   26
                    DS

Salutation   Dear Mr. Bates   28
          DS

Body of   This letter is written in what is called the "modified block   41
letter   style." It is the style we recommend for use in your office   53
for reasons I shall detail for you in the paragraphs below.   65

First, the style is a fairly efficient one that requires only   77
one tab setting--at center point--for positioning the current   90
date, the complimentary close, and the typed signature lines.   102
All other lines begin at left margin.   110

Second, the style is quite easy to learn. New employees will   123
have little difficulty learning it, and your present staff can   135
adjust to it without unnecessary confusion.   144

Third, the style is a familiar one; it is used by more busi-   156
ness firms than any other. It is conservative, and customers   168
and companies alike feel comfortable with it.   178

I am happy to enclose our booklet on the subject of letter   189
styles and special features of business letters.   199
                    DS

Complimentary   Sincerely yours   202
close   Operate return 4 times

Kathryn E. Bowers

Typed name   Ms. Kathryn E. Bowers   206
Official title   Senior Consultant   210
                    DS

Reference   xx   211
initials   DS
Enclosure   Enclosure   213
notation

Shown in pica type
60–space line

Style letter 3: modified block style, block paragraphs, open punctuation

17b ▶ 16
Learn new keyreaches:
8 4 0

Follow the "Standard procedure for learning new keyreaches" on page 10 (Lines 1–6 twice; Lines 7–10 once; repeat 7–10 if time permits).

Reach technique for 8	Reach technique for 4	Reach technique for 0

Note: Capitalize nouns that are identified by a number except for certain ones such as *page* and *verse* within a sentence.

8
1 k 8k 8k 8 8; 88 keys, 8 kegs, 8 kits, 888 kwh, 8 8
2 I took 8 keys to lock 8 kits in Truck 8 on Dock 8.

4
3 f 4f 4f 4 4; 4 fans, 4 fobs, 44 folk, 4 forks, 4 4
4 Tour 44 leaves at 4 p.m. to see 4 bays in 4 lakes.

0
5 ; 0; 0; 0 0; 30 paid, 70 posts, 30 pages, 10 plays
6 Send 30 palms to 30730 East 30th Street on May 30.

8/4/0
7 Page 10 of the program listed 48, not 84, members.
8 In 1840, the 84 men and 80 women walked to Toledo.

all figures learned
9 On June 30, we sent Check 184 to pay Invoice 7403.
10 In 1830, 14 feet of snow fell; in 1831, almost 18.

| 1 | 2 | 3 | 4 | 5 | 6 | 7 | 8 | 9 | 10 |

17c ▶ 7
Improve figure response patterns

each line once DS; repeat Lines 2, 4, and 6

all figures learned

1 I live at 418 East Street, not at 418 Easy Street.
2 *Memorize pages 137 to 148; omit pages 140 and 141.*
3 Tours 478 and 4781 travel to 10 cities in 30 days.
4 *Cy will be 18 on May 30; Jo, 17 on May 4 or May 7.*
5 English 348 meets in Room 710 at 10 a.m. each day.
6 *Memo 7481 says 7 pads and 8 pens were sent May 30.*

17d ▶ 8
Improve keystroking technique

each line twice SS; DS between 3-line groups; repeat if time permits

adjacent reaches
1 Teresa knew well that her opinion of art was good.

direct reaches
2 Herb Brice must hunt for my checks; he is in debt.

double letters
3 Anne stopped off at school to see Bill Wiggs cook.

long words
4 Debate concerned parochialism versus universalism.

| 1 | 2 | 3 | 4 | 5 | 6 | 7 | 8 | 9 | 10 |

35a ▶ 6
Preparatory practice

each line 3 times SS (slower, faster, slower); DS between 3-line groups; repeat if time permits

alphabet 1 The explorer questioned Jack's amazing story about unknown lava flows.

figures 2 I am sending 2,795 of the 4,680 sets now and the remainder on June 13.

capitalization 3 Is the notation on this memorandum Bob's, Edna's, Ralph's, or Myrna's?

easy 4 Work with vigor to shape a theory to make visible and audible signals.

| 1 | 2 | 3 | 4 | 5 | 6 | 7 | 8 | 9 | 10 | 11 | 12 | 13 | 14 |

35b ▶ 12
Use carbon paper

Materials needed:

1 original sheet
2 second sheets
2 carbon paper sheets
1 firm (5"×3") card

70-space line; DS; 2½" top margin; correct errors

1 Study the information and illustrations at the right.

2 Assemble a carbon pack and make an original and 2 carbon copies of the ¶ shown below the illustrations.

Assembling a carbon pack

1 Assemble letterhead, carbon sheets (uncarboned side up), and second sheets as illustrated below. Use one carbon and one second sheet for each copy desired.

2 Grasp the carbon pack at the sides. Turn it so that the letterhead faces away from you, the carbon sides of the carbon paper are toward you, and the top edge of the pack is face down. Tap the sheets gently on the desk to straighten.

3 Hold the sheets firmly to prevent slipping; insert pack into typewriter. Hold pack with one hand; turn platen with the other.

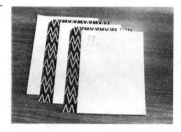  

Many companies no longer make carbon copies; of those that do, some do not erase errors on them. If you need to do so, pull the original forward and place a firm card in front of the carbon sheet. Erase the error on the original with a typewriter eraser; erase the carbon copy with a soft pencil eraser. For additional carbon copies, use the card to protect them by placing it between the sheet being erased and the next sheet of carbon paper.

35c ▶ 32
Format business letters in modified block style

3 plain full sheets; copy sheets

Problem 1

1 Study the information at the right and Style Letter 3, p. 71.
2 Type a copy of the letter; proofread; circle errors.
3 Type another copy of letter. Make one carbon copy; correct errors.

Problem 2

Type Problem 2, page 69, in modified block style. Make one carbon copy, no envelope. Proofread; correct errors.

As you study Style Letter 3, page 71, note that the block style has been "modified" by moving the dateline and the closing lines from block position at the left margin. In the modified block style, these lines begin at the center point of the page.

Because stationery with printed letterhead is either used or assumed, the dateline will be the first item typed in these letters. Type the dateline on about Line 15 and use a 60-space line for all letters in Section 8. Spacing between letter parts is the same as was used

with the block style. This spacing is standard for all business letters.

17e ▶ 12
Improve keyboarding continuity

1 Practice the ¶ once for orientation.
2 Take three 30" writings (30" *gwam* = words typed × 2).
3 Take three 1' writings.
4 Determine *gwam*.
Goal: *At least* 14 *gwam*.

Difficulty index

all letters/figures learned	E	1.2 si	5.1 awl	90% hfw

```
        .       2       .       4       .       6       .       8       .
Why did we not all realize that July 17 was a
    10      .      12      .      14      .      16      .      18      .
hot day?  For 30 days, still summer air had closed
    20      .      22      .      24      .      26      .      28      .
in on us.  Just to move was an effort; but here we
    30      .      32      .      34      .      36      .      38      .
stood, 48 quite excited people, planning our trek.
```

18

18a ▶ 7
Preparatory practice

each line twice SS (slowly, then faster); DS between 2-line groups; repeat selected lines if time permits

alphabet 1 One judge saw five boys quickly fix the prize elm.
p/x 2 Dixie, please have Pam fix the tax forms Hope has.
figures 3 Is it Channel 3, 8, or 10? Was the score 14 to 7?
easy 4 The girl may enamel the chair for the town chapel.

```
| 1 | 2 | 3 | 4 | 5 | 6 | 7 | 8 | 9 | 10 |
```

18b ▶ 16
Learn new keyreaches: 6 2 / (diagonal)

Follow the "Standard procedure for learning new keyreaches" on page 10 (Lines 1–6 twice; Lines 7–10 once; repeat 7–10 if time permits).

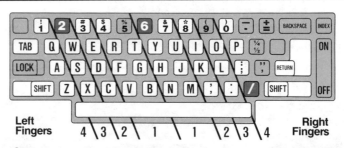

Left Fingers 4 \ 3 \ 2 \ 1 \ 1 / 2 / 3 / 4 **Right Fingers**

Reach technique for 6   Reach technique for 2   Reach technique for /

Reach *up* with *right first* finger.

Reach *up* with *left third* finger.

Reach *down* to / with *right little* finger.

6 1 j 6j 6j 6 6; 6 jobs, 6 jugs, 66 jays, 6 jokes, 6 6
   2 On July 6, 66 jumpers made 6 jumps of over 6 feet.

2 3 s 2s 2s 2 2; 2 skis, 2 sons, 22 sites, has 2 signs
   4 On May 2, Car 222 delivered 22 tons of No. 2 sand.

/ 5 ; /; /; / /; 1/3; and/or; 4/7/84; 4/14; 8 1/3; / /
   6 Type these mixed fractions: 1 3/8; 4 4/7; 1 3/14.

6/2/diag. 7 On May 26, I ordered 2 2/6 yards, not 6 2/6 yards.
           8 The recorder, Model 226/62, Serial 626/A, is mine.

all figures 9 Aida was 21 on 3/7/80. Bill will be 21 on 4/6/87.
learned   10 The terms for Invoice 7867/3 are 4/10, 2/30, n/60.

```
| 1 | 2 | 3 | 4 | 5 | 6 | 7 | 8 | 9 | 10 |
```

34d ▶ 25
Format business letters in block style

2 plain full sheets; 1 large envelope (LM p. 37); 60-space line; begin on Line 15

Problem 1

Prepare the letter; proofread and correct your copy before removing it from the machine.

words

(Current date) | Mr. Herbert B. Wymore, Jr. | Millikin & Descartes, Inc. | 800   15
Hazel Court | Denver, CO 80204-1192 | Dear Mr. Wymore | 25

(¶) In answer to his request, I am very happy to write a letter of recommenda-   40
tion for Mehti K. Boromand, who worked with our company for about fourteen   55
months.   56

(¶) Mr. Boromand's responsibilities, while he was employed here with us, in-   71
volved carrying important documents and packages from building to building.   86
He was responsible, prompt, and virtually tireless; cheerful, polite, and very   102
friendly; and above all, discreet and reliable. He was absolutely trustworthy.   118

(¶) He left our employ at the end of last summer to begin college studies, but he   134
will be welcomed back to our staff at any time that we have an opening in which   150
he might be interested and for which he might be qualified.   161

Sincerely | Miss Kim L. Schuyler | Assistant Vice President | xx   173

Problem 2

Make a corrected copy of the letter at the right. Insert the longer changes as numbered. Address an envelope.

Note: The total word count is shown as 173/186; the first figure is the letter count; the second is the letter plus the envelope.

June 16, 19--   3

Mr. Olin N. Werger   7
1640 Barnes Land--*e*   10
Wh*a*te Plains, NY 10604-3719   16
i
Dear Mr. Werger   19

    pleasure   *inform*
It is my ~~happy opportunity~~ to ~~tell~~ you/that the sug- ①   28
gestion you recently submitted ~~has been studied~~ by   38
our Management Board. The Management Board has recom-   52
mended to me its/immediate implementation.   64

      ②   *your* ③
I, too, have studied ~~the~~ suggestion, and I must tell   73
you that I am extremely enthusiastic about it. Your   84
explanations makes it quite obvious that by making   94
the changes in office layout you recommend, our com-   104
pany should be able to save a substantial expense.   116
    ④

Will you attend a brief ceremony to be held in my   126
office next Friday morning at 9? At that time it   136
will be my pleasure to award to you a check in the   147
amount of $4500 in appreciation of your excellent   157
money-saving recommendation.   162

Sincerely yours   166

    ① *for consideration*
    ② *has been accepted*
    ③ *adoption and*
Mrs. Cecelia P. Barbette ④ *amount of money*   171
President   173

xx   173/186

Compare skill: sentences

1 Take a 1' writing on Line 1; determine *gwam* and use this score for your goal as you take two 1' writings on Line 2 and two on Line 3.

2 Take a 1' writing on Line 4; determine *gwam* and use this score for your goal as you take two 1' writings on Line 5 and two on Line 6.

Goal: To have rates on Lines 2 and 3 and Lines 5 and 6 equal those on Lines 1 and 4.

words in line

1 Did the men enamel emblems on big panels downtown? 10

2 Pay the men to fix a pen for 38 ducks and 47 hens. 10

3 *They blame the chaos in the city on the big quake.* 10

4 Did the amendment name a city auditor to the firm? 10

5 He owns 20 maps of the 16 towns on the big island. 10

6 *Dian may make cocoa for the girls when they visit.* 10

18d ▶ 5

Proofread/revise as you keyboard

each line once DS; correct circled errors as you keyboard; read carefully

1 Court will not (ve) in session again until (august) 6.

2 Put more grass (sede) on the lawn at 307 Elm (Strett).

3 A team is (madeup) of 11 men; 12 were on (t he) field.

4 Liza and/or Dion (willldirect) the choir on (Tuseday).

5 (Theer) were (abuot) 10 or 11 pictures in the gallery.

18e ▶ 9

Improve keyboarding continuity

1 Practice the ¶ once for orientation.

2 Take three 30" writings.

3 Take three 1' writings.

4 Determine *gwam*.

Goal: *At least* 14 *gwam*.

Difficulty index

all letters/figures learned	E	1.2 si	5.1 awl	90% hfw

Volume 27 is quite heavy. Its weight must be
in excess of 10 pounds; yet I realize the only way
to complete this type of job is to study 164 pages
of Chapter 183 and all of the art in the big book.

34a ▶ 6
Preparatory practice

each line 3 times SS (slowly, faster, slower); DS between 3-line groups; repeat if time permits

alphabet 1 Ben Jackson will save the money required for your next big cash prize.

fig/sym 2 The 7 1/2% interest of $18.68 on my $249.05 note (dated May 3) is due.

double letters 3 Dell was puzzled by the letter that followed the offer of a free book.

easy 4 In Dubuque, they may work the rich field for the profit paid for corn.

| 1 | 2 | 3 | 4 | 5 | 6 | 7 | 8 | 9 | 10 | 11 | 12 | 13 | 14 |

34b ▶ 9
Compose at the keyboard

2 full sheets; 2″ top margin; DS

1 Center your name horizontally, then TS.

2 Answer the questions at the right in complete sentences.

3 Make pencil corrections on your copy, then retype it. Proofread; correct errors.

1 In what year were you graduated from high school?

2 How long have you been studying at your present school?

3 Have you attended any other postsecondary schools?

4 When do you plan to complete your formal schooling?

34c ▶ 10
Address large envelopes

3 large (No. 10) envelopes [LM pp. 35-37]

1 Read carefully the special placement information.

2 Address a large envelope to each addressee listed below; proofread; circle errors.

3 Fold a sheet of blank 8½″ × 11″ paper for insertion into a large envelope. Use the folding procedure shown for the Monarch envelope on page 63.

Placement information

Some businesses use small envelopes for 1-page letters and large envelopes for letters of 2 or more pages or letters with enclosures. Many firms, however, use large envelopes for all correspondence.

Study the placement of the letter address on the large envelope illustrated below. Set a tab stop about 5 spaces to the left of center or about 4″ from the left edge of the envelope. Space down about 14 lines from the top edge of the envelope and begin typing at the tab stop, thus positioning the address in approximately vertical center and slightly below the horizontal center. Learn to visualize this position so that you can type envelope addresses without special settings or measurements.

Type special messages for the addressee (*Please forward, Hold for arrival, Personal*, etc.) a TS below the return address and 3 spaces from the left edge of the envelope. Underline or type in ALL CAPS.

Type special mailing notations (such as REGISTERED, SPECIAL DELIVERY, etc.) in ALL CAPS below the stamp position.

MR MILO K DECKER PRESIDENT
POPULAR TOOL COMPANY
528 ESSEX LANE
DAVENPORT IA 52803-4163

BERA WALLPAPERS INC
7747 MC ARTHUR CIRCLE
EVANSVILLE IN 47714-3821

Miss Barbara B. Treece
Breummer & Joyner
6234 Reynolds Avenue
Columbus, OH 43201-6822

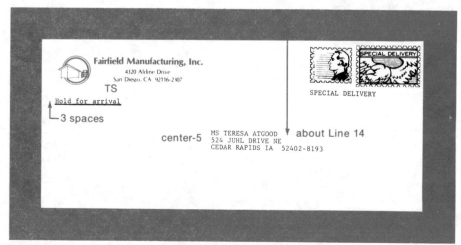

19a ▶ 7
Preparatory practice

each line twice SS (slowly, then faster); DS between 2-line groups; repeat selected lines if time permits

Space once after a question mark when the question is incomplete.

alphabet	1	Mavis Zeff worked quickly on the next big project.
q/?	2	Can you spell queue? quay? aqua? quavered? acquit?
figures	3	If 24 of the 87 boys go on May 10, 63 will remain.
easy	4	Fit the lens at a right angle and fix the problem.

| 1 | 2 | 3 | 4 | 5 | 6 | 7 | 8 | 9 | 10 |

19b ▶ 16
Learn new keyreaches: 9 5 - (hyphen) -- (dash)

Follow the "Standard procedure for learning new keyreaches" on page 10 (Lines 1–6 twice; Lines 7–11 once; repeat 7–11 if time permits).

Hyphen, dash: The hyphen is used to join closely related words or word parts. Striking the hyphen twice results in a dash--a symbol that shows sharp separation or interrup- tion of thought.

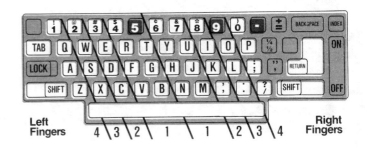

Reach technique for 9 — Reach *up* with *right third* finger.

Reach technique for 5 — Reach *up* with *left first* finger.

Reach technique for − — Reach *up* to - with *right little* finger.

9	1	l 9l 9l 9 9; 9 left, 9 lost, 9 loans, sell 99 lots
	2	On May 9, 99 buyers offered 99 bids for 999 lambs.
5	3	f 5f 5f 5 5; 5 fish, 5 fans, 5 forms, for 55 firms
	4	At 5 p.m., the 55 cars, 55 vans, and 5 jeeps left.
-	5	; -; -; - -- co-op; top-rate; in-depth; up-to-date
	6	Use a 5-inch line--50 pica spaces--for lines 1-10.
9/5/-	7	We--all 59 of us--have read pages 59, 95, and 595.
	8	All 95 girls--5 did not attend--voted on Item 599.
all figures/ symbols learned	9	Of 13,687 ex-workers, 2,481--or 9/50--had retired.
	10	Invoice 347/8--it is dated 2/9, not 2/10--is here.
	11	Do Problems 2-27, 8-35, and/or 16-42 before May 9.

| 1 | 2 | 3 | 4 | 5 | 6 | 7 | 8 | 9 | 10 |

Communications Design Associates

348 INDIANA AVENUE
WASHINGTON, DC 20001-1438
Tel: 1-800-432-5739

Dateline February 14, 19-- Line 15

Operate return 4 times

	total words	gwam 2'

Letter
address Mr. Harvey B. Barber — 8 | 4
Sunstructures, Inc. — 12 | 6
2214 Brantford Place — 16 | 8
Buffalo, NY 14222-5147 — 21 | 10
DS

Salutation Dear Mr. Barber — 24 | 12
DS

Body of This letter is written in what is called "block style." It — 36 | 18
letter is the style we recommend for use in your business office for — 48 | 24
reasons I shall detail for you in the following paragraphs. — 61 | 30

First, the style is a very efficient one. Because all lines — 73 | 6
(including the date) begin at the left margin, time is not — 85 | 12
consumed in positioning special parts of each letter. — 96 | 18

Second, this style is an easy one to learn. New employees — 107 | 23
should have little difficulty learning it, and your present — 119 | 29
staff should adjust to it without unnecessary confusion. — 131 | 35

Third, the style is sufficiently different from most other — 143 | 41
styles that it can suggest to clients that your company is a — 155 | 47
creative one. The style is interesting. It gains attention. — 168 | 54

I am pleased to enclose our booklet on the subject of letter — 180 | 6
styles and special features of business letters. — 190 | 11
DS

Complimentary Sincerely yours — 193 | 13
close Operate return 4 times

Kathryn E. Bowers

Typed name Ms. Kathryn E. Bowers — 197 | 15
Official title Senior Consultant — 201 | 17
DS

Reference
initials xx — 202 | 17
DS

Enclosure Enclosure — 203 | 18
notation

Shown in pica type
60–space line

Style letter 2: business letter in block style, open punctuation

19c ▶ 7

Improve figure response patterns

each line twice SS; DS between 2-line groups

Technique hint:

Work for continuity. Avoid any pause before or after figures.

all figures used

1 Send immediately *30* Solex cubes, Catalog No. *2748*.

2 As of *6/28*, your new extension number will be *375*.

3 Reserve for me Tape *640*. My identification: *819* .

4 Date of call: *2/7* . Time: *3:30* p.m. No message.

5 Top individual score: *87* . Top team average: *46* .

19d ▶ 5

Proofread/revise as you keyboard

each line once DS; correct circled errors as you keyboard; read carefully

1 Erin had ⓢ size 11/12 dress, but it was (two) large.

2 The figure he wrote--475-0is not a correct answer*o*

3 All that snow--(mroe) than 5(feat)--kept her at home.

4 Edna says 936 Valley (Rode) is (here) new home address.

5 He scored 80 on the first (test;he) must do(bet ter).

19e ▶ 5

Improve keystroking technique

each line twice SS; DS between 2-line groups

bottom row 1 Zach, check the menu; next, beckon the lazy valet.

home row 2 Sal was glad she had a flashlight; Al was as glad.

third row 3 Powell quit their outfit to try out for our troop.

| 1 | 2 | 3 | 4 | 5 | 6 | 7 | 8 | 9 | 10 |

19f ▶ 10

Improve keyboarding continuity

1 Practice the ¶ once for orientation.
2 Take three 30″ writings.
3 Take three 1′ writings.
Goal: *At least* 14 *gwam.*

Technique hint:

Work with confidence. Set your own "comfortable" rate and try to maintain it.

Difficulty index

all letters/figures used | E | 1.2 si | 5.1 awl | 90% hfw

Think with me back to a quite cold morning in
1984. It was just 7:50; I opened my door to leave
for work. Little did I realize that snow had been
expected--2/3 foot of it. I live at 6 Summer Way.

Learning goals
1 To prepare business letters in block and modified block styles.
2 To address large envelopes.
3 To develop composing skills.
4 To make carbon copies.
5 To learn to format half–page and full–page interoffice com–munications.

Machine adjustments
1 Check desk/chair adjustments.
2 Set ribbon control to type on upper half of ribbon.
3 Check placement of copy.
4 Set paper guide on 0.
5 Use a 70–space line unless otherwise directed.
6 SS drills; DS paragraphs.

33a ▶ 6
Preparatory practice

each line 3 times
SS (slowly, faster, slower);DS between
3-line groups; repeat if time permits

alphabet 1 One gray antique zinc box was the most favored object kept on display.

figures 2 Please turn to page 350 and answer Questions 2, 4, 6, 7, 8, 9, and 17.

hyphen 3 Pam thinks we have an up-to-the-minute plan for our out-of-town sales.

easy 4 When risk is taken by a giant firm, signs of visible profit may ensue.

| 1 | 2 | 3 | 4 | 5 | 6 | 7 | 8 | 9 | 10 | 11 | 12 | 13 | 14 |

33b ▶ 10
Compose at the keyboard

2 half sheets; 1″ top margin;
5-space ¶ indention; DS

1 Keyboard the sentences in ¶ form, inserting the needed infor-mation. Do not correct errors.
2 Remove the paper and make pencil corrections. Retype the ¶s. Proofread; correct errors.

(¶ 1) **My name is** (your name). **My home address is** (your complete home address, including ZIP Code). **I am a student at** (name of your school) **in** (city and state), **where I am majoring in** (major area of study). **My school address is** (street address, dormitory name, or other). (¶ 2) **The brand name of the typewriter I use is** (brand name). **I type at approximately** (state the rate in figures) **gwam. My greatest difficulty now seems to be** (name one, as: too many errors, not enough speed, poor techniques, lack of confidence).

33c ▶ 34
Format business letters in block style

plain full sheets

1 Read the special informa–tion at the right; then study the style letter on page 67.

2 Prepare a copy of the letter, following directions given on the letter. Correct errors.

3 Take three 2′ writings on opening lines and ¶1. Begin with paper out of the machine. Estimate placement of the date; move quickly from part to part to improve your speed.

Business letter placement information

Letter styles used for business letters are similar to styles used for personal letters, but note the following differences.

When letterhead paper (with a printed return address) is used, the return address is not typed above the date; begin the letter by typing the date.

If the letter is signed by a woman, the personal title she prefers (Ms., Miss, or Mrs.) may be included on the typed signature line. No title, per-sonal or professional, is needed if the writer is male.

The writer's official title may be typed directly beneath the typed signature line.

The initials of the typist may be shown at the left margin a DS below the typed name or title. (In Section 8 letters, ref-erence initials are indicated by xx; you should substitute your own initials.)

If an enclosure notation is used, type it a DS beneath the reference initials.

An attractive appearance is as essential for business let-ters as for personal letters. Proofreading and correcting must be done well if a letter is to have its desired effect.

The business letters in Sec-tion 8 are of average length; such letters fit well on a 60-space line. The date is usually typed on about Line 15, or 2½″ from the top of the page. This placement is recommended for all letters to be typed in Section 8.

20

Learning goals

1 To set margins.
2 To determine line endings using the warning bell.
3 To center copy horizontally and vertically.
4 To divide words at line endings.
5 To type short reports and an–nouncements.

Machine adjustments

1 Set paper guide at 0.
2 Set ribbon control to type on upper half of ribbon.
3 Use a 60–space line (center point −30; center point +30).
4 SS drills; DS paragraphs; indent first line of ¶ 5 spaces.
5 Insert half sheets long side first, unless otherwise directed.

20a ▶ 7
Preparatory practice

each line twice SS (slowly, then faster); DS between 2-line groups; repeat selected lines if time permits

alphabet 1 Freda Jencks will have money to buy six quite large topazes.

o/i 2 We take action from our position to avoid spoiling our soil.

figures 3 The 26 clerks checked Items 37 and 189 on pages 145 and 150.

easy 4 She bid by proxy for eighty bushels of a corn and rye blend.

| 1 | 2 | 3 | 4 | 5 | 6 | 7 | 8 | 9 | 10 | 11 | 12 |

20b ▶ 15
Learn to establish margin widths

study copy at right; then do the drills below

Margin release (31)
If the carrier locks, depress the margin release key with the little finger and complete the line.

Know your machine: margin stops

Typewriters (and other keyboarding machines) are usually equipped with one of two type sizes: pica or elite (some with both). Pica (10-pitch) is the larger—10 pica spaces fill a horizontal inch. Paper 8½ inches wide will accommodate 85 pica characters and spaces. Center point for pica type is 42 when left edge of paper is inserted at 0 on line-of-writing scale.

Elite (12-pitch) type is smaller—12 elite spaces fill a horizontal inch. Paper 8½ inches wide will accommodate 102 elite characters and spaces. Center point for elite type is 51 when left edge of paper is at 0 on line-of-writing scale.

Equal margin widths can be had either by (1) setting margin stops an equal distance in inches or spaces from extreme right and left edges of paper or by (2) setting the margin stops an equal distance right and left from center point. In lessons that follow, the second procedure will be used.

Drill 1

exact 60–space line (center − 30; center + 30); DS; make one copy, line for line

Note: A warning bell will sound as you approach the end of each line; listen for it.

If the margins are set correctly, if the paper guide is set at 0, and if you have made no mistakes which affect line length, each of these paragraphs can be typed with right and left margins which are exactly equal in width to each other.

| 1 | 2 | 3 | 4 | 5 | 6 | 7 | 8 | 9 | 10 | 11 | 12 |

Drill 2

exact 50–space line (center − 25; center + 25); DS; make one copy, line for line

If it is not already obvious to you, you will soon find that, while the left edge of a paragraph is even, the evenness on the right edge depends on your ability to decide where and how to end lines.

| 1 | 2 | 3 | 4 | 5 | 6 | 7 | 8 | 9 | 10 |

Supplemental communication activities

Spelling

70-space line; decide size of paper (full or half sheet), top margin (1″, 1½″, or 2″), and spacing (SS or DS)

1 Clear tab stops; set two new tab stops, one 29 spaces from left margin and one 58 spaces from left margin.

2 Type the first word at left margin as shown; tab and type the word again; then tab and type it a third time, this time without looking at the word in the book or on the paper.

3 Repeat this procedure for each word on the list. Proofread care–fully; correct errors.

4 Use the completed copy as a study list and for future reference.

5 Make comments about your placement decisions on the bot–tom of your typed copy.

SPELLING DEMONS

absence	absence	absence
accumulate		
already		
benefited		
convenience		
develop		
embarrass		
guarantee		
judgment		
likable		
noticeable		
parallel		
receive		
seize		

Capitalization

full sheet; 70-space line; DS; 1½″ top margin; set a tab 5 spaces to right of center point

1 Keyboard the data as shown; tab to type each example.

2 Proofread carefully and correct errors.

3 Study each line and its example from your copy.

Note: Some literary titles may be underlined or shown in all capital letters.

USING CAPITAL LETTERS

TS

		words
		4
Capitalize		9
the first word of a complete sentence:	She put the car in the garage.	23
the first word of a direct quotation:	Tio said, "That is my valise."	37
titles that precede personal names:	Introduce me to Senator Reese.	50
main words in literary titles:	I saw Anne of a Thousand Days.	67
adjectives derived from proper nouns:	We always enjoy Italian opera.	81
weekdays, months, and holidays:	Sunday, April 1, isn't Easter.	94
political and military organizations:	The Democrat left by Navy jet.	109
names of specific persons or places:	Jo jogs daily in Central Park.	123
nouns followed by identifying numbers:	They were assigned to Room 14.	137
	TS	
Do not capitalize		144
compass directions not part of a name:	I drive due north to Leesport.	158
a page if followed by a number:	Did he quote Milton on page 9?	171
a title that follows a name:	LeCare is captain of the ship.	183
commonly accepted derivatives:	Put french toast on the china.	196
geographic names made plural:	I sail on Moon and Fish lakes.	209
seasons (unless personified):	Sweet Summer gave way to fall.	221
generic names of products:	Try Magic Mugg instant coffee.	232

20c ▶ 5
Learn to use the backspacer and the margin release

exact 50-space line

Backspacer (20)

Use a quick, light stroke with the little finger. Depress the key firmly for repeated backspace action on an electric or electronic type-writer.

1 At the left margin of your paper, type the first word as it appears in the list at the right.

2 After typing the word, back-space and fill in the missing letter v.

3 Return, then repeat the proce-dure with each of the remaining words on the list.

lea e

har est

o ens

oli es

sa ings

Margin Release (31)

1 Before typing the sentence be-low, depress the margin release with the little finger and back-space 5 spaces into the left margin.

2 Type the sentence. When the carrier locks, depress the margin release and complete the line.

My typed work should be done neatly, correctly, and quickly.

20d ▶ 13
Learn to end lines

study copy at right; then do Drills 1 and 2

Drill 1

full sheet; begin on Line 10; DS copy

1 Set exact 60–space line.

2 Move right margin stop 5 or 6 spaces farther to the right.

3 Read the ¶ at the bottom of this page. Then, as you type it, listen for the bell. When it sounds, com-plete the word you are typing; re-turn immediately. If the machine locks on a long word, operate the margin release, complete the word, and return.

Your typed line endings will not match those in the textbook.

Drill 2

1 After typing Drill 1, return twice.

2 Set machine for a 50–space line with appropriate right margin bell adjustment.

3 Retype the ¶; follow the di-rections in Step 3 of Drill 1.

Know your machine: line ending warning bell

Margin stops cause the machine to lock at the point at which they are set. To bypass the lock, you must use the margin release (31), a time-consuming operation if used often.

Lines of a paragraph automatically align at the left margin, but they do not automati-cally align at the right margin. It is neces-sary, therefore, that the operator or typist ends lines at the right as evenly as possible.

To help you know when to end a line, a warning bell sounds 7 to 12 spaces before the margin stop is reached. Most typists

find that a warning of 5 or 6 spaces (a half inch) is adequate to maintain a fairly even righthand margin. Thus, after setting mar-gins for an exact line length, they move the right margin set 5 or 6 spaces farther to the right.

To use this procedure, set margin stops for an exact line length (50, 60, or 70 spaces); then move the right margin set another 5 or 6 spaces to the right. Doing so allows you to: (1) end a short word or (2) divide a longer one within 5 or 6 spaces after the bell rings.

When the bell sounds, you must decide just where to end that line and begin a new one. If the word you are typing as the bell rings can be finished within 5 letters, finish it. If it takes more, you may need to divide it. You will learn soon how and when to divide words.

Supplemental skill-building practice

Improve keystroking technique

60-space line; type 2 times SS; DS between 3-line groups

Technique hint:
Concentrate on each word as you type it.

direct reaches

1 ice cede gun herb deck mute nut shy grunt hunt hymn jump sun
2 Cecelia Haynes and John Lunce hunt in Greece every December.
3 A group of shy, hungry gnus munched on green jungle grasses.

adjacent reaches

4 folk three lion port trite quit pods ankle oil yule were art
5 Opal is prepared to buy gas and oil for her sporty roadster.
6 Tio has a new poncho for sale; it has beading and silk trim.

double letters

7 door veer err skiing lass committee odd off all success inns
8 Ella successfully crossed the creek at the foot of the hill.
9 Deer need access to green grass, weeds, and trees in summer.

Reach for new goals

1 Take a 1' writing on ¶1. Note your *gwam* base rate.

2 Add 4 words to base rate to set a new goal. Note your ¼' subgoals below.

3 Take a ½' writing on ¶1, guided by ¼' guide call. Try to reach your ¼' goal as each guide is called.

4 Take a 1' writing on ¶1, guided by ¼' guide call. Try to reach your ¼' goal as each guide is called.

5 Take two more ½' and two more 1' writings as directed above. If you reach your 1' goal, set a new one.

6 Type ¶2 as directed in 1–5.

7 Take a 3' writing on both ¶s without the call of the guide.

gwam	¼'	½'	¾'	Time
16	4	8	12	16
20	5	10	15	20
24	6	12	18	24
28	7	14	21	28
32	8	16	24	32
36	9	18	27	36
40	10	20	30	40
44	11	22	33	44
48	12	24	36	48

Difficulty index

all letters used	LA	1.4 si	5.4 awl	85% hfw

gwam 3'

Who is happier, a person with much education or one with little? 4

Which of the two is better adjusted, more satisfied, and better able to 9

realize goals? These are not easy questions. Education is no magic 14

elixir. It is only a tool that can help us to use knowledge to win out 19

over problems. The answer lies in how we use that tool. 22

Education will not bring about happiness any more than a hammer will 27

bring about a house. Yet we can use what we learn, through experience as 32

well as through school, to build the kind of lifestyle that will enable 37

us to recognize those values that have great significance for us. We can 41

use them in our best judgment to find the satisfaction we all seek. 46

gwam 3' | 1 | 2 | 3 | 4 | 5 |

20e ▶ 10

Learn to divide words

half sheet; insert (with long side up) to Line 9

1 Read the ¶; it explains basic rules for dividing words.

2 Use a 60–space line, ad–justed for bell warning.

3 As you type, listen for the bell. Complete or divide words as appropriate for a fairly even right margin.

As long as certain guides are observed, words may be divided in order to keep line lengths nearly even. For example, always divide a word between its syllables; as, care-less. Words of one syllable, however long, may not be divided, nor should short words --such as often--of five or fewer letters. The separation of a one- or two-letter syllable, as in likely or across, from the rest of a word must also be avoided.

21

21a ▶ 7

Preparatory practice

60-space line; each line twice SS (slowly, then faster)

Note: Line 3 has two ALL–CAP items. To type them, find the shift lock (27); depress the key with the left little finger; type the item; release the lock by striking either shift key.

alphabet 1 Jessie Quick believed the campaign frenzy would be exciting.

figures 2 The 2 buyers checked Items 10, 15, 27, 36, and 48 on page 9.

shift/lock 3 Titles of reports are shown in ALL CAPS; as, DIVIDING WORDS.

easy 4 Did they fix the problem of the torn panel and worn element?

| 1 | 2 | 3 | 4 | 5 | 6 | 7 | 8 | 9 | 10 | 11 | 12 |

21b ▶ 9

Learn to use the warning bell

half sheet; DS; begin on Line 9; 60-space line

Listen for the bell as you type. Make decisions about line endings. Avoid looking at the paper or typewriter as you type.

Learning to use a keyboard is worth our efforts. Few of us do so for the sheer joy of it. When most people type, they have a goal in mind--they want something in return. If we send a letter, we expect a reply--at least a reaction. If it is a job that we are doing for someone, we want approval--maybe payment. If it is for school, we hope for a top grade. What we get, though, will depend on what we give.

21c ▶ 9

Learn to center lines horizontally (side to side)

Drill 1

half sheet; DS; begin on Line 16

1 Insert paper (long side up) with left edge at 0.

2 Move each margin stop to its end of the scale. Clear all tab stops; set a new stop at center point of the page (elite, 51; pica, 42).

3 From center point, backspace once for each two letters, figures, spaces, or punctuation marks in the line.

4 Do not backspace for an odd or leftover stroke at the end of the line.

5 Begin to type where you com–plete the backspacing.

6 Complete the line; return; tab to center point. Type subsequent line in the same way.

Drill 2

half sheet; DS; begin on Line 14; center each line

Drill 1

LEARN TO CENTER LINES

Horizontally--Side to Side

Drill 2

You are invited

to attend the opening

of the new

JONES PUBLIC LIBRARY

Monday, May 3, 10 a.m.

32d ▶ 12
Address envelopes

1 Addressing envelopes is entirely a matter of visual placement. Read the following guides and study the illustrations to help you with the placement of addresses.

2 Type in United States Postal Service (U.S.P.S.) style a Monarch envelope (No. 9) and in standard style a small envelope (No. 6¾) for each address [LM pp. 29–33]. Use your own return address; proofread/circle errors.

Letter address

Vertically: Visualize a line drawn from side to side across the vertical center of the envelope. Begin the first line of the address just below such an imaginary line.

Horizontally: Visualize a line drawn from top to bottom across the horizontal center of the envelope. Align an address from 5 (for larger envelopes) to 10 (for smaller envelopes) spaces to the left of such an imaginary line.

Return address

Type the writer's name and address SS in block style in the upper left corner. Start about 3 spaces from the left edge on Line 2.

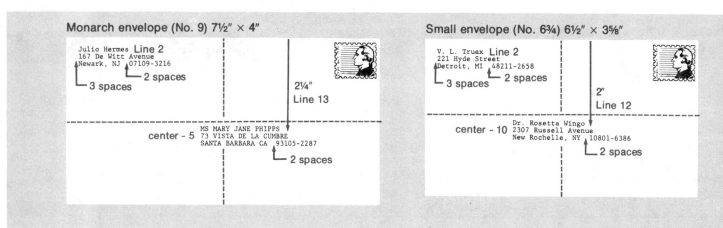

Monarch envelope (No. 9) 7½" × 4"

```
Julio Hermes   Line 2
167 De Witt Avenue
Newark, NJ  07109-3216
          └ 2 spaces
 └ 3 spaces
```
2¼"
Line 13
```
center - 5   MS MARY JANE PHIPPS
             73 VISTA DE LA CUMBRE
             SANTA BARBARA CA  93105-2287
                     └ 2 spaces
```

Small envelope (No. 6¾) 6½" × 3⅝"

```
V. L. Truax   Line 2
221 Hyde Street
Detroit, MI  48211-2658
          └ 2 spaces
 └ 3 spaces
```
2"
Line 12
```
center - 10  Dr. Rosetta Wingo
             2307 Russell Avenue
             New Rochelle, NY  10801-6386
                     └ 2 spaces
```

The envelope above is typed in ALL CAPS with no punctuation, the form recommended by the U.S. Postal Service.

Mrs. Arthur T. Werther
1321 Fairbanks Road
Concord, NH 03301-1789

Miss Grace Carveck
35 Fox Mill Lane
Springfield, IL 62707-7133

Mr. Brett Reymer
94 Mercer Street
Paterson, NJ 07524-5447

32e ▶ 8
Fold and insert letters

Study the illustrations below. Practice folding 8½" × 11" paper for small envelopes and 7¼" × 10½" paper for Monarch envelopes.

The folding procedure for Monarch envelopes is also used for large (No. 10) business envelopes.

Folding and inserting letters into small envelopes

Folding and inserting letters into Monarch envelopes

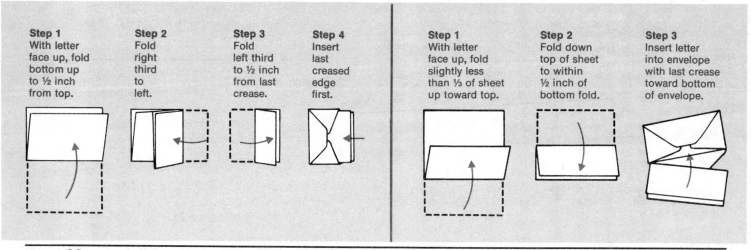

Step 1 With letter face up, fold bottom up to ½ inch from top.

Step 2 Fold right third to left.

Step 3 Fold left third to ½ inch from last crease.

Step 4 Insert last creased edge first.

Step 1 With letter face up, fold slightly less than ⅓ of sheet up toward top.

Step 2 Fold down top of sheet to within ½ inch of bottom fold.

Step 3 Insert letter into envelope with last crease toward bottom of envelope.

Format a short report on dividing words

full sheet; 60-space line; DS body; begin on Line 10; TS below heading; proofread and circle errors

To TS when machine is set for DS: DS, then by hand turn cylinder (platen) forward one space.

1 Read the report carefully.

2 Center heading on Line 10; then type the report.

3 Listen for the warning bell; decide quickly about line endings. Avoid looking up.

4 When finished, examine the margins critically; proofread your copy and circle errors.

> **Proofreading.** Conscientious keyboard operators always check carefully what they have keyboarded before they remove the paper from the machine. They *proofread* paragraphs; that is, they read them for *meaning*, as if they had not read them before. They double–check figures, proper names, and uncertain spellings against the original or some other source.

words

DIVIDING WORDS   3
TS

A word may be divided at the end of a line in order to keep   15
the margins as nearly equal in width as possible. Divided words,   28
of course, tend to be more difficult to read than undivided words;   41
so good judgment is needed. The following guides can help you   54
make sound decisions about word division.   62

Words that contain double consonants are usually divided be   74
tween consonants; as, bal-lots. However, if a word that ends in   87
double letters has a suffix attached, divide after the double let   100
ters; as, dress-ing or stuff-ing.   107

Words that contain an internal single-vowel syllable should   119
be divided after that syllable; as, miti-gate. If two internal   132
one-letter syllables occur consecutively in a word, divide between   145
them; as, situ-ation or gradu-ation.   153

Compound words that contain a hyphen should be divided only   165
at the hyphen; as, second-class. Compound words written without a   178
hyphen are best divided between the elements of the compound; as,   191
super-market.   194

Two final suggestions: Once you have decided to divide a   205
word, leave as much of that word as you can on the first line; that   219
way, a minimum of guesswork is required of the reader. Further,   232
when in doubt about how to divide a word, remember that a dictio   245
nary is still the best friend a writer can have.   254

Preparatory practice

60-space line; each line twice SS (slowly, then faster); DS between 2-line groups

alphabet 1 Roxy waved as she did quick flying jumps on the trapeze bar.

shift keys 2 Yang Woerman hopes Zoe Quigley can leave for Maine in March.

figures 3 Buy 25 boxes, 147 bags, 39 sacks, 68 cartons, and 10 crates.

easy 4 Did the girl make the ornament with fur, duck down, or hair?

| 1 | 2 | 3 | 4 | 5 | 6 | 7 | 8 | 9 | 10 | 11 | 12 |

32a ▶ 7
Preparatory practice

each line 3 times SS
(slowly, faster, still faster);
DS between 3-line groups;
repeat if time permits

alphabet 1 Perry might know I feel jinxed because I have missed a quiz.

figures 2 Buy 147 fish, 25 geese, 10 ponies, 39 lambs, and 68 kittens.

hyphen 3 He won the first-class ribbon; it was a now-or-never effort.

easy 4 The neighbor owns a fox, six foals, six ducks, and six hens.

| 1 | 2 | 3 | 4 | 5 | 6 | 7 | 8 | 9 | 10 | 11 | 12 |

32b ▶ 10
Align and type

It is sometimes necessary to reinsert the paper to correct an error.
The following steps will help you
learn to do so correctly.

1 Type this sentence, but do not
make the return:

I can align this copy.

2 Locate aligning scale (16),
variable line spacer (2), and paper
release lever (13) on your
machine.

3 Move the carrier (carriage) so
that a word containing an i
(such as align) is above the align-

ing scale. Note that a vertical line
points to the center of i.

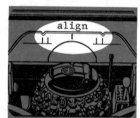

4 Study the relation between top
of aligning scale and bottoms of
letters with downstems (g,p,y).

Get an exact eye picture of the
relation of typed line to top of
scale so you will be able to adjust
the paper correctly to type over a
character with exactness.

5 Remove paper; reinsert it.
Gauge the line so bottoms of letters are in correct relation to top of
aligning scale. Operate the variable line spacer, if necessary, to
move paper up or down. Operate
paper release lever to move paper
left or right, if necessary, when
centering the letter i over one of
the lines on the aligning scale.

6 Check accuracy of alignment by
setting the ribbon control (28) in
stencil position and by typing over
one of the letters. If necessary,
make further alignment adjustments.

7 Return ribbon control to normal
position (to type on upper half of
ribbon).

8 Type over the characters in the
sentence, moving paper up or
down, to left or right, as necessary
to correct alignment.

32c ▶ 13
Personal letter
in block style

1 personal-size sheet [LM p.
27] or plain paper; SS ¶s; DS
between ¶s; proofread/correct
errors

1 Format the letter at the right,
making corrections as marked.

2 For special parts, use:

Return address and date

334 Pittman Street
Olathe, KS 66061-1678
March 22, 19--

Letter address

Miss Evelyn Guione
1352 Pilgrim Place
Pasadena, CA 91108-3307

Salutation **Dear Evelyn**

Closing lines

Sincerely

(Return 4 times)

Trevor Hunter

	words
opening lines	26

As I told you I might, I have changed my plans. I shall be — 38

taking *several* morning classes *there in Pasadena* at the University during — 52

July and august. — 55

My expenses would be eased considerably if I could find a — 67

part-time job where I might work afternoons or evenings. — 78

So, would you be kind enough to let me know if you *should* — 89

learn of such a position? May I use your name *as a reference* if I make the — 104

application? — 106

I value you friendship Evelyn; and I shall be very gratful — 119

for any assistance *stet* that you may provide. — 127

	words
closing lines	129

22b ▶ 13
Review procedure for horizontal centering

half sheet (long side up); begin on Line 13; DS body; TS below heading; proofread and circle errors

1 Review steps for centering lines horizontally (see 21c).
2 Center each line of the announcement shown at right.

EASTERN HILLS GOLF CLUB
TS
Annual Awards Banquet

The Nineteenth Hole

October 10, 6:30 p.m.

22c ▶ 30
Learn to center copy vertically

half sheet

Study the guides for vertical centering given at the right; then format and type Problem 1 below and Problem 2 on p. 45.

Guides for vertical centering

1 Count all lines and blank line spaces required by the problem (1 blank line space between DS lines; 2 blank line spaces between TS lines).

Note. Both pica and elite type require 1" for 6 lines of copy.

2 Subtract the total lines required by the problem from the number of lines on the paper (33, half sheet; 66, full sheet).

3 Divide the resulting number by 2 to determine number of lines to be left in top margin. *Disregard any fraction that may result from the division.*

4 From the top edge of the paper, space down 1 more than the number of lines figured for the top margin; begin typing on that line.

5 Center each line of the problem horizontally.

Calculation check

Lines available:	33
Lines required:	12
Lines remaining:	21
Top margin: (20 ÷ 2)	10
(Begin on Line 11)	

This procedure places copy in what is called "exact center."

Problem 1

```
1
2
3
4                              Center
5                                |
6                                |
7                                |
8                                |
9                                |
10                               ↓
11            HISAKO GIBSON HARROW
12                                    TS
13
14      will read selections from her book
15                                        DS
16            ONE GRAY MORNING
17
18    on Friday evening, August 9, at eight
19
20            in Benjamin Court
21
22      The Art Institute of Jersey City
23
24
25
26
27
28
29
30
31
32
33
```

Personal letters in block style

3 personal-size sheets [LM pp. 21-25] or plain paper; see pages 58 and 59 for guides to letter placement; proofread/correct errors

Postal authorities recommend using 2–letter state abbreviations (always with ZIP Code). For a complete list of such abbreviations, see the Reference Guide, p. iv at the back of this book.

Personal titles

As a courtesy to the person to whom a letter is addressed, a letter writer may use a personal or professional title—Miss, Mr., Dr., etc.—with the name in the letter address and on the envelope.

A letter writer, if male, does not ordinarily give himself a title in the signature lines. A female writer, however, may properly use a title before her typed name or, when she writes it, in parentheses before her signature to indicate her preference.

Problem 1

words

900 Beecher Street | Montgomery, AL 36108-4473 | May 18, 19-- | 12
(Operate return 4 times) | Mr. Lymon S. Bohn | 890 Crestview   18
Drive | Rockford, IL 61107-2317 | DS | Dear Lymon | DS   26

(¶) This morning I talked with Debra Tredsaw, a member of the   38
school reunion committee; and I heard a bit of great news--that   51
you plan to attend our class reunion next month.   61

(¶) More great news! Herb Dobynski will also be here, and he   72
and I want to play a little golf that afternoon. Can you arrange   85
to be in town early enough to join us? Maybe I can persuade   98
Jimmy Geddes or Ted Oxward to make it a foursome.   108

(¶) Let me know when you are arriving, Lymon. I'll be glad to   120
pick you up at the airport or to make any other arrangements for   133
you.   133

Cordially | (Operate return 4 times) | Mike Stavros   138

Problem 2

890 Crestview Drive | Rockford, IL 61107-2317 | May 25, 19-- | Mr.   12
Michael Stavros | 900 Beecher Street | Montgomery, AL 36108-   24
4473 | Dear Mike   26

(¶) I do indeed plan to attend the Monroe High reunion of the   38
Class of '78. I wouldn't miss it--nor would I pass up a chance to   51
give you and Herb a drubbing on the golf course.   61

(¶) The trip to Montgomery will also involve taking care of some   74
business. I shall drive down, arriving there during the late   86
afternoon or early evening of the 16th. I have made reserva-   98
tions at the Graymoor for three days. I'll call you when I get in.   112

(¶) I'm really looking forward to this trip, Mike, and to the oppor-   125
tunity to visit many old friends.   131

Cordially | Lymon Bohn   135

Problem 3

900 Beecher Street | Montgomery, AL 36108-4473 | May 27, 19-- | 11
Mr. Herbert Dobynski | 8098 Fairwater Drive | Norfolk, VA   23
23508-6172 | Dear Herb   27

(¶) I have tried to reach you several times by phone, but I have   39
not been successful; hence, this brief note.   48

(¶) Lymon Bohn has confirmed that he'll be in town for the re-   60
union on June 17, and he has agreed to join us for golf that after-   73
noon. Ted Oxward will also join us.   81

(¶) Because I expect things might be hectic at my club that day,   93
I called the pro, Jill Nyles, today and asked her to save us a   105
tee-off time of 1 p.m. If for any reason this time is not good   118
for you, let me know.   123

Cordially | Mike Stavros   127

22c, continued

Problem 2

half sheet; DS; center each line horizontally and the entire an- nouncement vertically; proofread; circle errors

Calculation check

Lines on half sheet	33
Lines in announcement	12
Unused lines	21
Top margin	10
(Begin on Line 11)	

THE RUGBY SHOP
TS

invites you to attend

a special unadvertised sale

of sweaters, slacks, and shirts

one day only

Saturday, March 13, from 9 to 9

23

23a ▶ 7

Preparatory practice

60-space line; each line once DS; two 1' writings on Line 4

alphabet	1	Merry will have picked out a dozen quarts of jam for boxing.
d/s	2	Eddie Deeds sold daisy seeds to a student from East Dresden.
figures	3	Your 3:15 p.m. show drew 49 men, 72 women, and 680 children.
easy	4	As usual, Len bid and paid for a quantity of big world maps.

| 1 | 2 | 3 | 4 | 5 | 6 | 7 | 8 | 9 | 10 | 11 | 12 |

23b ▶ 10

Measure straight-copy skill

two 1' writings
two 3' writings

Difficulty index

all letters used | E | 1.2 si | 5.1 awl | 90% hfw

gwam 3'

By this time, you must realize that there are many rules   4

you should learn about line endings and word division. Add   8

to your store of rules those that explain when you ought to   12

avoid dividing a word at the end of a line. Unless you must,   16

for example, you should not divide a figure, a proper name, a   20

date, or the last word on a page. If you learn these rules   24

and combine them with just a little common sense, you will be   28

able to handle problems of word division quickly and wisely.   32

| 1 | 2 | 3 | 4 |

31a ▶ 7
Preparatory practice

each line 3 times SS (slowly, faster, slower); DS between 2-line groups; then as many 30″ writings on Line 4 as time permits

Goal: Finish Line 4 in 30″.

alphabet 1 Max Jurez worked to improve the quality of his basic typing.

adjacent reaches 2 Bert quickly pointed to where onions grew in the sandy soil.

fig/sym 3 Veronica bought 16 7/8 yards of #240 cotton at $3.59 a yard.

easy 4 The formal gowns worn by the girls hang in the civic chapel.

| 1 | 2 | 3 | 4 | 5 | 6 | 7 | 8 | 9 | 10 | 11 | 12 |

31b ▶ 15
Correct errors

1 Read the information at the right.

2 Keyboard the lines below the information exactly as they appear DS; correct the errors *after* you have typed each line.

Truly finished work contains no errors. Most individuals rely upon an "inner sense" to tell them when they have made an error, and they stop keyboarding at once and correct it. This "inner sense," however, is fallible; and even an expert typist should carefully proofread completed work for undetected mistakes while the paper is still in the machine. Correcting errors before the paper is removed is easier than reinserting paper and trying to realign lines of copy.

There are several acceptable methods that can be used to correct errors, and they are explained below. Whichever one of them is used, one should keep in mind that an error must be repaired skillfully enough so that neither the error nor evidence of the correction can be observed.

Automatic correction

If your machine is equipped with an automatic correcting ribbon, consult with your instructor or the manufacturer's manual for operating instructions.

Correction paper ("white carbon")

1 Backspace to the error.
2 Place the correction paper in front of the error, coated side toward the paper.
3 Retype the error. The substance on the correction paper will cover the error.
4 Remove the correction paper; backspace; type the correction.

Correction fluid ("liquid paper")

1 Be sure the color of the fluid matches the color of the paper.
2 Turn the paper forward or backward to ease the correction process.
3 Brush the fluid on sparingly; cover only the error, and it lightly.
4 The fluid dries quickly. Return to correction point and make the correction.

Rubber eraser

1 Use a plastic shield (to protect surrounding type) and a typewriter (hard) eraser.
2 Turn the paper forward or backward in the typewriter to position the error for easier correction.
3 To keep bits of rubber out of the mechanism, move the carrier away from the error (or move carriage to the extreme left or right).
4 With a sharp edge of the eraser, erase ink from the paper. Move the eraser in one direction only to avoid cutting the paper.

1 Concentrate when you type; fongers can "telegraph" an error.

2 Just as soon as a mistade is made, it ought to be corrected.

3 It pays to be sure that you find evrey error and correct it.

4 Proofread carefully; then remove your work from the nachine.

23c ▶ 15
Center announcements

Problem 1

half sheet; DS; use exact vertical center; center each line hori–zontally (not aligned as shown); proofread/circle errors

Problem 2

full sheet; DS; use directions for Problem 1, but center in *reading position*

Reading position

Reading position places data slightly higher on a page than exact vertical center. Find top margin for exact center, then sub-tract 2 lines. Reading position is generally used only for full sheets (or half sheets with short side up— long edge at the left).

THE ELMIRA CONCERT SOCIETY _{TS}

proudly presents

the eminent Latin American pianist

Jorge Cabrara

in concert

Saturday afternoon, April 30, at 4:00

Carteret Auditorium

23d ▶ 9
Center data on special-size paper

half sheet, short side inserted first; DS; begin on Line 22; center information requested for each line

---

Finding horizontal center

To find the horizontal center of special-size paper or cards

1 Insert the paper or card into the machine. From the line-of-writing scale, add the numbers at the left and right edges of the paper.

2 Divide this sum by 2. The result is the horizontal center point for that size paper or card.

Your name

Your street address

Your city and state

The name of your college

Current date

23e ▶ 9
Center on a card

use a 5" × 3" card or paper cut to size; insert to type on 5" width; center the data verti-cally and horizontally DS; proofread/circle errors

Calculation checks

There are 6 horizontal lines to a vertical inch. A 3" card, therefore, holds 18 lines.

Lines available	18
Lines required	9
Lines remaining	9
Top margin	4
(Begin on Line)	5

John and Mary Dexter _{DS}

announce the arrival of

Meredith Anne

Born December 8

7 pounds 8 ounces

gwam 1' (total words)

gwam 2'

Return address
Dateline

101 Kensington Place   Line 13   4
Brockton, MA 02401-5372   9
August 3, 19-- 2 spaces   12

Operate return
4 times

Letter address

Ms. Viola Bargas   15
6776 Heidelberg Street   20
Durham, NC 27704-4329   25
                       DS

Salutation

Dear Viola   27
        DS

Body of letter

It will be great to have you living in Brockton   36
again. Your promotion to vice-president of the   46
marketing division is certainly well deserved.   55

You will find that our town has changed consider-   65
ably since your last visit three years ago. It is   75
still a small, close-knit community; but the newly   86
established Arts Commission has begun to promote   95
the efforts of many local artists. As a result,   105
our little village has taken on a bohemian air.   115

Let me show you one way that Brockton has changed.   125   5
I should like you to be my guest on August 23 when   135 10
the local theater group presents SCHOOL FOR SCANDAL   146 15
at the Whitmore Playhouse. Two of our sorority   155 20
members are directing the production.   163 24

As you requested, I shall meet you at the airport   173 29
(Gate 11) on August 23 at 8:25 a.m. You can spend   183 34
the afternoon apartment hunting, and you can relax   193 39
in the evening during dinner and the play.   202 44

I am very eager to see you, Viola!   209 47
                              DS

Complimentary close
Signature

Cordially   211 48

Amanda

This letter is typed with
"open" punctuation; that is,
no punctuation follows the
salutation or complimentary
close.

Style letter 1: personal letter in block style

Learning goals

1 To learn symbol keystrokes.
2 To improve facility on figure keyreaches.
3 To improve proofreading and revision skills.
4 To learn proofreader's marks and their uses.
5 To improve keyboarding continuity.

Machine adjustments

1 Set paper edge guide at 0.
2 Set ribbon control to type on upper half of ribbon.
3 Use a 60–space line (adjusted for bell) unless otherwise directed.
4 SS drills; DS paragraphs.
5 Space problems as directed.

24a ▶ 6
Preparatory practice

each line twice SS (slowly, then faster); DS between 2-line groups; repeat selected lines as time permits

alphabet	1	John Quigley packed the zinnias in twelve large, firm boxes.
n/m	2	Call a woman or a man who will manage Minerva Manor in Nome.
figures	3	Of the 13 numbers, there were 4 chosen: 29, 56, 78, and 90.
easy	4	An auditor may handle the fuel problems of the ancient city.

| 1 | 2 | 3 | 4 | 5 | 6 | 7 | 8 | 9 | 10 | 11 | 12 |

24b ▶ 12
Learn new keyreaches: $ &

$ = dollars
& = ampersand (and)

> **Technique hint**
> Pace your shift–type–release technique when practicing the symbol reaches. Straighten the appropriate finger; avoid as much as you can moving the hands and arms forward.

Reach technique for $

Shift; then reach *up* to $ with *left first* finger.

Left Fingers 4 \ 3 \ 2 \ 1 \ \ 1 \ 2 \ 3 \ 4 Right Fingers

Reach technique for &

Shift; then reach *up* to & with *right first* finger.

Follow the "Standard procedure for learning new keyreaches" on page 10 (Lines 1–4 twice; Lines 5–7 once; repeat 5–7 if time permits).

$
1 $ $ $4 $4, if $4, 4 for $44, her $444 fur, per $4, $4 tariff
2 The items cost them $174, $184, and $54. They paid $14 tax.

&
3 & & J & J, Jory & Jones, Bern & James, H & U Co., Foy & Hope
4 We buy pipe from Smith & Jones, Li & Hume, and Clay & Young.

all fingers/ new symbols
5 The $185 check is from J & J. The $192 check is from B & B.
6 Send $274 to Fish & Heath; deposit $300 with Booth & Hughes.
7 Hecot & Ryne charged us $165; Carver & Hunt charged us $340.

| 1 | 2 | 3 | 4 | 5 | 6 | 7 | 8 | 9 | 10 | 11 | 12 |

Learning goals

1 To prepare personal letters in block style.
2 To correct keyboarding errors.
3 To improve ability to keyboard unedited copy.
4 To address envelopes.
5 To align and type over words.

Machine adjustments

1 Position desk and chair at com–fortable heights.
2 Elevate book.
3 Set ribbon control to type on upper half of ribbon.
4 Use 60–space line for drills; 50–space line for letters.
5 SS drills; DS paragraphs.
Materials: Monarch–size sheets and envelopes; plain sheets; supplies for correcting errors.

30a ▶ 7
Preparatory practice

each line 3 times SS (slowly, faster, slower); DS between 3-line groups; re-peat if time permits

alphabet 1 Jayne Coxx puzzled over the workbooks required for geometry.

a/s 2 This essay says it is easy to save us from disaster in Asia.

figures 3 The box is 6 5/8 by 9 1/2 feet and weighs 375 to 400 pounds.

easy 4 The city auditor paid the proficient man for the fine signs.

| 1 | 2 | 3 | 4 | 5 | 6 | 7 | 8 | 9 | 10 | 11 | 12 |

30b ▶ 43
Prepare personal letters in block style

7¼" × 10½" personal station-ery [Laboratory Materials pp. 17-19]; 50-space line; 2" top margin; proofread/circle errors

If personal–size stationery or plain paper cut to size is not available, use full sheets (8½" × 11"); 50–space line; 2½" top margin.

1 Study the explanatory para–graphs at the right. Refer to the style letter on page 59 for further illustration.

2 Prepare the letter illustrating the block style shown on page 59. Follow spacing directions given on the letter.

3 On a plain full sheet, do two 1' writings on the opening lines (return address through saluta–tion) and two 2' writings on the closing lines (last 3 ¶s through complimentary close).

4 Retype the letter; omit ¶3.

Letter placement information

Many personal letters are prepared on personal-size stationery (Monarch); and Style Letter 1, page 59, is shown with pica (10-pitch) type on that size stationery.

Good letter placement results from the ability to make judgments based on the length of letter, style of stationery, and size of type. Therefore, while it is suggested that letters in Section 7 be started on Line 13 when personal stationery is used (which al-lows approximately a 2" top margin) or on Line 16 if full sheets are used (approxi–mately a 2½" top margin), the starting point can be raised for a longer letter or lowered for a shorter one if you believe it is wise to do so.

Every letter must have a return address. On business stationery, the return address is part of the letterhead. When personal stationery is used, a return address must be typed as part of the letter. The most appro-priate place for this address, according to common usage, is on the two lines imme-diately above and aligned with the date.

It is standard procedure to operate the return 4 times, leaving 3 blank line spaces between the date and the letter recipient's address. This procedure is repeated after the complimentary close, leaving 3 blank line spaces for the signature to be written between the complimentary close and the writer's typed name. (For a personal letter, a typed name is not necessary.) These placement procedures should be followed with all letters in Section 7.

For smaller personal stationery, side margins should be no less than 1" and no more than 1½". A 50-space line, pica or elite, fits within this standard. It is recom-mended, therefore, that a 50-space line be used with Section 7 letters regardless of type size.

24c ▶ 8
Reach for new goals

1 Two 30" writings on each line; try to pace yourself to end each writing just as time is called.

2 Three 1' writings on Line 4; determine *gwam* on each writing.

gwam 30"

1 The six girls paid $81 to visit the old city. 18

2 Lana paid the man the $94 due for the work he did. 20

3 Coe & Wu may sign the form for the auditor of the firm. 22

4 If Torke & Rush paid $730, then Corlan and Aldorn paid $637. 24

| 1 | 2 | 3 | 4 | 5 | 6 | 7 | 8 | 9 | 10 | 11 | 12 |

24d ▶ 7
Use the warning bell/ divide words

two half sheets; begin on Line 12; once with 70-space line, once with 60-space line

Take time to evaluate your completed work. Look carefully at what you have done. Would you be impressed with it if you were a reader? Is it attractive in form and accurate in content? If it does not impress you, it will not impress anyone else.

24e ▶ 9
Proofread/revise as you keyboard

each line twice SS; DS between 2-line groups; identify and correct the circled errors *as you keyboard*

1 He chose 12 to 14 dozen cards for my all-prupose card shelf.

2 The expert quick ly listed 23 sources of information forher.

3 I drove my new jeep at an average ratt of 56 miles per hour?

4 Minimum spedd on that part of Route 789 is 35 miles an horu.

5 The whit pine frame is 15 x 20 inches; there is no picture.

24f ▶ 8
Improve keyboarding continuity

1 Practice the ¶ once for orientation.

2 Take three 30" practice writings on the ¶. Determine *gwam*: words typed × 2.

3 Take three 1' speed writings on the ¶. Determine *gwam*: total words typed = 1' *gwam*.

Goal: 20 or more *gwam*.

Difficulty index

| all letters used | E | 1.2 si | 5.1 awl | 90% hfw |

    2   4   6   8   10

We purchased our computer from the Jeff & Zorne Company

  12   14   16   18   20   22

for $500. That is quite a lot of money; but I think it will

  24   26   28   30   32   34

be a good investment if I can use the machine and all of the

  36   38   40   42   44   46

parts--figures and symbols, for example--in the correct way.

25a ▶ 7
Preparatory practice

each line twice SS (slowly, then faster); DS between 2-line groups; repeat selected lines if time permits

25

alphabet 1 Why did the judge quiz poor Victor about his blank tax form?

t/r 2 Bart had trouble starting his truck for a trip to Terrytown.

figure/ symbol 3 Buy 103 ribbons and 45 erasers from May & Muntz for $289.67.

easy 4 Did she rush to cut six bushels of corn for the civic corps?

| 1 | 2 | 3 | 4 | 5 | 6 | 7 | 8 | 9 | 10 | 11 | 12 |

LEVEL TWO
Formatting/typing basic communications

Let's be elemental. A keyboard is made up of several rows of buttons, or keys, which, when struck, operate your machine. This activity of striking is called keyboarding.

Keyboarding certainly seems commonplace enough. It takes on added meaning when you consider that your keyboard is identical to those used to operate an increasingly large number and variety of technical machines, such as computers, microcomputers, word processors, and electronic typewriters. As part of such equipment, the keyboard becomes the instrument through which are transmitted thoughts and ideas, facts and figures, and all sorts of business, academic, social, and scientific data.

How efficiently any machine functions, of course, depends directly upon how skillfully the operator uses it. Its utility increases in ratio to a user's knowledge about it and ability to operate it rapidly and accurately.

By successfully completing Level 1 work, you have gained ability to keyboard by touch and to enter data attractively on a page. Now you are ready to begin a new level of learning, one in which you will learn to put these important skills to professional use.

You will learn, for example, to format and input personal and business correspondence, tables, data sheets, and reports; and you will gain more experience using printed, rough-draft, and handwritten input materials.

In addition, as you enter the practice and problem data, your keyboarding speed should increase; and, with concentrated effort, your accuracy should also improve.

Learning to keyboard and format with skill is a significant accomplishment. From now on, you should realize that future output from equipment you use depends on the input abilities you develop now.

25b ▶ 12
Learn new keyreaches
( )

Follow the "Standard procedure for learning new keyreaches" on page 10 (Lines 1–4 twice; Lines 5–8 once; repeat 5–8 if time permits.)

= number/pounds
( ) = parentheses

Left Fingers   4 3 2 1   1 2 3 4   Right Fingers

Reach technique for #	Reach technique for (	Reach technique for)
 Shift; then reach *up* to # with *left second* finger.	 Shift; then reach *up* to (with *right third* finger.	 Shift; then reach *up* to) with *right little* finger

#	1 # # #3 #33 Card #3, File #3, Car #33, #3 grade. Try #3 now.
	2 Memo #169 says to load Car #3758 with 470# of #2 grade sand.
( )	3 (1 (1);); (90) two (2); type (1) and (2); see (8) and (9).
	4 He (John) and his cousin (Lynne) are both the same age (17).
#/( )	5 Pay the May (#34) and June (#54) bills soon (before July 1).
	6 We lease Car #84 (a white sedan) and Car #86 (a blue coupe).
all figures/ new symbols	7 Our Check #230 for $259 paid Owen & Cobb (auditors) in full.
	8 Deliver the $78 order (collect) to Fox & Tucker (Room #416).

| 1 | 2 | 3 | 4 | 5 | 6 | 7 | 8 | 9 | 10 | 11 | 12 |

25c ▶ 8
Proofread/revise as you keyboard

each line twice SS; DS between 2-line groups; correct circled errors as you type

1   I saw them fill the (Baskets) full of (appels) (form) the orchard.

2   None of (use) took that (specal) train to Cincinnati (adn) Dayton.

3   They (paln) an intensive (campaing) for television and/or (raido)

4   (Teh) two leaders (Betty and Luis) left at 2--not 1:30 today.

5   (put) a fork, knife, and (sppon) at each informal place setting.

29c ▶ 5
Develop concentration with fill-ins

each line once DS; proofread and mark with proofreader's marks any errors you make; retype from your edited copy

1 Rent in the amount of $185 is payable the 5th of each month.

2 In response, refer to Invoice #187-3 and the date, April 21.

3 Plant seedlings 3 inches deep, 12 inches apart, after May 1.

4 On 3-17-85 Bands 7746-7789 were used to band Canadian geese.

5 Shipments left Dock 15 via Atlantic Express May 29 at 3 p.m.

29d ▶ 6
Improve response patterns

once as shown; repeat if time permits

Lines 1-2: Say and type each word as a unit.

Lines 3-4: Spell each word as you type it letter by letter at a steady pace.

Lines 5-6: Say and type short, easy words as units; spell and type longer words letter by letter.

word
1 Their goal is to do social work downtown for a city auditor.
2 Did the men cut the eight bushels of corn down by the field?

stroke
3 He acts, in my opinion, as if my cards gave him greater joy.
4 Jimmy deserves my extra reward; few cars ever tested better.

combination
5 Based on my theory, she decreased that quantity of protozoa.
6 They sign with great care several of their formal abstracts.

| 1 | 2 | 3 | 4 | 5 | 6 | 7 | 8 | 9 | 10 | 11 | 12 |

29e ▶ 9
Improve keystroking technique

each line twice SS; DS between 2-line groups; keep wrists low, eyes on copy

bottom row
1 Did six brave, zany exhibitors and/or bakers climb Mt. Zemb?

home row
2 Sada and Jake had a dish of salad; Gail had a glass of soda.

3d row
3 At her party, a quiet waiter poured tea as I wrote a letter.

figures
4 On June 24, Flight 89 left at 1:30 with 47 men and 65 women.

| 1 | 2 | 3 | 4 | 5 | 6 | 7 | 8 | 9 | 10 | 11 | 12 |

29f ▶ 13
Measure skill growth: straight copy

60-space line; DS

three 1' writings
three 3' writings

Goal:

1'—25 or more gwam
3'—21 or more gwam

Difficulty index

all letters used	E	1.2 si	5.1 awl	90% hfw

gwam 3'

Do we care about how people judge us? Most of us do. 4 | 26

We hope and expect that other people will recognize quality 8 | 30

in what we do, what we say, and the way we act. Is it not 12 | 34

true, though, that what others think of us results from some 16 | 38

image that we have created in their minds? In other words, 20 | 42

are we not really our own creation? 22 | 44

gwam 3' | 1 | 2 | 3 | 4 |

25d ▶ 8
Improve keyboarding continuity

1 Practice the ¶ once for orienta-tion.

2 Take three 30″ writings and three 1′ writings.

Goal: At least 14 *gwam*.

```
            .      2      .      4      .      6      .      8      .     10      .
     Issue #27 of a recent (1/9/85) magazine told how an ex-
            12     .     14      .     16      .     18      .     20      .     22      .
     ecutive got her first job with a top-level firm (Roe & Roe):
            24     .     26      .     28      .     30      .     32      .     34      .
     She knew how to keyboard.  Paid merely $140 a week at first,
            36     .     38      .     40      .     42      .     44      .     46      .
     she moved up quickly; now she is making about $1,360 a week.
```

25e ▶ 15
Review centering an announce-ment on special-size paper

half sheet; insert short side first; DS; center vertically in reading position; center each line horizontally; proofread/ circle errors

Calculation checks:

The page is 8½″ long. There are 6 lines in one vertical inch. 8½ × 6 = 51 available lines.

Lines in problem: 14
Exact top margin: 18
Reading position
    top margin: 16

Add right paper edge reading to left paper edge reading; divide by 2. The result is the center point of the page.

Members of THE CHORALIERS
                          TS

Arvid Badger

Muriel Ann Bressuyt

Bertram Garrett, Jr.

Wayne L. Jewell

Phillip R. Runyun

Bette Lee Yamasake

26

26a ▶ 7
Preparatory practice

each line twice SS (slowly, faster); as many 30″ writ-ings on Line 4 as time permits

Goal: Complete Line 4 in 30″.

alphabet **1** Jewel quickly explained to me the big fire hazards involved.

space bar **2** is by it do in be of am my go me an us so if to or ad on and

figure symbol **3** Silva & Stuart checked Items #2346 and 789 (for a $150 fee).

easy **4** The auditor did the rush work right, so he risks no penalty.

```
     ‵    |  1  |  2  |  3  |  4  |  5  |  6  |  7  |  8  |  9  | 10  | 11  | 12  |
```

28d ▶ 23
Improve keyboarding continuity

full sheet; DS; 60-space line; 1½" top margin

1 Prepare the report once, making the corrections designated by the proofreading symbols.

2 Correct any new errors using proofreader's marks.

3 Prepare a final copy from your marked paragraphs; proofread; circle errors.

words

my ARIZONA HIDEAWAY   4
TS

In arizona, there is a small hotel that is locatd near   15

six high green and white mountains. I like it there, for I 27
to visit   stet

enjoy the quite of that palce. The morningview is special, 40

and each day there i feel better that I fell the day before. 52

The six mountains are quite high, green just so far up;   63

then they turn white. They reach into the azure beyond like 75

human hands; and when a cloud appears, it seems as if one of 88

the hands has flung a small piece of vapor into the heavens. 100

Rates are excellent. The hotel provides two (2) large-   111

size rooms and a tasty dinner for just $65 daily. The hotel 123

has only 134 rooms; therefore, I call early for reservations 136

when I visit this area--as I did last April 7, 8, 9, and 10. 148

29a ▶ 7
Preparatory practice

each line twice SS (slowly, then faster); DS between 2-line groups; 1' writings on Line 4 as time permits

alphabet	1	Bob realized very quickly that jumping was excellent for us.
fig/sym	2	Ann's 7% note (dated May 23, 1985) was paid at 4690 J Drive.
double letters	3	Will Buzz and Lee carry the supplies across the street soon?
easy	4	He paid for the endowment, and he owns the giant coal field.

| 1 | 2 | 3 | 4 | 5 | 6 | 7 | 8 | 9 | 10 | 11 | 12 |

29b ▶ 10
Improve symbol keyreaches

each line twice SS; DS between 2-line groups; repeat lines that seemed difficult

Keep eyes on copy; keep keystroking smooth and continuous.

'	1	Ray's brother didn't plan for the day's work; it's not done.
-	2	A pay-freeze plan on so-called full-time jobs is well-known.
( )	3	All of us (including Vera) went to the game (and it rained).
"	4	They read the poems "September Rain" and "The Lower Branch."
$	5	His weekly checks totaled $128.35, $96.20, $114.80, and $77.
/	6	The Sr/C Club walked and/or ran 15 1/2 miles in 6 3/4 hours.

26b ▶ 12
Learn new keyreaches:
% ' !

% = percent
' = apostrophe/single quote
! = exclamation point

Note: If you are using a nonelectric machine, refer to page 3; see directions for reach to '.

Reach technique for %

Shift; then reach *up* to % with *left first* finger.

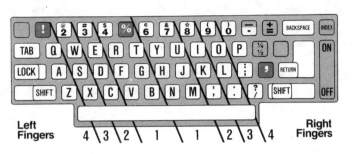

Left Fingers 4 3 2 1   1 2 3 4 Right Fingers

Apostrophe (')

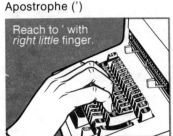

Reach to ' with *right little* finger.

Follow the "Standard procedure for learning new keyreaches" on page 10 (Lines 1–4 twice; Lines 5–8 once; repeat 5–8 if time permits).

Exclamation point:

If your machine has an exclamation point key, strike it with the nearest little finger. If it does not, refer to page 3. Space twice after an exclamation point when used after an emphatic interjection or as end–of–sentence punctuation.

%
1 % % 5%, off 5%, if 5%, save 15%, ask 15%, less 50%, 5% force
2 Mark prices down 15% on coats, 5% on hats, and 10% on shoes.

,
3 ' ' 10's, it's, Bob's, Sec'y, Ok'd; It's summer. I'm going.
4 It's time for Ann's party. I don't have Melanie's notebook.

!
5 Fire! Ouch! Oh wow! Keep out! They offer a big discount!
6 Their slogan reads THINK! They used the headline OOPS SALE!

%/'/!
7 Don't give up! Keep on! We're over the top! We have $950!
8 Uhl & Co. had a 16% profit! Their third quarter showed 20%!

| 1 | 2 | 3 | 4 | 5 | 6 | 7 | 8 | 9 | 10 | 11 | 12 |

26c ▶ 10
Proofread/revise as you keyboard

Errors are often circled in copy that is to be retyped. More frequently, perhaps, the copy is marked with special symbols called "proofreader's marks" which indicate changes desired by an editor.

Some commonly used proofreader's marks are shown at the right. Study them; then type each drill line at least twice, SS; DS between 2–line groups.

Concentrate on copy content as you keyboard.

Proofreader's marks

Symbol	Meaning	Symbol	Meaning
Cap or ‗	Capitalize	#	Add horizontal space
∧	Insert	/ or *lc*	Lowercase letters
ℓ	Delete (remove)	⌒	Close up space
⊏	Move to left	⌣	Transpose
⊐	Move to right	*stet*	Leave as originally written

1 patience pays; the espert's goalis 1% every day improvement.

2 do today's work today; tommorrow's work will be 100T lighter.

3 One's best isusually enough; Few are expect ed to give 101%.

4 It's easier to risk 10%, but return depends on risk.

5 We miss life's pleasures I know because we refuse to sample.

6 I'll be lucky if at anytime I can so lve 50% of my problems.

Learning goals

1 To achieve smooth, continuous keystroking.

2 To improve ability to concen-trate on copy.

3 To improve proofreading skills.

4 To improve facility with figure and symbol reaches.

5 To type script and rough-draft copy smoothly.

Machine adjustments

1 Set paper guide at 0.

2 Set ribbon control to type on upper half of ribbon.

3 Use 60-space line throughout.

4 SS drills; DS paragraphs.

28a ▶ 7
Preparatory practice

each line three times SS (slowly, faster, still faster); DS between 3-line groups; repeat selected lines if time permits

alphabet 1 My wife helped fix a frozen lock on Jacque's vegetable bins.

difficult reaches 2 Beverly sneezed even though she ate a dozen square lozenges.

figures 3 Do Problems 6 to 19 on page 275 before class at 8:30, May 4.

easy 4 Did the form entitle Jay to the land at the end of the lane?

| 1 | 2 | 3 | 4 | 5 | 6 | 7 | 8 | 9 | 10 | 11 | 12 |

28b ▶ 10
Control machine parts

once as shown DS; repeat if time permits

Lines 1-4: Clear all tabs; set tab at center point; tab and type. Keep eyes on book copy.

Line 5: Supply appropriate spac-ing after punctuation.

Line 6: Release margin; back-space 5 spaces into left margin to begin.

Line 7: Depress shift/lock keys firmly.

center

1 ──────────────▶ The tab key should be operated

tab and return 2 quickly. ──────────▶ One quick flick of your finger

3 should suffice. ──────▶ Avoid pauses; do not slow down

4 or look up when you tab.

space bar 5 Was it Mary? Judy? Pam? It was a woman; she wore a big hat.

margin release/ backspacer 6 When you type from copy, elevate the copy to make reading easier.

shift/lock 7 Al read A TALE OF TWO CITIES; Vi read THE MILL ON THE FLOSS.

28c ▶ 10
Improve response patterns

1 Once as shown; checkmark the three most difficult lines.

2 Repeat the lines you checked as difficult.

3 Take a 1' writing on Line 2, next on Line 4, and then on Line 6. Determine *gwam* on each writing.

word 1 Did the antique map of the world also hang by the oak shelf?
2 Did they pay the auditor the duty on eighty bushels of corn?

stroke 3 Holly tests fast race cars; we get oil at my garage in Juno.
4 Johnny erected a vast water cascade on my acreage in Joplin.

combination 5 She paid the extra debt and the taxes on their land in Ohio.
6 Lynn sewed the nylon flaps on the six burlap bags with care.

| 1 | 2 | 3 | 4 | 5 | 6 | 7 | 8 | 9 | 10 | 11 | 12 |

26d ▶ 11
Reach for new goals

1 Take a 1' writing on Line 1.

2 Take a 1' writing on Line 2, try-ing to type as many lines as on Line 1.

3 Practice each of the other pairs of lines in the same way to im-prove figure/symbol keyboarding speed.

words in line

1	Did the girls make soap in a handy clay bowl?	9
2	They spent $85 on a visit to Field & Co.	8
3	Did the men visit the dismal shanty on the island?	10
4	Form #72 is title to the island (their half).	9
5	I turn the dials on the panel a half turn to the right.	11
6	She may pay me for my work, and I make 40% profit.	10
7	It is a shame he spent the endowment on a visit to the city.	12
8	She paid 20% down for the $18 formal tie; it's apricot.	11

| 1 | 2 | 3 | 4 | 5 | 6 | 7 | 8 | 9 | 10 | 11 | 12 |

26e ▶ 10
Improve keyboarding continuity

1 Practice the ¶ for orientation.

2 Take three 30" writings and three 1' writings.

3 Proofread/circle errors after each writing.

Goal: At least 14 gwam.

Avoid looking at the keyboard when you encounter figures and symbols.

Difficulty index

| all letters/symbols learned | E | 1.2 si | 5.1 awl | 90% hfw |

Sales Report #38/39 of the modern firm of Wenz & Jelkes states that, if they are to remain in business, they are re-quired to clear a profit of 10% on all sales (net)--or $1 on each $10. They don't expect the figure to change very soon.

27

27a ▶ 7
Preparatory practice

each line twice SS (slowly, then faster); DS between 2-line groups; take a 1' writ-ing on Line 4 if time per-mits

alphabet	1	Jacky Few's strange, quiet behavior amazed and perplexed us.
shift	2	Lily read BLITHE SPIRIT by Noel Coward. I read VANITY FAIR.
fig/sym	3	Invoice #38 went from $102.74 to $97.60 after a 5% discount.
easy	4	They may go to a town social when they visit the big island.

| 1 | 2 | 3 | 4 | 5 | 6 | 7 | 8 | 9 | 10 | 11 | 12 |

27b ▶ 8
Practice long reaches

each line twice SS; DS be-tween 2-line groups; repeat lines you find most difficult

Keep eyes on copy as you strike figures and symbols.

$	1	He spent $25 for gifts, $13 for dinner, and $7 for cab fare.
( )	2	We (my uncle and I) watched his sons (my cousins) play golf.
%	3	If I add 3% to the company discount of 8%, I can deduct 11%.
&	4	Send the posters to Bow & Held, Mans & Tow, and Wick & Jens.
'	5	It's time to send Hale's credit application to Land's Store.

| 1 | 2 | 3 | 4 | 5 | 6 | 7 | 8 | 9 | 10 | 11 | 12 |

27c ▶ 20
Learn new keyreaches:
" __

" = quotation marks
__ = underline

Quotation (")

Shift; then reach to " with *right little* finger.

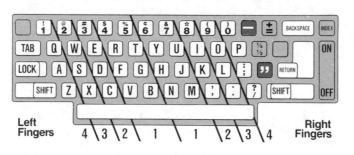

Left Fingers   4 \ 3 \ 2 \ 1 \   \ 1 \ 2 \ 3 \ 4   Right Fingers

Underline (__)

Shift; then reach *up* to __ with *right little* finger.

Follow the "Standard procedure for learning new keyreaches" on page 10 (Lines 1–6 twice; the ¶ once, then again if time permits).

Note: If you are using a non–electric machine, see page 3 directions for reach to ".

To underline: Type the word, backspace to first letter, then strike underline once for each letter in the word.

" 1 ; "; "; James was "Jim"; Mary was "Mo"; and Janis was "Jan."
2 "We are," he said, "alone." "Wrong," said I, "Lee is here."

__ 3 There is a <u>right</u> way and a <u>wrong</u> way; then there is <u>her</u> way.
4 I ordered <u>hose</u>, not hoes, and soda for <u>baking</u>, not <u>drinking</u>.

"/__ 5 "This," she stated, "is the <u>antique</u>; <u>that</u> is the facsimile."
6 She said, "I know that I <u>should</u> go, but I cannot do it <u>now</u>."

Wenz & Jelkes tell us too (in their Report #3) that the margin figure, 10%, is not "very high" for what a major firm makes. The profit this year ($1.5 million) isn't so high as it could have been, but the firm hopes to improve <u>next</u> year.

| 1 | 2 | 3 | 4 | 5 | 6 | 7 | 8 | 9 | 10 | 11 | 12 |

27d ▶ 15
Type a short report
full sheet; DS; 60-space line; 2" top margin; make corrections as you type; proofread/circle errors

SOME FACTS TO REMEMBER (Center)   words 4

TS
one horizontal

There are 10 pica and 12 elite spaces to ∧an inch. With   18
size
either ∧style of type, six lines comprise a vertical inch.   30
horizontal   sheet,
To find the ∧center point of a given ∧area add the readings   44
its   edges
for ∧the left and right ∧limits from the line ∧of writing scale; 56
sum
divide the ∧total by 2.   61
determine   for vertical centering
to ∧set top and bottom margins, subtract the number of   79
to format   on
lines needed ∧for the problem from the number available of ∧the 91
the remaining lines
page; divide ∧by 2 to find exact top margin. Subtract 2 if   107
reading position. After computing lines to be left   120
you desire
one   line
in the top mar gin, space down ∧once more ∧and begin the first   133
line of the problem.   137

Capitalize

1 The first word of a complete sentence.

I have the final page of the report.

2 The first word of a direct quotation.

She said, "Let's work together."

3 The first and main words in titles or headings in books, poems, reports, songs, etc.

I read portions of Leaves of Grass.

4 Titles that precede personal names.

I met Major Busby and Mayor Lopez.

5 Titles of distinction that follow a personal name.

Ms. Chu is a U.S. Senator from Idaho.

6 Names of specific persons and places.

My friend Larry lives in Baltimore.

7 Words derived from the names of specific persons and places.

Barry, a Scot, wore an Edwardian costume.

8 Names of weekdays, months, holidays, and historic periods.

Thursday, November 27, is Thanksgiving.

9 Most nouns followed by identifying numbers.

Issue Check #7813 to pay Invoice 785-J.

10 The first word after a colon if it begins a complete sentence.

Notice: No running is permitted.

11 Seasons of the year if they are personified, and compass points if they designate definite regions.

The icy breath of Winter chilled the Midwest.

12 Trademarks, brand names, and names of commercial products.

My Peerless radio uses Rayovac batteries.

Do not capitalize

1 Compass points when they indicate direction.

We drove north to South Brunswick.

2 *Page* and *verse*, even when followed by a number.

The quotation is in verse 72 on page 512.

3 A title following a name that is not a title of distinction.

Rana was elected secretary of our club.

4 Commonly accepted derivatives of proper nouns.

Why not go dutch treat tonight?

5 The common noun following the name of a product.

I have a Silvertone radio; Jan has an SRE tape deck.

6 Generic terms when they appear in the plural to describe two or more names.

Meet me where Oak and Maple roads cross.

See also page 65 of the textbook.

Numbers: Type as words

1 A figure that begins a sentence.

Three of the runners were disqualified.

2 Numbers ten and lower, unless used as part of a series of figures, some of which are above ten.

I carried five books with me today.
Only 9 of the 27 ducks had been banded.

3 Expressions of time with the word *o'clock*.

Dinner will be served at seven o'clock.

4 The smaller of two numbers used together.

Buy two 5-gallon containers of gasoline.

5 Isolated fractions or indefinite amounts.

Only one third of almost six hundred members attended.

6 Names of small-numbered (ten and under) streets.

He moved from First Street to Seventh Avenue.

7 Large even numbers.

My chances of winning are one in a million.

Numbers: Type as figures

1 Numbers preceded by most nouns.

Check Column 3 of the Volume 2 appendix.

2 Expressions of time followed by *a.m.* or *p.m.* and days and years used as part of a date.

We will meet again at 2 p.m., May 5, 1989.

3 House numbers (except One) and high-numbered street names (with *d* and *th*).

Deliver the flowers to 45 East 72d Street.
My temporary address is 340--39th Street.

4 Numbers used with abbreviations, symbols, or dimensions.

For a 2% solution, add 4 tsp. salt to 4 qts. of water.

5 Dates (with *d* and *th*) that precede the month and are separated from it by words.

We signed a lease on the 23d or 24th of April.

See also pages 77-78 of the textbook.

Word-division guides

A word may correctly be divided between syllables as defined in a dictionary or word-division manual. In special cases, the guidelines below will be helpful.

Short words. Do not divide words of five or fewer letters, even if they have two or more syllables.

area   bonus   alien   aroma   truth   ideal

Double consonants. Divide between double consonants unless the division involves a word that ends in double con-sonants.

excel-lent   call-ing   win-ner   add-ing

One- or two-letter syllables. Do not divide a one-letter sylla-ble at the beginning of a word.

enough   ideal   opened   aboard   ozone

Do not separate a two-letter syllable at the end of a word.

friendly   shaker   nickel   groggy   fluid

Divide after a one-letter syllable within a word; if two single-letter syllables occur together, divide between them.

tele-vision   ele-ment   gradu-ation   idi-omatic

Hyphenated words. Divide at the hyphens only.

self-centered   off-white   soft-spoken

Figures. Do not divide figures presented as a unit.

2,785,321   127,100   #3290533   150/371

Avoid if possible. Try to avoid dividing proper names, dates, and the last word on a page.

See also page 43 of the textbook.

ZIP Code abbreviations

Alabama, AL	Kentucky, KY	Ohio, OH
Alaska, AK	Louisiana, LA	Oklahoma, OK
Arizona, AZ	Maine, ME	Oregon, OR
Arkansas, AR	Maryland, MD	Pennsylvania, PA
California, CA	Massachusetts, MA	Puerto Rico, PR
Colorado, CO	Michigan, MI	Rhode Island, RI
Connecticut, CT	Minnesota, MN	South Carolina, SC
Delaware, DE	Mississippi, MS	South Dakota, SD
District of Columbia, DC	Missouri, MO	Tennessee, TN
Florida, FL	Montana, MT	Texas, TX
Georgia, GA	Nebraska, NE	Utah, UT
Guam, GU	Nevada, NV	Vermont, VT
Hawaii, HI	New Hampshire, NH	Virgin Islands, VI
Idaho, ID	New Jersey, NJ	Virginia, VA
Illinois, IL	New Mexico, NM	Washington, WA
Indiana, IN	New York, NY	West Virginia, WV
Iowa, IA	North Carolina, NC	Wisconsin, WI
Kansas, KS	North Dakota, ND	Wyoming, WY

Margins/Date Placement. The average letter, business or per-sonal, fits well on an 8½" × 11" page if 1½" side margins are used. When letterhead paper is not used, type a return address on Lines 14 and 15. Type the date on Line 16, just below the return ad-dress (or alone on letterhead paper). With a short or long letter, adjust the margins in or out ½"; lower or raise the return address and date as needed.

Horizontal placement of the date varies according to letter style. In block and AMS Simplified styles, type the date at left margin; in modified block style, begin the date at center point. Other letter parts, when they are used, are formatted at left margin, unless otherwise noted.

Mailing notation: on the second line space between the date and letter address. See Letter 2 below.

Letter address: on the fourth line space below the date. Type any official title on the same line as the name or below it, whichever gives better balance. A personal title (as *Ms.* or *Mr.*) precedes an individu-al's name.

Attention line: as the second line of the letter address. The saluta-tion corresponds with the letter address, not the attention line. See Letter 1 below.

Subject line: a double space below the salutation. An introduc-tion such as *Re.* or *SUBJECT:* is optional. See Letter 3 below.

Salutation: a double space below letter address or subject line. The salutation corresponds with the first line of the letter address. If the first line of the letter address, use *Ladies and Gentlemen or Dear Sir or Madam.* See Letters 1 and 3 be-low.

Company name in closing: on the second line space below the complimentary close, in ALL CAPS, at center point for modified block style. See Letter 2 below.

Writer's typed name/official title: on the fourth line space below the complimentary close or company name. With the exception of the AMS style, the writer's title may go on either the same line as the name or below it—whichever gives better balance. A female may indicate personal title preference; a male does not, as *Mr.* is always acceptable. See Let-ters 1–4 below.

Reference initials: a double space below the name and official title in lower case. See Letters 1–4 below.

Enclosure notation: a double space below the reference initials: See Letters 1 and 2 below.

Copy notation (cc, bcc, pc): a double space below the reference initials or enclosure notation, fol-lowed by the recipient's name. See Letter 1 below.

Postscript: a double space below the last letter item, in the same style as was used for other para-graphs. The letters P.S. are rarely used. See Letter 3 below.

Multiple pages: If a letter is too long for one page, at least 2 lines of the body of the letter should be carried to the second page. Begin the sec-ond and subsequent pages on Line 7; leave two blank line spaces below page headings. Use the same side margins as the first page.

Second-page headings

block form

```
Leslie Moll, Inc.
Page 2
October 23, 19--
TS
1"
     and it would seem appropriate for the remainder of the shipment
1"   to be kept in storage at the Dubuque depot until the conditions
```

horizontal form

```
Leslie Moll, Inc.          2          October 23, 19--
TS
1"
     and it would seem appropriate for the remainder of the shipment
1"   to be kept in storage at the Dubuque depot until the conditions
```

Communications Design Associates

348 INDIANA AVENUE
WASHINGTON, DC 20001-1438
Tel: 1-800-432-5739

February 14, 19--

Sunstructures, Inc.
Attention Mr. Harvey Bell
2214 Brantford Place
Buffalo, NY 14222-5147

Ladies and Gentlemen

This letter is written in what is called "block style."
It is the style we recommend for use in your business
office for reasons detailed in the following paragraphs.

First, the style is a very efficient one. All lines
(including date) begin at the left margin, and time is
not consumed in positioning special parts of letters.

Second, the style is easy to learn. New employees will
have little difficulty learning it, and your present
staff can adjust to it without unnecessary confusion.

Third, the style is sufficiently different from most
other styles that it can suggest to clients that your
company is creative. The style gains attention.

At the request of Thomas Wray, I am enclosing his booklet about business letter styles and special features.

Sincerely

Kathryn E. Bowers

Ms. Kathryn E. Bowers
Senior Consultant

xx

Enclosure

pc Mr. Thomas Wray

1 Block, open

Communications Design Associates

348 INDIANA AVENUE
WASHINGTON, DC 20001-1438
Tel: 1-800-432-5739

November 28, 19-- .

SPECIAL DELIVERY

Mr. Otto B. Bates, President
Third Bank and Trust Company
9080 Reservoir Avenue
New Brunswick, NJ 90901-4476

Dear Mr. Bates

This letter is written in the "modified block style."
It is the style we recommend for use in your office for
reasons detailed for you in the paragraphs below.

First, the style is an efficient one that requires only
one tab setting--at center point--for positioning the
date, complimentary close, and typed signature lines.

Second, the style is easy to learn. New employees will
have little difficulty learning it, and your present
staff can adjust to it without unnecessary confusion.

Third, the style is a familiar one; it is used by more
business firms than any other. It is conservative, and
customers and companies alike feel comfortable with it.

A booklet about business letter styles and special features is enclosed. Use the reply card, also enclosed,
if you need additional information.

Sincerely yours

COMMUNICATIONS DESIGN ASSOCIATES

Kathryn E Bowers

Ms. Kathryn E. Bowers
Senior Consultant

xx

Enclosures: 2

2 Modified block, open

Communications Design Associates

348 INDIANA AVENUE
WASHINGTON, DC 20001-1438
Tel: 1-800-432-5739

November 2, 19--

Office Manager
Ramsey Engineering, Inc.
4799 Hamner Drive
Amarillo, TX 79107-6359

Dear Sir or Madam:

    MODIFIED BLOCK STYLE LETTER

    I am pleased to answer your letter. As you can
see, we use the modified block style, indented paragraphs, and mixed punctuation in our correspondence.
It is the style used in this letter.

    The spacing from the top of the page to the date
varies with the length of the letter. Other spacing in
the letter is standard. The date, complimentary close,
and name and official title of the writer are begun at
horizontal center.

    Please write to me again if I can help further.

                    Very truly yours,

                    Allen M. Woodside

                    Allen M. Woodside
                    Marketing Manager

xx

    Our new LETTER STYLE GUIDE will be sent to you as
soon as it comes from the printer.

3 Modified block, indented ¶'s, mixed

                    4885 Crescent Avenue, N.
                    Chicago, IL 60656-3781
                    April 6, 19--

Ms. Alice Trent-Rockler
Personnel Manager
Leisure Life Inns
1000 East Lynn Street
Seattle, WA 98102-4268

Dear Ms. Trent-Rockler

The Placement Office at Great Lakes College tells
me that your company has employment available this
summer for students.

I am now in my junior year as an economics major.
Although my educational background has been mostly
in the liberal arts, I have learned to keyboard;
and I have taken two accounting courses. In past
summers I have worked successfully at a variety of
jobs; in fact, I have accepted responsibility for
most of my college expenses. I travel as much as
I can; I like to meet new friends; and I have a
friendly, outgoing personality.

Your interest in providing summer employment for
students is much appreciated, Ms. Trent-Rockler.
I am sure I would enjoy working at Leisure Life
Inns. May I send you a complete resume and a list
of my references?

                    Sincerely yours

                    Lance J. Mykins

                    Lance J. Mykins

4 Personal letter on Monarch paper

Reference guide: letter styles

Folding and inserting procedure

Small envelopes (No. 6¾, 6¼)

Step 1 With letter face up, fold bottom up to ½ inch from top.

Step 2 Fold right third to ½ inch from last crease.

Step 3 Fold left third last.

Step 4 Insert last creased edge first.

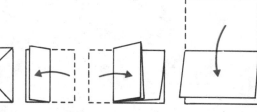

Large envelopes (No. 10, 9, 7¾)

Step 1 With sheet face down, fold up less than ⅓ of sheet up toward top.

Step 2 Fold down top of sheet slightly less than ½ inch to within ½ inch of bottom fold.

Step 3 Insert letter into envelope with last crease toward bottom of envelope.

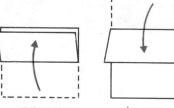

Window envelopes (letter)

Step 1 With sheet face down, fold upper third down.

Step 2 Fold lower third up toward you, so address is showing.

Step 3 Insert sheet into envelope with last crease at bottom.

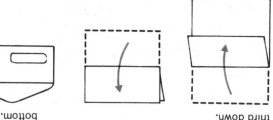

Window envelopes (invoices and other forms)

Step 1 Place sheet face down, top toward you.

Step 2 Fold back top so address shows.

Step 3 Insert into envelope with crease at bottom.

Addressing procedure

Envelope address. Set a tab stop (or margin stop if a number of envelopes are to be addressed) 10 spaces left of center for a small envelope or 5 spaces for a large envelope. Start the address here on Line 12 from the top edge of a small envelope and on Line 14 of a large one.

Style. Type the address in *block style*, single-spaced. Type the city name, state name or abbreviation, and ZIP Code on the last address line. The ZIP Code is usually typed 2 spaces after the state name.

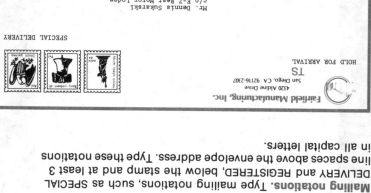

Addressee notations. Type addressee notations, such as *Hold for Arrival, Please Forward, Personal*, etc., a triple space below the return address and about 3 spaces from the left edge of the envelope. These notations may be underlined or typed in all capitals. If an *attention line* is used, type it immediately below the company name in the address line.

Mailing notations. Type mailing notations, such as SPECIAL DELIVERY and REGISTERED, below the stamp and at least 3 line spaces above the envelope address. Type these notations in all capital letters.

Ergonomics Consultants, Inc.

INTEROFFICE COMMUNICATION

TO: All Communication Processors
FROM: Rachel Darboro, Director
DATE: June 13, 19--
SUBJECT: Interoffice Memoranda

The exchange of information within a company is frequently typed on interoffice forms, either half or full sheets, depending upon the length of the message. The following points describe unique features of this form of memorandum.

1. Space twice after a printed heading; set the left margin stop for typing heading items and the body. Set the right margin stop an equal distance from the right edge. These margin adjustments will usually provide side margins of 1 inch.

2. Full addresses, the salutation, the complimentary close, and the signature are omitted.

3. Personal titles, such as Mr., are usually omitted from the memo heading. They are included on the envelope, however.

4. TS between the heading and the message; SS the paragraphs, but DS between them.

5. Reference initials, enclosure notation, and carbon copy notation are included if needed.

Special colored envelopes are often used for interoffice memos. Type the addressee's personal title, name, and business title or name of department for the address. Type COMPANY MAIL (in caps) in the postage location.

xx

pc Paul Glass, Assistant to the President

1 Interoffice memorandum

Sally Ann Dupois
123 Poinciana Road
Memphis, TN 38117-4121
(901-365-2775)

PRESENT CAREER OBJECTIVE

Eager to accept part-time position that provides opportunities for additional training and potential for full-time employment.

MAJOR QUALIFICATIONS

Knowledge of merchandising, management, inventory control, and related areas of a retail clothing store. Cheerful, outgoing personality and a dependable, cooperative worker.

EDUCATION

Junior at Memphis State University, Memphis, Tennessee, majoring in Marketing.

AA degree (associate degree/advertising; honors), State Technical Institute, Memphis, Tennessee.

Graduate (honors), East High School, Memphis, Tennessee.

EXPERIENCE

Assistant Manager, The Toggery, 100 Madison Avenue, Memphis, TN 38103-4219, June 1985 - Present.

Inventory Clerk and Cashier, Chobie's, 1700 Poplar Avenue, Memphis, TN 38104-2176, June 1984 - September 1984.

Clerk and Assistant to the Buyer, Todds, 1450 Union Avenue, Memphis, TN 38104-5417, June 1983 - September 1983.

REFERENCES

Mrs. Evelyn J. Quinell
Manager, Chobie's
1700 Poplar Avenue
Memphis, TN 38104-2176

Professor Aldo R. MacKenzie
Marketing Department
Memphis State University
Memphis, TN 38114-3285

Ms. Lanya Roover
The Toggery
100 Madison Avenue
Memphis, TN 38103-4219

Mr. Robert E. Tindall, Jr.
Attorney-at-Law
1045 Quin Avenue
Memphis, TN 38106-4792

2 Personal data sheet

Cap or ≡	Capitalize
⌣	Close up
ℓ	Delete
∧	Insert
⌃	Insert comma
# or / #	Insert space
⌄	Insert apostrophe
⌄⌄	Insert quotation marks
⎯⎯	Move right
⎯⎯	Move left
⎿⎾	Move down; lower
⎾⎿	Move up; raise
lc or /	Set in lowercase
¶	Paragraph
no new ¶	No new paragraph
‖	Set flush; align type
⊙ sp	Spell out
stet	Let it stand; ignore correction
∿ or tr	Transpose
⎯⎯⎯⎯	Underline or italics

Proofreader's marks
Preliminary copy may be corrected with proofreader's marks. The typist must be able to interpret correctly these marks when retyping the corrected (rough-draft) copy. The most commonly used marks are shown above.

Formatting reports (See illustrations below)

Margins. Use 1" top, side, and bottom margins, except for the first page, which has a 1½" or 2" top margin.

Binding. Allow an extra ½" for side or top binding.

Spacing. Double spacing for the body of a report and 5-space paragraph indentions are usual.

Quotations. Single-space quotations of 4 or more lines and indent them 5 spaces from each margin; otherwise, enclose the quotations in quotation marks and include them double-spaced as part of the body of the report.

Ellipsis. An ellipsis, an intentional omission of part of a quotation, is indicated by 3 periods with one space between each of the periods. If the omission ends a sentence, use 4 periods.

Leaders. If the report contains tabular copy, the columns may be separated by leaders. Leaders (spaced periods) can help a reader to move from one column to another. After typing the first item in the first column, space once and then alternate a period and a space to a point 2 or 3 spaces short of the next column. Note whether you type the periods on odd or even line-of-writing numbers; align subsequent rows by starting on an odd or even number as you did in the first line.

Justifying the right margin (manually). A preliminary copy must be typed to determine how many extra spaces must be added between words to insure an even right margin in a final copy. The normal procedure for the preliminary typing is to type as close to the end of each line as possible and then fill the remaining spaces with diagonals until the machine locks. Interpret diagonals as spaces to be added to each line in the final copy.

Footnotes. Footnotes may be placed at the end of a report, or they may be placed at the foot of the page on which reference is made.

Use a superior figure or symbol in the text of the report as reference to a footnote. Repeat the reference with the footnote.

Separate footnotes from the body of a report with a single underline 1½" long; single-space below the last line of the report to type the underline, type the underline, and double-space below the underline to begin the first line of the footnotes.

Single-space footnotes; double-space between them. Calculate footnote placement to insure a 1" bottom margin.

Formatting outlines

Data may be reduced to a more functional form through the use of an outline. Use the following suggestions.

Separate divisions and subdivisions of various orders with 4-space indentions.

Type first order divisions in ALL CAPS; capitalize main words only in second-order divisions; capitalize only the first word in third- and subsequent-order divisions.

Use the margin release and backspacer to type all Roman numerals other than I, V, and X.

The line length chosen must accommodate the longest line but must not exceed 70 spaces.

There must be at least two parts to any division.

```
                    HEADING

                                              TS
I.  FIRST-ORDER DIVISION
                                              DS
    A.  Second-Order Division
    B.  Second-Order Division
        1.  Third-order division
        2.  Third-order division
    C.  Second-Order Division
                                              DS
II. FIRST-ORDER DIVISION
                                              DS
    A.  Second-Order Division
        1.  Third-order division
        2.  Third-order division
        3.  Third-order division
            a.  Fourth-order division
            b.  Fourth-order division
    B.  Second-Order Division
```

1 Unbound report, page 1

PREPARING REPORTS: THE PROFESSIONAL TOUCH

Both the writer and keyboard operator, or compositor, share concern for the preparation and ultimate success of a report, but usually the writer must accept final accountability. The compositor's contribution, however, is a vital one; and she or he should proceed cautiously. For example, before starting to prepare a final copy of a report, the compositor should determine

1. the specified purpose of the report and whether some particular format is required;
2. the number, kind, and grade of copies required;[1] and
3. deadlines for completion.

The keyboard operator should be prepared to work from script, rough-draft, or printed copy and yet give the report a final presentation that is as professional as it is functional.

"Tricks of the Trade"

Those with experience in preparing reports have found that there are special procedures they can use to simplify their tasks. The following paragraphs contain samples of some procedures that can be especially helpful to a person who has not previously keyboarded reports. (Anyone who plans to prepare more than a few reports, however, should read several good books on the subject.)

Right margins. Attractive right margins result when good judgment is exercised. Using the warning bell judiciously ensures right margins that approximate left margins in width.

---
[1] For further information, see The Chicago Manual of Style, 13th ed. (Chicago: The University of Chicago Press, 1982), p. 40.

2 Unbound report, page 2

2

Reference characters. To keystroke a superior figure, turn the platen back a half line and type the figure. Asterisks and other reference symbols require no such adjustment. Keyboards with special symbol keys for report writing are available.

Page endings. A few simple guides become important whenever a report has more than one page. For example, never end a page with a hyphenated word. Further, do not leave a single line of a paragraph at the bottom of a page or at the top of a page (unless the paragraph has only one line, of course).

Footnote content. Underline titles of complete publications; use quotation marks with parts of publications. Thus, the name of a magazine will be underlined, but the title of an article within the magazine will be placed in quotation marks. Months and locational words, such as volume and number, may be abbreviated.

Penciled guides. A light pencil mark can be helpful to mark approximate page endings, planned placement of page numbers, and potential footnote locations. When the report has been finished, erase any visible pencil marks.

Conclusion

With patience and skill, the keyboard operator can give a well-written report the professional appearance it deserves. Says Lesikar[2],

Even with the best typewriter available, the finished work is no better than the efforts of the typist. But this statement does not imply that only the most skilled typist can turn out good work. Even the inexperienced typist can produce acceptable manuscripts simply by exercising care.

---
[2] Raymond V. Lesikar, Basic Business Communication (Homewood: Richard D. Irwin, Inc., 1979), p. 364.

3 Title page

TRENDS IN OFFICE COMMUNICATION

Bernadette E. Blount
Northern Illinois University

January 11, 19--

4 Bibliography

BIBLIOGRAPHY

Blum, Lester. "Computer Generated Graphic Tutorials In Economics." Collegiate Microcomputer 4 (Winter 1983): 289-97.

Crawford, T. James, et al. Basic Keyboarding and Typewriting Applications. Cincinnati: South-Western Publishing Co., 1983.

Hess, M. Elizabeth. Printing Manager, Effective Office Systems, New Orleans, Louisiana. Interviewed by Lois Walker, March 20, 1985.

Ray, Patrick V. "Electronic Printing Applications." Class handout in BADM 487, Central University, 1985.

Toffler, Alvin. The Third Wave. New York: William Morrow and Company, Inc., 1980.

Correcting errors

There are several methods that can be used to correct errors, and they are explained below.

Correction paper ("white carbon")
1 Backspace to the error.
2 Place the correction paper in front of the error, coated side toward the paper.
3 Retype the error. The substance on the correction paper will cover the error.
4 Remove the correction paper; backspace; type the correction.

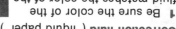

Rubber eraser
1 Use a plastic shield to protect surrounding and a typewriter (hard) eraser.
2 Turn the paper forward or backward in the machine to position the error for easier correction.
3 To keep bits of eraser out of the mechanism, move the carrier away from the error (or move carrier to the extreme left or right).
4 Move the eraser in one direction only to avoid cutting the paper.

Correction fluid ("liquid paper")
1 Be sure the color of the fluid matches the color of the paper.
2 Turn the paper forward or backward to ease the correction process.
3 Brush the fluid on sparingly; cover only the error, and it lightly.
4 The fluid dries quickly. Return to correction point and make the correction.

Automatic correction
If your machine is equipped with an automatic correcting ribbon, consult with your instructor or with the manufacturer's manual for operating instructions.

Horizontal centering

1 Move the margin stops to extreme ends of the scale.
2 Clear tab stops; then set a tab stop at center of paper.
3 Tabulate to the center of the paper.
4 From center, backspace once for each 2 letters, spaces, figures, or punctuation marks in the line.
5 Do not backspace for an odd or leftover stroke at the end of the line.
6 Begin to type where backspacing ends.

Example

Scale reading at left edge of paper	0
+Scale reading at right edge of paper	102
	102
Total ÷ 2 = Center point	102 ÷ 2 = 51

Spread headings

1 Backspace from center once for each letter, character, and space except the last letter or character in the heading. Start typing where the backspacing ends.
2 When typing a spread heading, space once after each letter or character and three times between words.

Vertical centering

Roll-back-from-center method
From vertical center of paper, roll platen (cylinder) back once for each 2 lines, 2 blank spaces, or line and blank line space. Ignore odd or leftover line.

Steps to follow:
1 To move paper to vertical center, start spacing down from top edge of paper:
a half sheet down 6 TS (triple spaces) −1 SS (Line 17)
b full sheet down 11 TS +1 SS (Line 34)
2 From vertical center:
a half sheet, SS or DS; follow basic rule, back 1 for 2.
b full sheet, SS or DS; follow basic rule, back 1 for 2; then back 2 SS for reading position.

Mathematical method
1 Count lines and blank line spaces needed to type problem.
2 Subtract lines to be used from lines available (66 for full sheet and 33 for half sheet).
3 Divide by 2 to get top and bottom margins. If fraction results, disregard it. Space down from top edge of paper 1 more than number of lines to be left in top margin.
For reading position, which is above exact vertical center, subtract 2 from exact top margin.
Formula for vertical mathematical placement:

$$\frac{\text{Lines available} - \text{lines used}}{2} = \text{top margin}$$

Prepare

1 Insert and align paper.
2 Clear margin stops by moving them to extreme ends of the scale.
3 Clear all tab stops.
4 Decide the number of spaces to be left between columns (for intercolumns).

Plan vertical placement

Follow either of the vertical centering methods explained on page viii.

Headings. Double-space (count 1 blank line space) between main and secondary headings, when both are used. Triple-space (count 2 blank line spaces) between the last heading (either main or secondary) and the first horizontal line of column items or column headings. Double-space between column headings (when used) and the first line of the columns.

Plan horizontal placement

Backspace from center of paper 1 space for each 2 letters, figures, symbols, and spaces in the *longest item* of each column and for each 2 spaces between columns. Set the left margin stop of the longest item when backspacing, carry it forward to the next column. Ignore an extra space at the end of the last column. (See illustration below).

An easy alternate method is to backspace for the longest item in each column first, *then* for the spaces to be left between columns.

Note. If a column heading is longer than the longest item in the column, it may be treated as the longest item in determining placement. The longest column item must then be centered under the heading, and the tab stop set accordingly.

Set tab stops. From the left margin stop, space forward 1 space for each letter, figure, symbol, and space in the longest item in the first column and for each space in the first intercolumn. Set a tab stop. Follow this procedure for each additional column to be typed.

To center column headings

Backspace-from-column-center method

From the point at which the column begins (tab or margin stop), space forward (→) once for each 2 letters, figures, or spaces in the longest item in the column. This leads to the column center point; from it, backspace ( ) once for each 2 spaces in the column heading. Ignore an odd or leftover space. Type the heading at this point; it will be centered over the column.

Mathematical method

1 To the number of the cylinder (platen) or line-of-writing scale immediately under the first letter, figure, or symbol of the longest item of the column, add the number shown under the space following the last stroke of the item. Divide this sum by 2; the result will be the center point of the column. From this point on the scale, backspace to center the column heading.
—or—
2 From the number of spaces in the longest item, subtract the number of spaces in the heading. Divide this number by 2; ignore fractions. Space forward this number from the tab or margin stop and type the heading.

To type horizontal lines

Depress the shift lock; strike the underline key.

To draw vertical lines

Operate the automatic line finder. Place a pencil or pen point through the cardholder (or the type bar guide above the ribbon or carrier). Roll the paper up until you have a line of the desired length. Remove the pencil or pen and reset the line finder.

```
              MAIN HEADING

            Secondary Heading


   These        Are      Column      Heads

  xxxxxx      longest    xxxx       xxxxx
  xxxx        item       longest    xxx
  xxxxx       xxxxx      item       longest
  longest     xxxxxx     xxxxx      item
  item        xxxx       xxx        xxx

 |lo|ng|es|t1|23|4|lo|nge|st|12|34|lo|ng|es|t1|23|4|lo|nge|st|
```

List of illustrations

List of drills and timed writings

Basic techniques

Business letters

TECHNIQUE CHECK SHEET

		Rating periods											
		1	2	3	4	5	6	7	8	9	10	11	12

Position at typewriter . . . . **Rating**

1. Sits in a comfortable, relaxed position directly in front of typewriter.
2. Keeps feet on floor for proper body balance.
3. Keeps elbows in relaxed, natural position at sides of body to provide correct hand position.
4. Keeps wrists low and relaxed, but off frame of typewriter.
5. Keeps fingers well curved, upright, and in typing position.

Keystroking . . . . **Rating**

1. Keeps fingers curved and upright over home keys.
2. Makes quick, snappy keystrokes with immediate key release.
3. Maintains uniform keystroking action (force).
4. Keeps hands and arms quiet, wrists low.
5. Strikes each key with proper finger.

Space bar . . . . **Rating**

1. Keeps right thumb curved—on or close to space bar.
2. Strikes space bar with a quick, down-and-in (toward palm) motion of right thumb.
3. Releases space bar instantly.
4. Does not pause before or after spacing stroke.

Carriage (element) return . . . . **Rating**

1. Returns carriage (element) quickly at ends of lines.
   Manual: Quick, flick-of-hand motion.
   Electric: Quick, little finger reach.
2. Keeps eyes on copy during and following return.
3. Starts new line without break or pause.

Shift keys . . . . **Rating**

1. Reaches quickly with little fingers; keeps other fingers in typing (home-key) position.
2. Holds shift key all the way down as the letter key is struck—capitals are uniformly on the line of writing.
3. Releases shift key quickly after letter is struck.
4. Does not pause before or after shift-key stroke.

Tabulator key or bar . . . . **Rating**

1. Reaches quickly with controlling finger; keeps other fingers near typing (home-key) position.
2. Uses minimum hand and arm motion.
3. Continues typing immediately after tabulating— without pause or interruption.

TECHNIQUE CHECK SHEET, continued

RATINGS		Rating periods											
Excellent . . . 4 points Good . . . . . 3 points Average . . . . 2 points Acceptable . . 1 point		1	2	3	4	5	6	7	8	9	10	11	12

Reading/typing response patterns . . . . | **Rating**

1. Keeps eyes on copy—concentrates on copy to be typed. . . .
2. Keeps carriage (element) moving without jerks and
   pauses—maintains continuous keystroking
   by reading slightly ahead in the copy. . . . .
3. Types one-hand letter combinations and words quickly
   and with keystroking action in fingers. . . . .
4. Types balanced-hand words by *word* response. . . . . . .
5. Uses a smooth, fluent rhythm pattern which varies
   according to difficulty of copy being typed. . . . . . .

Mind-set . . . . | **Rating**

1. Follows directions carefully. . . . .
2. Gives attention to technique cues and goals. . . . .
3. Makes effort to reach suggested goals. . . . .
4. Practices with a purpose at assigned practice level. . . . .
5. Shows alert attention, but shows no evidence of tenseness
   in shoulders, arms, and hands. . . . .

SUGGESTED EVALUATION/GRADING PLAN

Grade range
A = 3.6–4.0
B = 2.6–3.5
C = 1.6–2.5
D = 0.6–1.5
F = 0–0.5

1. Observe and rate the student on each major technique listed on this Check Sheet (or those that are currently appropriate), using point scores of 4 = A; 3 = B; 2 = C; 1 = D. Enter the appropriate point score opposite the word *Rating* for each technique being rated.

2. When observing and rating the student, place a check mark opposite each numbered item that needs immediate improvement.

3. After all currently appropriate techniques have been evaluated and rated, enter the *Rating* scores in a table such as the one illustrated below.

4. Add (across) the *Rating* scores awarded the student for each technique and enter the total in the *Total* column opposite the student's name.

5. Divide the total by the number of techniques rated (8 in the illustrative examples) and enter the average in the *Average* column opposite the student's name.

6. Award A-B-C-D-F grades on the basis of the *Grading range* scale given in the block above.

Name of student	Position	Essential Motions					Response patterns	Mind-set	Total	Average
		Key-stroking	Space bar	Carriage return	Shift keys	Tabu-lator				
Allan, Marcia	4	4	2	3	4	4	3	4	28	3.5
Cardona, Eduardo	3	3	3	4	3	3	2	3	24	3.0
Isobe, Keiko	2	2	1	1	2	1	1	2	12	1.5
Taylor, David	2	3	2	2	3	3	3	3	21	2.6

Speed growth charts

use in Division 1
(Lessons 1–50)

The charts given here may be used to record *gwam* on 1', 3', and 5' straight-copy, timed writings.

To plot *gwam* on each writing to be recorded, place a dot on the vertical line at the point opposite the proper number (*gwam*).

To show your progress, connect the dots with a solid line.

1' straight-copy sentences

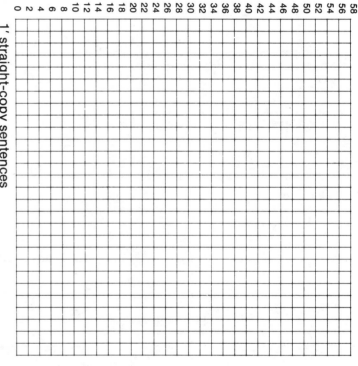

58
56
54
52
50
48
46
44
42
40
38
36
34
32
30
28
26
24
22
20
18
16
14
12
10
8
6
4
2
0

3' straight-copy paragraphs

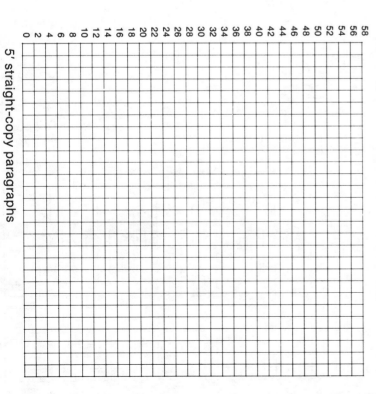

58
56
54
52
50
48
46
44
42
40
38
36
34
32
30
28
26
24
22
20
18
16
14
12
10
8
6
4
2
0

1' straight-copy paragraphs

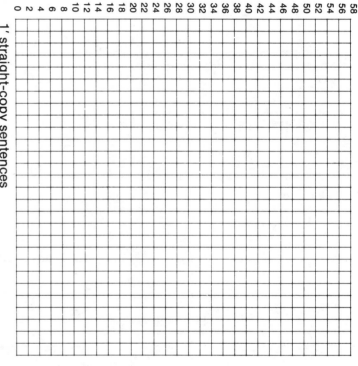

58
56
54
52
50
48
46
44
42
40
38
36
34
32
30
28
26
24
22
20
18
16
14
12
10
8
6
4
2
0

5' straight-copy paragraphs

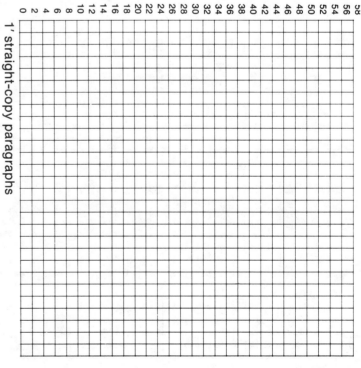

58
56
54
52
50
48
46
44
42
40
38
36
34
32
30
28
26
24
22
20
18
16
14
12
10
8
6
4
2
0

Accuracy growth charts

use in Division 1 (Lessons 1–50)

The charts given here may be used to record gwam on 1', 3', and 5' straight-copy timed writings.

To plot gwam on each writing to be recorded, place a dot on the vertical line at the point opposite the proper number (gwam).

To show your progress, connect the dots with a solid line.

Note: Use the "Extracts from International Typewriting Contest Rules" on page 6 to identify your errors.

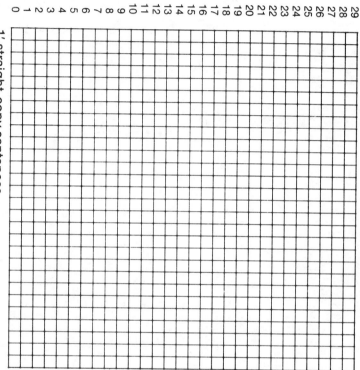

1' straight-copy sentences

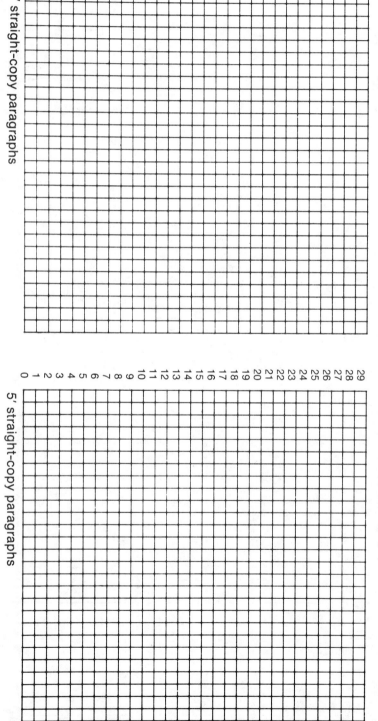

3' straight-copy paragraphs

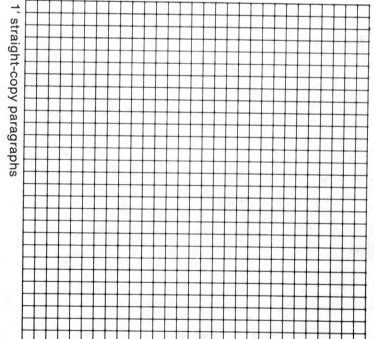

1' straight-copy paragraphs

5' straight-copy paragraphs

PROGRESS RECORD FOR DIVISION 1

PROCEDURE Keep a lesson-by-lesson completion record on the form given below, indicating your speed and accuracy on timed writings and the number of problems completed.

LESSON	DATE	GWAM (Gross Words a Minute)/ERRORS				NUMBER OF PROBLEMS COMPLETED
		1' Timing	3' Timing	5' Timing	Other Timing	
15						
16						
17						
18						
19						
20						
21						
22						
23						
24						
25						
26						
27						
28						
29						
30						
31						
32						
33						
34						
35						
36						
37						
38						
39						
40						
41						
42						
43						
44						
45						
46						
47						
48						
49						
50						

Learn to to use word-count columns and scales with paragraphs

The column at the right of the paragraphs shows the cumulative line-by-line gross words for each paragraph. The 1' *gwam* scale below the last line shows the number of words keyboarded for a partial line during a 1' writing. Thus, if you take a 1' writing on ¶1 and keyboard through the word *so* in the second line, you will have reached 18 *gwam*. If you complete the paragraph in 1', you will have reached 19 *gwam*.

Complete Items 1–3; then check correct answers below.

	gwam 1'
Just how much effort is expected of me? Why	9
do I acquiesce when others seem to demand so much?	19
I know that when I have finished a difficult	9
job, often a still more difficult one needs doing.	19
Yet that is the way I grow. Lazy people are	9
pleased at an easy job; hard jobs make us stretch.	19

gwam 1' | 1 | 2 | 3 | 4 | 5 | 6 | 7 | 8 | 9 | 10 |

Answers

1. If you take a 1' writing on the second ¶ and keyboard through the word *more* in the second line, your *gwam* will be (a) 5; (b) 15; (c) 14. ____

2. If you take a 1' writing on the third ¶ and complete the ¶, your *gwam* will be: (a) 9; (b) 19; (c) 20. .... ____

3. If you take a 1' writing on the first ¶ and complete the ¶ and keyboard through the word *much* on the first line a second time, your *gwam* will be: (a) 23; (b) 13; (c) 4. .... ____

Learn to use superior figures, word-count columns, and scales with paragraphs

The superior dots and figures in each paragraph indicate the number of words keyboarded during a 1' writing of each paragraph (the count increases in 2-word increments). The columns at the right of the paragraphs show the cumulative line-by-line gross words keyboarded during a 2' writing of both paragraphs. The 2' *gwam* scale below the last line shows the number of words keyboarded for a partial line during a 2' writing. Thus, if you take a 1' writing on the first paragraph and keyboard through the word *in* in the second line, you will have reached 16 *gwam*. If you take a 2' writing on both ¶s and keyboard through the word *our* in the second line of the second paragraph, you will have reached 21 *gwam*.

Complete Items 4–6; then check correct answers at the right.

			gwam 2'
.	4	. 8	
We must be able to express our thoughts with			5 | 34
. 12	. 16	.	
ease if we desire to find success in the world of			10 | 39
20	. 24	. 28	
business. It is there that sound ideas earn cash.			15 | 44
.	4	. 8	
It makes good sense to decide that we should			19 | 49
. 12	. 16	.	
stop to get our thoughts in order before we begin			24 | 54
20	. 24	. 28	
to talk. Talk before thought is often just noise.			29 | 59

gwam 2' | 1 | 2 | 3 | 4 | 5 |

Answers

4. If you take a 1' writing on the first ¶ and keyboard through the word *ideas* in the third line, your *gwam* will be: (a) 11; (b) 20; (c) 27........ ____

5. If you take a 2' writing on both ¶s and type through the word *thought* in the third line of the second ¶, your *gwam* will be: (a) 25; (b) 26; (c) 27.. ____

6. If you take a 2' writing on both ¶s and complete them and keyboard through the word *desire* in the second line of the first ¶ a second time, your *gwam* will be: (a) 36; (b) 31; (c) 34. .... ____

Answers
(1)c; (2)b; (3)a; (4)c; (5)c; (6)a

**Enrichment activity:
keyboarding review**

may be used after completing
Lesson 12, p. 28
Keyboard each line twice (slowly,
then faster); repeat selected lines.

a Barbara arranged ten asters in the alabaster vase.
b Bob bravely lobbed the bouncing ball back to Babs.
c Cara hurt her coccyx in a car accident in Chicago.
d Indeed, her dad did deed the Denver land to Addie.
e There is an eagle's aerie eighteen feet above her.
f In effect, four of the five offices are different.
g Greg dragged a gigantic log up a gorge in Georgia.
h Hannah's headache hurt her; she had to rush lunch.
i I had a quick trip from Cincinnati to Mississippi.
j Jojo judged just the jars of jam or jelly in June.
k Frank kicked a rock and knocked down a weak plank.
l Molly lulled little Billy to sleep with a lullaby.
m Sometimes Emma mumbles, but her grammar is better.
n Nancy had a tuna sandwich and a banana for dinner.
o The old school stood at the foot of the oak grove.
p Pepe happily applied plenty of pepper to the soup.
q Quint quickly quieted the quarrels in Albuquerque.
r Harry arranged for a carrier to reroute our order.
s These professors assessed the basis of the system.
t The telltale rattle of the reptiles startled Kitt.
u The bus to Albuquerque is usually four hours late.
v Favoring vibrant hues, Vi's van is a vivid violet.
w We want to win an award; we will wait a few weeks.
x Rex is not lax; he waxed my taxi next to the exit.
y They may simply try analyzing Yuma's very dry air.
z Dizzy and puzzled, Zina took a zany, zigzag route.
alphabet Jan Kimby gave six prizes to qualified white cats.
alphabet One judge saw five boys quickly fix the prize elm.
alphabet Did Peg Linway quiz Jack Vance about his tax form?
alphabet Mavis Zeff worked quickly on the next big project.

gwam 1' | 1 | 2 | 3 | 4 | 5 | 6 | 7 | 8 | 9 | 10 |

Enrichment activity: keyboarding goal sentences

may be used during Section 2 (Lessons 13–15)

1 Keyboard each line of Set 1 once without being timed.

2 Take two 30″ writings on each line in Set 1. Try to reach the end of the line as "return" is called.

3 Take a 1′ writing on each line without the call to "return."

4 Keyboard Set 2 using Set 1 directions.

Set 1 (balanced-hand words)

		gwam 1′	30″
1	Did the corps visit the firms?	6	12
2	She cut the usual quantity of corn.	7	14
3	Zoe risks a penalty for the dismal work.	8	16
4	She did fix the height and angle of the maps.	9	18
5	Jane paid for the right to dig coal by the bushel.	10	20

gwam 1′ | 1 | 2 | 3 | 4 | 5 | 6 | 7 | 8 | 9 | 10 |

Set 2 (balanced-hand and one-hand words)

		gwam 1′	30″
1	We saw the pair of rare vases.	6	12
2	We got bread and milk in the city.	7	14
3	Tex set the bags of corn in the freezer.	8	16
4	John paid for a quantity of nylon gear cases.	9	18
5	Did he pay for the gas and oil only at the garage?	10	20

gwam 1′ | 1 | 2 | 3 | 4 | 5 | 6 | 7 | 8 | 9 | 10 |

Enrichment activity: keystroking precision

may be used during Section 2 (Lessons 13–15)

Each line emphasizes a letter combination that is a frequent source of error. Keyboard each line twice SS (slowly, then faster) with attention to the sequence of letters and finger movements.

m/n Minimum numbers of them mind their dinner manners.

r/t We first start to cart the trays to the red truck.

o/i I toiled to ship my ration of oil to Iowa or Ohio.

e/r We are very aware their papers are free of errors.

s/d He adds an address to goods he sends on to Odessa.

a/s She has asked Sara to shop at sales and save cash.

v/b The bridge vibrated as Bev braved the vast ravine.

d/e Ed desired to ride in a rodeo; does he dare do it?

f/g Flag flying, the freighter fought through the fog.

o/l An old soldier slowly folds her gold nylon blouse.

a/e As agreed, we have named each leader of the teams.

u/i Did you dilute each unit of the juice as required?

d/f A diffident Fred offered to find fodder for a doe.

l/k Kelly talked quickly about weekly walks she takes.

gwam 1′ | 1 | 2 | 3 | 4 | 5 | 6 | 7 | 8 | 9 | 10 |

Enrichment activity: keyboarding figures

may be used after Lesson 19, p. 39

Keyboard each line twice SS (slowly; faster); DS between 2-line groups. Repeat selected lines.

Figure review

1 We found 11 machines and 11 operators in Room 112.

2 On August 22, we sent 232 pounds of No. 22 cotton.

3 Only 33 of the 333 letters were sent on August 23.

4 I need 44 desks and 44 chairs to furnish Room 454.

5 She delivered the 55 bags to 545 East 55th Street.

6 The 66 buses drove 776 miles, not 666 as reported.

7 Engine 778 pulled 77 cars and 77 tons of iron ore.

8 The 889 settlers walked about 88 miles in 88 days.

9 The 99 men and 99 women joined 990 other marchers.

0 Their Model 009 uses Grades 00 sand and 00 pumice.

all figures Send Checks 320 and 789 to 56 Lynn Lane on May 14.

all figures At 7:30 on May 15, 1836, the 249 settlers arrived.

all figures Of 13 members, 4 were chosen: 29, 56, 78, and 90.

gwam 1' | 1 | 2 | 3 | 4 | 5 | 6 | 7 | 8 | 9 | 10 |

Enrichment activity: keyboarding goal sentences

Keyboard each line of each 2-line group as a 1' writing with the 20" call to "return." Try to reach the end of each line as "return" is called.

		words in line	gwam 20"
straight copy	I am not free to go right now.	6	18
figures	He scored 23 of the 78 points.	6	18
straight copy	She plans to arrive today by train.	7	21
figures	I know only 5 or 6 of the 123 boys.	7	21
straight copy	Where are the trees you want me to trim?	8	24
figures	Dave took Route 890 north for 678 miles.	8	24
straight copy	I wonder why you did not do well on the quiz?	9	27
figures	Their score was not 10 to 3; it was 10 to 13.	9	27
straight copy	My friend moved to this city just over a year ago.	10	30
figures	Bill worked on May 23 and 24; Ruth, May 27 and 28.	10	30

gwam 1' | 1 | 2 | 3 | 4 | 5 | 6 | 7 | 8 | 9 | 10 |

Enrichment activity: keyboarding symbols

may be used after Lesson 27, p. 53

Keyboard each line 3 times SS (slowly, faster, slower); DS between 3-line groups.

Symbol review

$ Post $41.18 and $4.27 today; post $21.56 and $8.90 tomorrow.

& Lee & Lee, Ain & Sak, Day & Foh, and Yi & Lear represent us.

Check Card #12 and Card #13 to find Load #10 of #33 decking.

() They (Jess and Jane) paid the debt twice (in June and July).

% Note our discounts: coats, 25% and 30%; shoes, 10% and 15%.

' I can't read Bob's writing; he isn't following Ty's example.

! Ready! You may begin! Keep the treadmill going! Now stop!

" "Are you ready," I asked, "for the party?" "No," said Tina.

_ Order the paper products this week; canned goods, next week.

- An ex-student--Dan Lee--writes our end-of-the-month reports.

/ Pay by 3/10, and 1/2 of the savings goes to Jane and/or Kay.

gwam 1' | 1 | 2 | 3 | 4 | 5 | 6 | 7 | 8 | 9 | 10 | 11 | 12 |

Enrichment activity: goal sentences

Keyboard each line of each 3-line group as a 1' writing with the 20" call of the return. Try to reach the end of each line as "return" is called.

		words	gwam
straight copy	Place some value on your time.	6	18
figures	I have done pages 1, 4, and 9.	6	18
fig/sym	Did Joe pay you $14 on July 9?	6	18
straight copy	Time and money are close relatives.	7	21
figures	Mickey is 32, but Helen is only 20.	7	21
fig/sym	Pay Cort & Hile the $33 I owe them.	7	21
straight copy	Both time and money need wise investing.	8	24
figures	Of 600 men surveyed, 57 did not respond.	8	24
fig/sym	I paid $75 for the Model #60-7 computer.	8	24
straight copy	Just like money, time can be spent only once.	9	27
figures	Jack read pages 2 to 8; Anne, pages 16 to 18.	9	27
fig/sym	Jo-Ann will pay the $25 she owes Kim & Lopez.	9	27
straight copy	When I give my time to something, I give it value.	10	30
figures	Flight 498 should leave Omaha in 15 or 20 minutes.	10	30
fig/sym	Pam got a 3% discount ($7) on Drake's Invoice #36.	10	30

gwam 1' | 1 | 2 | 3 | 4 | 5 | 6 | 7 | 8 | 9 | 10 |

Enrichment activity: figure/symbol review

Self-check questions 1

use after Lesson 27, p. 53

NAME _____

DATE _____ SCORE _____

1 Write the answer to each item in the blank provided at the right.

2 When you have answered all items, check the accuracy of your answers with the key below.

Answers

1. a
2. b
3. a
4. b
5. c

Text Page

20
5,42
4
17,33
41

Answers

6. a
7. b
8. b
9. c
10. c

Text Page

51
17,26,51
4
51
4

Answers

11. c
12. a
13. b
14. c
15. a

Text Page

40
5,40
4
44
5,40

Answers

16. c
17. a
18. b
19. a
20. c

Text Page

44
42
26
21
17

		Answers	Score

1. One standard typewritten word contains (a) five strokes; (b) eight strokes; (c) varies from word to word. .... ___ 1.___

2. The horizontal center point is (a) 51 pica, 42 elite; (b) 42 pica, 51 elite; (c) 42 for pica and elite. .... ___ 2.___

3. For routine keyboarding, the paper guide should be set at (a) 0; (b) a certain number of spaces to the left of center point; (c) various places, depending on the problem. .... ___ 3.___

4. Following a period (.) after an initial in a name, there is/are (a) no space; (b) one space; (c) two spaces. .... ___ 4.___

5. To bypass the margin lock, use the (a) margin set; (b) tab clear; (c) margin release. .... ___ 5.___

6. Which of the following proofreader's marks means to "capitalize"? (a) Cap on ≡; (b) ⌒ ; (c) ⊏ .... ___ 6.___

7. The number of spaces that follow any mark of punctuation at the end of a sentence (a) is one; (b) is two; (c) depends on the mark of punctuation. .... ___ 7.___

8. The part of the typewriter that reads from 0 to at least 110 for machines with elite type or from 0 to at least 90 for machines with pica type is known as a (a) line-space selector; (b) line-of-writing scale; (c) center point indicator. .... ___ 8.___

9. Which of the following proofreader's marks means "close up space"? (a) ⊏ ; (b) # ; (c) ⌒ .... ___ 9.___

10. A horizontal inch of elite type has (a) 8 spaces; (b) 10 spaces; (c) 12 spaces. .. ___ 10.___

11. Paper that is 8½″ wide has (a) 85; (b) 100; (c) 102 elite spaces. .... ___ 11.___

12. To center a 60-space line horizontally on a sheet of paper 8½″ wide, set the left margin stop (a) 30; (b) 35; (c) 40 spaces to the left of the horizontal center..... ___ 12.___

13. To type with one blank line space between lines, set the line-space selector on (a) SS; (b) DS; (c) TS. .... ___ 13.___

14. To have a 1″ top margin, begin keyboarding on Line (a) 5; (b) 6; (c) 7. .... ___ 14.___

15. Paper that is 8½″ wide has (a) 85; (b) 100; (c) 102 pica spaces. .... ___ 15.___

16. A sheet of paper that is 11″ long has the following number of vertical lines: (a) 52; (b) 50; (c) 66. .... ___ 16.___

17. To center data horizontally, backspace from center point (a) once for each two characters or spaces; (b) once for each character or space; (c) twice for each character or space. .... ___ 17.___

18. After a colon is used as punctuation, except at the end of a line, (a) space once; (b) space twice; (c) do not space. .... ___ 18.___

19. After a comma is used as punctuation, except at the end of a line, (a) space once; (b) space twice; (c) do not space. .... ___ 19.___

20. When a period falls at the end of a line, (a) space once; (b) space twice; (c) do not space. .... ___ 20.___

Progress checkup 1: Basic skills

use after Lesson 27, p. 53

1a▶14
Measure basic skill: straight copy

1 Set margins for 60-space line. Take two 1' writings on each ¶; proofread and circle any errors; determine *gwam*.

2 Take two 3' writings on both ¶s; proofread and circle any errors; determine *gwam*.

all letters used

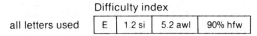

Difficulty index			
E	1.2 si	5.2 awl	90% hfw

	gwam 1'	3'

	1'	3'
Men or women who are a success will give the best that	11	4 | 43
they can give. They do not do this just because their egos	23	8 | 47
order it. They do it because they are oriented to succeed;	35	12 | 51
they fail to recognize that they could put forth any effort	47	16 | 55
that is not first class. They just expect to do their best.	59	20 | 59
The top men and women in their fields seem to realize,	11	23 | 63
though, that success has to mean a lot more than just doing	23	27 | 67
quality work. To be a real success, they say, we must look	35	31 | 71
at the work we do and rate it against our own standards for	47	35 | 75
excellence. Success is bound up with a belief in ourselves.	59	39 | 79

gwam 1' | 1 | 2 | 3 | 4 | 5 | 6 | 7 | 8 | 9 | 10 | 11 | 12 |
3' | 1 | 2 | 3 | 4 |

1b▶14
Measure basic skill: statistical copy

1 Set margins for 60-space line. Take two 1' writings on each ¶; proofread and circle any errors; determine *gwam*.

2 Take two 3' writings on both ¶s; proofread and circle any errors; determine *gwam*.

all letters/ figures used

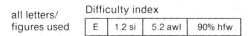

Difficulty index			
E	1.2 si	5.2 awl	90% hfw

	gwam 1'	3'

	1'	3'
Thank you for your request of the 29th. I am sorry we	11	4 | 39
could not reply to it before now, but the letter was mailed	23	8 | 43
to 3478 Xenia--not 658 Zinnia Drive (which is now our local	35	12 | 47
mailing address). We did not get your letter until June 10.	47	16 | 51
We are pleased to reserve for you a single room (#794)	11	19 | 55
for August 26 to 30. If you believe you might arrive after	23	23 | 59
4, won't you please forward a 50% deposit of $38.50 to hold	35	27 | 63
the room. We shall be happy to serve you and hope you will	47	31 | 67
enjoy your 5-day visit with us here at the Hotel Washington.	59	35 | 71

gwam 1' | 1 | 2 | 3 | 4 | 5 | 6 | 7 | 8 | 9 | 10 | 11 | 12 |
3' | 1 | 2 | 3 | 4 |

Self-check questions 2

for use after Lesson 32, p. 63

NAME _____

DATE _____   SCORE _____

1 Write the answer to each item in the blank provided at the right.

2 When you have answered all items, check the accuracy of your answers with the key below.

	Answers	Score

1. For an odd or leftover stroke at the end of a line you are centering (a) backspace once; (b) do not backspace; (c) either answer—(a) or (b)—is an acceptable procedure. . . . .   ____   1.____

2. When two one-letter syllables occur together within a word (grad-u-a-tion), divide the word (a) before the one-letter syllables; (b) between the one-letter syllables; (c) after the one-letter syllables. . . . .   ____   2.____

3. Words that contain double consonants (million) are (a) usually divided between the consonants; (b) usually divided after the consonants; (c) never divided. . . .   ____   3.____

4. A half sheet of typing paper contains (a) 33 vertical lines; (b) 85 vertical lines; (c) 102 vertical lines. . . . .   ____   4.____

5. To center a problem that contains 8 double-spaced lines of copy in exact vertical center on a full sheet of paper, begin keyboarding on Line (a) 10; (b) 25; (c) 26. . . . .   ____   5.____

6. To center in reading position a problem that contains 10 double-spaced lines of copy, begin keyboarding on Line (a) 20; (b) 22; (c) 13. . . . .   ____   6.____

7. To help you know when to end a line, a warning bell sounds (a) 7 to 12 spaces; (b) 5 spaces; (c) 13 to 15 spaces before the margin stop is reached. . . . .   ____   7.____

8. Every letter must have a (a) return address; (b) an envelope addressed in all caps; (c) typed signature. . . . .   ____   8.____

9. It is standard procedure to leave between the date and the letter address (a) 3 blank lines; (b) 2 blank lines; (c) 4 blank lines. . . . .   ____   9.____

10. The main heading of a report is followed by a (a) single blank line; (b) double space; (c) triple space. . . . .   ____   10.____

11. A word such as *through* that has only one syllable (a) may be divided; (b) may not be divided; (c) may be divided in special situations. . . . .   ____   11.____

12. The proofreader's mark "*stet*" means (a) include statistic; (b) leave as originally written; (c) study the material before continuing. . . . .   ____   12.____

13. *Horizontal* means (a) side to side; (b) top to bottom; (c) diagonally. . . . .   ____   13.____

14. For reading position, the number to be subtracted from the exact top margin figure is (a) 0; (b) 2; (c) 4. . . . .   ____   14.____

15. A 3″ card can hold (a) 12; (b) 15; (c) 18 vertical lines. . . . .   ____   15.____

16. The following is an *ampersand*: (a) &; (b) #; (c) $. . . . .   ____   16.____

17. If the scale at the left edge of the paper shows 20 and the scale at the right edge shows 86, the center of the paper will be (a) 43; (b) 53; (c) 106. . . . .   ____   17.____

18. A problem with a main heading and 10 lines of copy in the body that are double-spaced and typed on a half sheet in exact center would begin on Line (a) 5; (b) 6; (c) 10. . . . .   ____   18.____

19. If no punctuation follows the salutation or complimentary close of a letter, the punctuation form is called (a) open; (b) modified; (c) aligned. . . . .   ____   19.____

20. Most keyboard operators find an adequate bell warning for the end of a line to be (a) 5 or 6 spaces; (b) 7 to 12 spaces; (c) a various number, depending on the copy being keyboarded. . . . .   ____   20.____

Answers	Text Page
1.b	42
2.b	43
3.a	43
4.a	44
5.c	44

Answers	Text Page
6.b	46
7.a	41
8.a	58
9.a	58
10.c	43

Answers	Text Page
11.b	43
12.b	51
13.a	42
14.b	46
15.c	46

Answer	Text Page
16.a	47
17.b	46
18.b	44
19.a	59
20.a	41

Progress checkup 2: Basic skills

for use after Lesson 32, p. 63

2a▶14
Measure basic skill: straight copy

1 Set margins for a 60-space line. Take a 1' writing on each ¶; proofread and circle any errors; determine *gwam*.

2 Take two 3' writings on both ¶s; proofread and circle any errors; determine *gwam*.

all letters used

Difficulty index

LA	1.4 si	5.4 awl	85% hfw

	gwam 1'	3'
It seems that not very much can go on without some kind	11	4	47
of leadership being exerted, although it is not really clear	23	8	51
in each case whether leadership caused a thing to happen or	35	12	55
whether a leader just arose to take charge of it. However,	47	16	59
it's quite clear that unless somebody takes charge of a situ-	60	20	64
ation, it simply fizzles out in a short time.	69	23	67
No group organization can exist very long without its	11	26	70
leader, as it is vital that such a group be given both pur-	23	30	74
pose and direction. Most of the time, the leadership role is	35	35	78
acquired by the general agreement of members of the group;	47	38	82
but at times a leader can take charge just by force of his or	59	43	86
her personality.	62	44	87

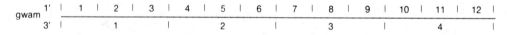

2b▶14
Measure basic skill: statistical copy

1 Set margins for a 60-space line. Take a 1' writing on each ¶; proofread and circle any errors; determine *gwam*.

2 Take two 3' writings on both ¶s; proofread and circle any errors; determine *gwam*.

all letters/figures used

Difficulty index

LA	1.4 si	5.4 awl	85% hfw

	gwam 1'	3'
If you will refer to my Memorandum #67-8 dated the first	11	4	56
week of July, you will notice that I quote the manager of the	24	8	60
Surf & Turf (a restaurant at 1139 Zodiac Street) who says that	36	12	64
her food costs are "very high this year; in fact, they are up	49	16	69
23.4%." Her standard daily food costs, she goes to some length	62	21	73
to explain, were approximately $275 last year. This year, they	74	25	77
are usually more than $300 a day.	81	27	79
Food costs are alluded to again on page 3 of the memoran-	11	31	83
dum--where it mentions that a family can save $7 to $8 a month	24	35	87
by buying food in larger quantities to be used in the future.	37	39	92
To buy 12 of something, rather than 4 or 5, can save 9% to 10%	49	43	96
on food bills (over several months, of course). Another wise	62	48	100
"tip" to the thrifty consumer says, "Buy when goods are in	73	51	104
high supply."	76	52	105

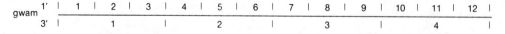

Progress checkup **3**: Applications

for use after Lesson 32, p. 63

3a ▶ 14
Word division

words

Problem 1

half sheet; DS; 34-space line; begin on Line 10

1 Keyboard the first word; space twice.

2 Keyboard the word again, this time with diagonals that show the dictionary divisions of the word. Space twice.

3 Keyboard the word again; insert a hyphen at the preferred point for end-of-line word division. Return.

4 Repeat with the next and subsequent words.

reception	re/cep/tion	recep-tion	7
copyright	cop/y/right		14
remission	re/mis/sion		21
flippancy	flip/pan/cy		28
aforesaid	a/fore/said		35
paragraph	par/a/graph		42
equipment	e/quip/ment		49
separates	sep/a/rates		56

Problem 2

2 half sheets; 60-space line; DS; begin on Line 10

1 Keyboard the ¶. Listen for the bell; divide words as necessary.

2 Before keyboarding the ¶ again, examine the right margin of your first copy and make any advisable adjustments.

While some keyboard operators say they don't like to divide words, doing 15
so is vital if attractive right margins are to be maintained. Keyboarded ma- 30
terial that does not seem to be well placed on the page detracts from the 45
importance of the message contained in the copy. Caution ought to be exer- 60
cised, however, not to divide a word incorrectly; errors detract from a mes- 75
sage as much as ragged margins do. 82

3b ▶ 15
Personal letter

plain full sheet
Format/keyboard the letter in the style of your choice. Use a 50-space line; begin on Line 16. Correct all errors.

250 Cliftgate Pass | Fort Wayne, IN 46804-2110 | May 27, 19-- | Ms. Helene 14
Grasse | 9 Iroquois Avenue | Atlantic City, NJ 08402-3387 | Dear Helene 27

¶ When I spoke with your sister Tris a week ago, she told me that you had 42
applied for the Barton-Felder Scholarship, which is one of the truly presti- 57
gious awards in the field of journalistic study. Today I talked with Tris 72
again, and she told me that you had won the Scholarship! 84

¶ This was thrilling news, and I congratulate you on this remarkable 97
achievement. Since I know Tris so well, I share the pride your whole family 112
feels in this fine honor. 118

¶ Tris tells me, too, that you will be visiting here in Fort Wayne in July. I hope 134
I shall have an opportunity to meet you at that time. 145

Sincerely yours | Jon J. Nunnally 151

3c ▶ 8
Centering
an invitation

half sheet; keyboard as
shown; center each line
horizontally; center problem
vertically in exact center;
proofread; circle errors

words

We   1

hope you   3

will come to   5

our holiday party   9

at 8 o'clock December 22   14

906 Skyline Terrace, Apartment 8   20

Nikki   21
and   22
Steve   23

3d ▶ 13
Personal letter
in rough draft

plain full sheet

Format/keyboard the
letter in block style. Use a
50-space line; begin on
Line 16.

6776 Buckthorne Street | Inglewood, CA 90301-4529| May 1, 19--| 12
Mr. Howard Stein | 2999 Del Mar Avenue| Long Beach, CA 90806-   24
7532 | Dear Howie   27

¶ sending me tickets for the opening night performance of of   38

"Otello" was very thoughtful, for you know that it is one   50

of my favorite shakespearean plays. Yes, I rmember very well   63

when we saw that great performance in Chicago.   72

¶ My calendar, however, has taken an unfortunate turn; And I   84

shall not be able to use the tickets. Since there is no time   96

left to re turn the tickets to you, I am asking cal and Verna   109

Rossmann to go. You will rmember that you met them at our cottage   122

last july.   125

¶ I look froward to seeing you at the show in Dayton on the 21st.   138

Give my regards to Dana.   142

Sincerely | Tyrone Askins   147

Tear along perforated lines.

32d, page 63

32d, page 63

Tear along perforated lines.

32d, page 63

32d, page 63

32d, page 63

Tear along perforated lines.

extra envelope

32d, page 63

32d, page 63

32d, page 63

Tear along perforated lines.

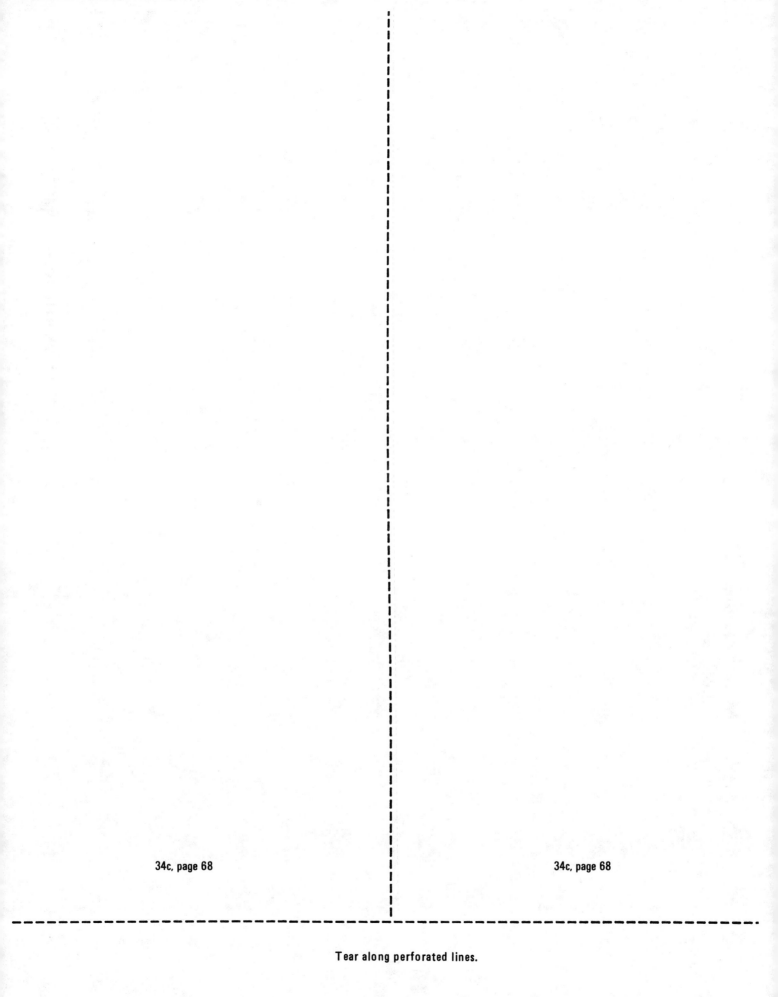

34c, page 68

34c, page 68

Tear along perforated lines.

34c, page 68

LM-35

Fairfield Manufacturing, Inc.

4320 Aldine Drive
San Diego, CA 92116-2307

Fairfield Manufacturing, Inc.

4320 Aldine Drive
San Diego, CA 92116-2307

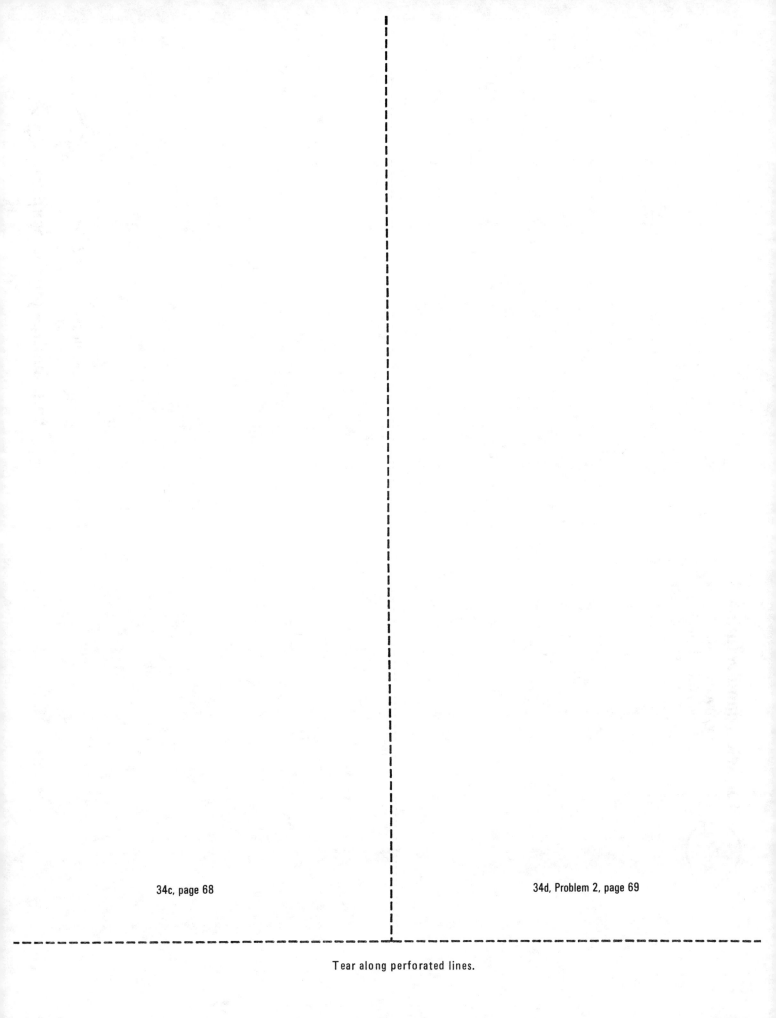

34c, page 68

34d, Problem 2, page 69

Tear along perforated lines.

Fairfield Manufacturing, Inc.

4320 Aldine Drive
San Diego, CA 92116-2307

Fairfield Manufacturing, Inc.

4320 Aldine Drive
San Diego, CA 92116-2307

Grafton's Department Store

1398 Duncan Avenue   Macon, GA   31201-4588

36c, page 72

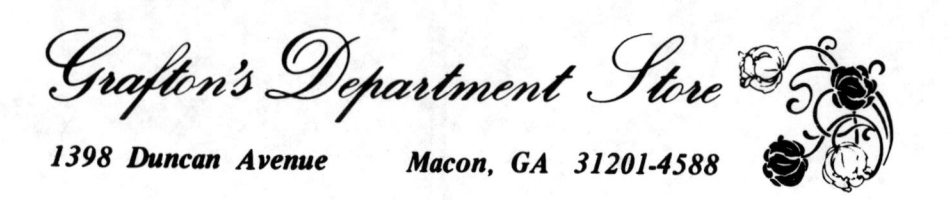

Grafton's Department Store

1398 Duncan Avenue   Macon, GA 31201-4588

36d, page 73

ic Industrial Consulting, Inc.

1225 WESTERN AVENUE
CHICAGO, IL 60608-5228
(312) 841-7330

INTEROFFICE COMMUNICATION

TO:

FROM:

DATE:

SUBJECT:

37d, Problem 3, page 75 **LM-43**

Tear along perforated line.

37c, page 74

EXECUTIVE OFFICES

THE HOUSE BY THE SIDE OF THE ROAD
1712 ANSON AVENUE   ABILENE, TX 79603-4951

INTEROFFICE COMMUNICATION

TO:

FROM:

DATE:

SUBJECT:

SUBJECT:

DATE:

FROM:

TO:

*Clark &
Jones, inc.*
655 Jefferson Avenue   Sioux Falls, SD 57104-3257   INTEROFFICE COMMUNICATION

EXECUTIVE OFFICE

THE HOUSE BY THE SIDE OF THE ROAD
1712 ANSON AVENUE   ABILENE, TX 79603-4951

37d, Problem 1, page 75

EXECUTIVE OFFICES   (915) 922-7300

THE HOUSE BY THE SIDE OF THE ROAD
1712 ANSON AVENUE   ABILENE, TX 79603-4951

37d, Problem 2, page 75

cp

CLEO PRODUCTS, INC.
18 Woodbury Avenue   Reno, NV 89103-6211

Self-check questions 3
for use after Lesson 37, p. 75

NAME _____

DATE _____ SCORE _____

1 Write the answer to each item in the blank provided at the right.

2 When you have answered all items, check the accuracy of your answers with the key below.

		Answers	Score

1. Which sentence has correct capitalization? (a) Drive north to Fell City; (b) I camp in Pike and Fuller Parks; (c) It was a cold Winter day. . . . .   _____ 1._____

2. A standard interoffice memorandum never includes the following: (a)enclosure notation; (b) reference initials; (c) complimentary close. . . . .   _____ 2._____

3. Which word is spelled correctly? (a) absense; (b) already; (c) convience. . . . . . .   _____ 3._____

4. Postal authorities recommend 2-letter state abbreviations (a) in all circumstances where state names are abbreviated; (b) only with ZIP Codes; (c) for letter addresses, but not for envelope addresses. . . . .   _____ 4._____

5. Folding a letter for a large envelope involves making (a) 2; (b) 3; (c) 4 creases in the letter. . . . .   _____ 5._____

6. Standard procedure requires the keyboard operator to leave how many blank lines below the date and above the letter address? (a) 3; (b) 4; (c) depends on the length of the letter. . . . .   _____ 6._____

7. Standard procedure is to operate the return how many times after the complimentary close and before the typed name: (a) 3; (b) 4; (c) 5. . . . .   _____ 7._____

8. Folding a letter for a small envelope involves making (a) 2; (b) 3; (c) 4 creases in the letter. . . . .   _____ 8._____

9. The placement of the envelope address on a small envelope is approximately how far from the top edge of the envelope? (a) 3"; (b) 3½"; (c) on Line 12. . . . . .   _____ 9._____

10. Average-length business letters on standard-size stationery fit well on a (a) 50-space line; (b) 60-space line; (c) 70-space line. . . . .   _____ 10._____

11. An average-length business letter on standard-size stationery usually begins on about Line (a) 10; (b) 15; (c) 20. . . . .   _____ 11._____

12. The letterhead on letter stationery functions primarily as (a) advertising; (b) a return address; (c) decoration. . . . .   _____ 12._____

13. Following the salutation in a letter with open punctuation there is (a) a colon; (b) a comma; (c) no punctuation. . . . .   _____ 13._____

14. Standard procedure is to operate the return how many times after the official title of the writer of a letter to type the reference initials? (a) 1; (b) 2; (c) 3. . . . . .   _____ 14._____

15. Type addressee notations (Hold for Arrival, Personal, Please Forward, etc.) a TS below (a) the stamp position; (b) the mailing address; (c) the return address.   _____ 15._____

16. Type mailing notations (SPECIAL DELIVERY, REGISTERED, etc.) in all caps below (a) the return address; (b) the mailing address; (c) the stamp position.   _____ 16._____

17. When using blank paper, such as personal stationery, for a letter, the first item typed is the (a) date; (b) name; (c) return address. . . . .   _____ 17._____

18. The dateline, complimentary close, and typed name on a modified block style letter appear at (a) the right margin; (b) the center point; (c) the left margin. . . .   _____ 18._____

19. Vertical spacing between parts on a block style letter and modified block style letter is (a) standard for all business letters; (b) modified according to the letter style; (c) left to the preference of the writer. . . . .   _____ 19._____

20. Reference initials represent the initials of the individual who is (a) receiving the letter; (b) sending the letter; (c) typing the letter. . . . .   _____ 20._____

Progress checkup 4: Letters

for use after Lesson 37, p. 75

		words
4a ▶ 12 **Personal letter in block style** plain sheet; 50-space line; begin on Line 16; proofread; correct errors	240 Eva Lane I Greensboro, NC 27405-3211 I March 20, 19-- I Mr. Leo Brice I 1080 Park Road I Lynn, MA 01906-6142 I Dear Mr. Brice	14 24
	¶1 Yesterday afternoon I arrived back in Greensboro after a very pleasant New England trip--pleasant, that is, except for the difficulty I had with my automobile near Lynn.	38 54 58
	¶2 I want to tell you again how grateful I am for the assistance you gave me under very difficult circumstances. I thought I would be alone for a very long time on that back road in Massachusetts until you offered to drive me to the repair shop in Lynn.	73 89 104 109
	¶3 Thank you again for your kindness. I hope that if you are ever in the Greensboro area you will call me and let me repay you with a bit of southern hospitality.	123 138 141
	Sincerely I Albert W. Hilbrand	147

4b ▶ 12 **Business letter in block style** plain sheet; 60-space line; begin on about Line 15; proofread; correct errors	February 27, 19-- I Mr. Raymond E. Balthous I Manager, McCellan's I 2020 Rosedale Avenue, SE I Washington, DC 19809-4311 I Dear Mr. Balthous	13 26
	¶1 I saw a robin this afternoon, and I realized that spring is just around the corner. That's why I want to send you our new brochure featuring our Cypress Belle rustic lawn furniture.	42 56 63
	¶2 Each piece of Cypress Belle is handcrafted to have a smooth, polished finish that looks interestingly rough hewn. The beauty of natural wood is there--and it looks so comfortable. Available pieces include lawn swings, arm-chairs, end tables, and stools.	77 92 108 115
	¶3 Why not use the card that is enclosed to send for our full-color brochure; then you can stock Cypress Belle for immediate delivery, or you can order it especially for customers who are sure to like this furniture when they picture it on their lawns.	130 145 161 165
	Sincerely I Rosella Murphy I Director of Sales I xx I Enclosure	176

4c ▶ 10 **Business letter in modified block style** plain sheet; 60-space line; begin on about Line 15; proofread; correct errors	April 26, 19-- I Ms. Dorotha Langsu I 6201 Myrtle Lane I Poughkeepsie, NY 12601-7396 I Dear Ms. Langsu	14 19
	¶1 I have two rabbits that live in my backyard, and they eat the nice green foliage it contains. I like those foolish bunnies, but I wish they could live somewhere else.	34 49 53
	¶2 All of us have things around the house that we don't want to throw away, but we wish they could live somewhere else. I have a solution: Why not bring your "treasures" to The Attic, the shop at 62 Main Street. We'll help you to price them, and we'll sell them on consignment for you; or we will give you a receipt when they are sold, and the income will be given to one of the charities on our list.	67 83 99 114 131 133
	¶3 If you have no such articles, just drop by to see us. Who knows; you might find a bargain! We have lots of them.	149 156
	Sincerely yours I Edwin Jacobs I Director I xx	164

Self-check questions 4

for use after Lesson 47, p 98

NAME _____

DATE _____ SCORE _____

1 Write the answer to each item in the blank provided at the right.

2 When you have answered all items, check the accuracy of your answers with the key below.

Answers — Score

1. The line length for an outline should be (a) 45 spaces; (b) 50 spaces; (c) set to accommodate the longest line in the outline, but not more than 70 spaces. .... ____ 1.____

2. If one stroke is left over when backspacing by 2's to center columnar items of a table, (a) disregard it; (b) backspace one additional time; (c) neither method is acceptable......................... ____ 2.____

3. As standard procedure for spacing between a main or secondary heading and columns of a table, (a) single space; (b) double space; (c) triple space......... ____ 3.____

4. To align numbers in a column, adjust the margin and tab settings for the digit that requires (a) the least forward spacing; (b) the least backspacing; (c) the least forward and backward spacing. .... ____ 4.____

5. A main heading is separated from a secondary heading by a (a) single space; (b) double space; (c) triple space. .... ____ 5.____

6. To determine the centerpoint of the longest item in a column when centering column headings, space forward from the starting position of the column (a) once for every two strokes or spaces; (b) twice for every one stroke or space; (c) once for every one stroke or space. .... ____ 6.____

7. In a bibliography, surnames (a) are listed first; (b) follow the first name; (c) are enclosed in parentheses. .... ____ 7.____

8. A personal data sheet should (a) be at least 2 pages long; (b) rarely use complete sentences; (c) stress aspirations, not just capabilities. .... ____ 8.____

9. An important factor in deciding intercolumn widths in tables is (a) whether the table is in reading position or exact center; (b) the length of the table; (c) the width of the table.. ____ 9.____

10. If the column heading is longer than its column, (a) shorten it; (b) treat it as the longest columnar item; (c) divide it and place it on 2 lines. .... ____ 10.____

11. Reading position is recommended for tables that are (a) on a half sheet; (b) double-spaced; (c) on a full sheet. .... ____ 11.____

12. First-order divisions in outlines are keyboarded (a) in all caps; (b) with only important words capped; (c) with only the first word capped.................. ____ 12.____

13. The side and bottom margins for an unbound report are (a) 1" side margins, 2" bottom margin; (b) 2" side margins, 1" bottom margin; (c) 1" side and bottom margins. .... ____ 13.____

14. In written reports, quoted material of four or more lines is (a) single spaced and indented 5 spaces from left margin; (b) double-spaced and not indented; (c) single-spaced and indented 5 spaces from both margins. .... ____ 14.____

15. When a carbon pack is assembled on a desk, the carbon paper is placed (a) carbon side down; (b) carbon side up; (c) at the bottom of the pack. .... ____ 15.____

16. To keyboard a spread heading, after each letter or character space (a) once; (b) twice; (c) three times. .... ____ 16.____

17. An elite line with 1" side margins on standard-size paper will contain (a) 78 spaces; (b) 60 spaces; (c) 65 spaces. .... ____ 17.____

18. In footnotes, surnames (a) are listed first; (b) follow the first name; (c) are enclosed in parentheses. .... ____ 18.____

19. Footnotes are typed at the foot of the page on which their reference numbers appear or at the end of the report and (a) are double spaced; (b) are single spaced with a blank line between them; (c) may be single spaced or double spaced depending whether the body of the report is single or double spaced. ____ 19.____

20. On unbound reports, the second and subsequent pages are numbered on (a) Line 4; (b) Line 7; (c) Line 13. .... ____ 20.____

Skill-performance checkup

for use after Lesson 47, p. 98

SPC 1: Outline

half sheet, long side up; 40-space line; exact center; correct errors

	words
MADRIGAL CONCERT SERIES	5

I. BALLET COMPANIES — 9

    A. Royal MacKenzie Ballet Company — 16
    B. DuBaugh Ballet Company — 21
    C. Florida Ballet Ensemble — 27

II. SINGERS — 30

    A. Robert Swindell, baritone — 36
    B. Allison Mason-McCardle, soprano — 43

SPC 2: Table

half sheet, long side up; SS; begin on Line 12; 8 spaces between columns

NORTHWESTERN HIGH SCHOOL — 5

Additions to Fall Class Schedule — 12

Subject	Teacher	Time	
			19
Algebra I	Davenport	10:05 a.m.	26
German Literature	Mays	1:40 p.m.	32
Business Mathematics	Scordone	8:20 a.m.	40

SPC 3: Footnote

full sheet; DS last ¶ of the report; 1" side margins; begin on Line 44

Frank Garcia, an amateur paleontologist, has spent many days digging — 14
at a beach site in Florida and has discovered fossils millions of years old. — 29
Asked why he spends so much of his own time digging for remains of the — 44
past, Begley[1] reports him as saying — 51

    The fossils are like time travelers, story-tellers from another life. — 65
I can stand on the site just imagining what life was like then. The — 79
reward I get is simply one of discovery--to me, that's what living on — 93
earth is all about. — 97

    — 100

[1]Sharon Begley with Bill Belleville, "A Treasure Trove of Fossils," — 113
Newsweek, (April 2, 1984), p. 72. — 122

SPC 4: Center lines

half sheet, long side up; DS; center lines vertically and horizontally; center main heading as spread heading

C E N T R A L   S T A T E   U N I V E R S I T Y — 10

"Home of the Hornets" — 14

Department of Athletics — 19

Progress
checkup 5: Basic skills

for use after Lesson 47, p. 98

5a▶12
**Measure
basic skill:
straight copy**
three 3' writings;
proofread
carefully; circle
errors

all letters used

Difficulty index

A	1.5 si	5.7 awl	80% hfw

gwam 3' | 5'

		3'	5'
Words are the tools used to communicate with others--orally as		4	3
well as in writing--and just like structural tools, words must be used		9	5
carefully; or they cannot do the job. The length of a word, its famil-		14	8
iarity, and any poetic qualities it may possess, while very important,		18	11
are secondary to the exactness of its meaning in conveying an idea.		23	14
A large and varied vocabulary, like a supply of fine tools, is		27	16
necessary for a person who works at a job that depends on communication.		32	19
For such a person, words can be almost a hobby; new words can be col-		37	22
lected, polished, analyzed, and used when just the right moment presents		42	25
itself. Words give concrete meaning to abstract ideas.		45	27
Words are everywhere; and, fortunately, they cost nothing. When we		50	30
are quiet, we hear them. When we read, we see them. Upon finding a new		55	33
word, the avid collector studies it to determine its exact meaning and		60	36
then practices using it in some practical way--in conversation or writ-		64	39
ing. If it works, a new tool is added to the collection.		68	41

gwam 3' | 1 | 2 | 3 | 4 | 5 |
       5' | 1 | 2 | 3 |

5b▶12
**Measure
basic skill:
statistical copy**
three 3' writings;
proofread
carefully; circle
errors

all letters/
figures used

Difficulty index

A	1.5 si	5.7 awl	80% hfw

gwam 3' | 5'

		3'	5'
An interesting addition to the news, a big city paper recently		4	3
carried an article (#3 of a series) that presented a panorama of the		9	5
city in figures. According to the article, the area baseball club won		13	8
a game 11 to 2. For the evening, known in the area as "family night,"		18	11
31,309 people turned out to attend an event that took 2 hours and 58 min-		23	14
utes to play. The happy customers, the article said, purchased 23,000		28	17
Sojia & Quent (a local firm) hot dogs, 12,000 ice cream bars, and 4,200		33	20
bags of peanuts; and they were served 29,000 soft drinks and 30,000		37	22
other beverages. Food expenses: <u>more</u> than $76,000. They saw 4 pitchers		42	25
turn 322 pitches into 191 strikes (59.3%) and 131 other pitches as the		47	28
teams turned 26 hits into 13 runs. The number of baseballs used: 15.		52	31

gwam 3' | 1 | 2 | 3 | 4 | 5 |
       5' | 1 | 2 | 3 |

Progress checkup 6: Letters

for use after Lesson 47, p. 98

6a▶12
Personal letter in block style

Monarch sheet and envelope [LM p. 55], 50-space line; begin on Line 13; proofread; correct errors

	words
2258 Summey Avenue I Charlotte, NC 28205-2411 I October 25, 19-- I Miss	13
Dorna Felice I 1859 San Fernando Way I Sacramento, CA 95818-7388 I Dear	27
Dorna	28

¶1 I was happy to receive your letter stating that you will be visiting in | 42
Charlotte next month to interview for a position with the <u>Charlotte News</u>. | 60
The <u>News</u> is a fine newspaper, and I know you would be a great addition to | 76
the staff. | 78
¶2 I know Eleanor Bennett, the business editor, quite well; and if you think it | 94
would be worthwhile, I'll be glad to speak to her about you. | 106
¶3 In any event, I want you to be my house guest when you are in Charlotte. If | 121
you let me know when you are arriving, I'll arrange to meet you. | 135
Sincerely I Janet Marcus | 139

6b▶10
Business letter in block style

plain sheet; 60-space line; begin on Line 15; proofread; correct errors

January 9, 19-- I Mr. Frank E. Guerra I 9460 Cedarwood Court I Mansfield, OH | 14
44906-4298 I Dear Mr. Guerra | 20

¶1 Your account is in arrears. | 25
¶2 I know this is not news to you, for we have written to you about this | 39
obligation on two previous occasions. We can understand that you might be | 54
having financial difficulties at the present time; all of us face that problem | 70
from time to time. What we cannot understand is why you have not been | 84
willing to talk with us about your situation. | 94
¶3 If we do not have some response to this letter, we shall have no choice but | 109
to begin other action. Why not contact us and explain your problem; or, better | 125
still, send us your check for $87.50. A stamped, addressed envelope is en- | 140
closed for your convenience. | 146
Sincerely I Alden R. Taylor I Credit Manager I xx I Enclosure | 157

6c▶12
Business letter in modified block style

plain sheet; 60-space line; begin on Line 15; proofread; correct errors

March 10, 19-- I Mrs. Celia Myota I 5061 Linda Lane, W. I Peoria, IL 61605-5814 | 15
I Dear Mrs. Myota | 18

¶1 It is my very great pleasure to inform you that you have been chosen to | 33
receive one of the Woman of the Year Awards to be given to three Peoria | 47
women at The Commonwealth Club's annual awards banquet on May 5. | 60
Please accept my congratulations. | 67
¶2 You will be recognized for your outstanding community work; specifically, | 82
your organization of the Library Association, your assistance with the Child | 97
Safety Group, and your service at the Emergency Warehouse. | 109
¶3 You have made Peoria a better place to live, Mrs. Myota; and we are | 123
pleased to honor you with our Woman of the Year Award. I shall telephone | 138
you in a few days to complete arrangements. | 146
Sincerely yours I Kimberly Scott I Secretary I xx | 155

PC 6, 6a, Workbook, page LM-54

Tear along perforated lines.

Progress
checkup 7: Reports and tables
for use after Lesson 47, p. 98

7a▶30
Two-page report

2 plain full sheets

Make placement decisions appropriate for a two-page unbound report.

Reminders

1 Leave a 1½″ top margin for pica type, 2″ for elite.

2 Allow 3 lines for the footnote if elite type is used; 4, if pica.

3 Number page 2 at the top of the page; do not number the first page.

words

THE WORKER OF THE FUTURE | 5

Some of us can picture "the office of the future" as one awash in won- | 19
drous equipment representative of the Age of Technology; and facilities, as | 34
we can see if we look closely, will have been designed to house to the best | 49
advantage all these marvelous, expensive, sensitive machines. This is a true | 65
picture of things to come. | 70

But if we take an even closer look at the picture, we should see women | 85
and men doing all the tasks that no machine--no matter how marvelous, | 99
expensive, or sensitive--can perform. The workers will be manipulating dials, | 114
switches, and keys; feeding information, and analyzing machine-generated | 129
data and making decisions based upon it. What thought, we might ask, will | 144
have been given to the comfort and welfare of these <u>human</u> elements of | 159
production: In one word, <u>plenty</u>. Enter "ergonomics." | 171

What is ergonomics? Clark[1] tells us | 179

> First of all, ergonomics is merely another word for human factor | 192
> design or human engineering--sciences that have been around for | 204
> some time. Designers applying these sciences attempt to reduce op- | 218
> erational fatigue and other forms of discomfort, both physiological | 231
> and psychological, in a man/machine environment. Properly done, | 244
> this results in machines which we can operate, utilize, or handle | 258
> with minimum physical problems and fewer machine-induced diffi- | 270
> culties. | 272

Although they are probably little different than before, the needs of the | 287
"worker of the future" are being studied now, even as new equipment is being | 302
developed. Management is rediscovering a concept that includes the worker | 317
as an integral part of the office environment and recognizes that if human | 332
factors are to function with maximum efficiency--the level expected of | 346
equipment--the physiological and psychological needs of the worker are | 361
important factors to be managed. | 368

| 371

[1]Jim Clark, "Preventing the Office of the Future from Being a Pain in the | 385
Neck, Back, Eye . . .," <u>The Balance Sheet</u> (March/April 1984), p. 4. (Reprinted | 404
with permission from <u>The Directory of Office Information Systems</u>.) | 426

(continued on page LM-58)

words

Such management is called ergonomics. It includes lighting that pre- 440
vents eyestrain; furniture that deters physical fatigue; temperature controls 455
that ensure comfort; environmental layouts and decor that provide a relaxed, 471
safe, efficient atmosphere; and such psychological factors as privacy, quiet, 486
work breaks, and space. 491

Ergonomics is not a form of pampering; rather, it attempts to recognize 506
the worker as a functional partner with the equipment of the modern office. 521
And this is as it should be; for is not the worker, too, a marvelous, expensive, 537
sensitive machine? 541

7b▶8
**2-column
table**

half sheet, long side up

Center and keyboard (SS) the
table in exact vertical and
horizontal center; allow 10 spaces
between columns. Center title as
a spread heading.

C A N A D A   2

Provinces and Capitals   7

Alberta	Edmonton	10
British Columbia	Victoria	16
Manitoba	Winnipeg	19
New Brunswick	Fredericton	24
Newfoundland	St. John's	29
Nova Scotia	Halifax	33
Ontario	Toronto	36
Prince Edward Island	Charlottetown	43
Quebec	Quebec City	47
Saskatchewan	Regina	51

7c▶13
**3-column
table**

full sheet

Center and keyboard (DS) the
table in reading position; decide
intercolumn spacing.

STATE NICKNAMES AND CAPITALS   6

(Selected States)   9

State	Nickname	Capital	
			18
Colorado	Centennial State	Denver	25
Idaho	Gem State	Boise	29
Iowa	Hawkeye State	Des Moines	35
Maine	Pine Tree State	Augusta	41
Montana	Treasure State	Helena	47
New York	Empire State	Albany	53
Oregon	Beaver State	Salem	58
Texas	Lone Star State	Austin	64
Virginia	Old Dominion	Richmond	70
Wyoming	Equality State	Cheyenne	76

48c, Problem 1, page 100

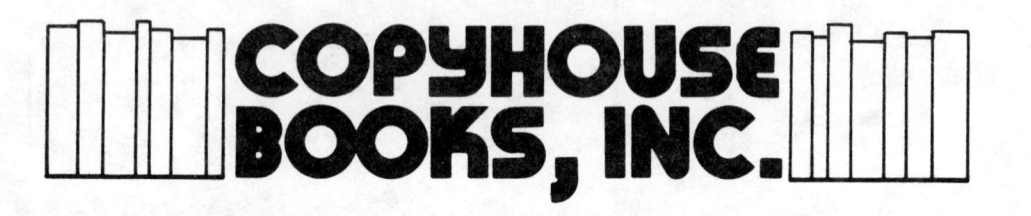

COPYHOUSE BOOKS, INC.

2112 BELMONT AVENUE   JAMAICA, NY 11417-2988   (212) 478-2400

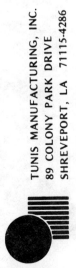

TUNIS MANUFACTURING, INC.
89 COLONY PARK DRIVE
SHREVEPORT, LA 71115-4286

48c, Problem 2, page 100

TUNIS MANUFACTURING, INC.
89 COLONY PARK DRIVE
SHREVEPORT, LA   71115-4286

(318) 591-6500

48c. Problem 3, page 100